PRACTICING

ETHNOGRAPHY

A Student Guide to Method and Methodology

PRACTICING

ETHNOGRAPHY

A Student Guide
to Method and Methodology

Edited by

Lynda Mannik and Karen McGarry

 UNIVERSITY OF TORONTO PRESS

Library and Archives Canada Cataloguing in Publication

Practicing ethnography : a student guide to method and methodology / edited by Lynda Mannik
    and Karen McGarry.

Includes bibliographical references and index.
Issued in print and electronic formats.
ISBN 978-1-4875-9313-1 (hardcover).—ISBN 978-1-4875-9312-4 (softcover).—
ISBN 978-1-4875-9315-5 (PDF).—ISBN 978-1-4875-9314-8 (EPUB)

    1. Ethnology—Methodology—Textbooks. 2. Textbooks. I. Mannik, Lynda, 1957–, editor
II. McGarry, Karen Ann, 1972–, editor

GN316.P73 2017   306.01   C2017-903412-X
                                                       C2017-903413-8

We welcome comments and suggestions regarding any aspect of our publications—please feel free
to contact us at news@utphighereducation.com or visit our Internet site at www.utorontopress.com.

North America	UK, Ireland, and continental Europe
5201 Dufferin Street	NBN International
North York, Ontario, Canada, M3H 5T8	Estover Road, Plymouth, PL6 7PY, UK
	ORDERS PHONE: 44 (0) 1752 202301
2250 Military Road	ORDERS FAX: 44 (0) 1752 202333
Tonawanda, New York, USA, 14150	ORDERS E-MAIL: enquiries@nbninternational.com

ORDERS PHONE: 1–800–565–9523
ORDERS FAX: 1–800–221–9985
ORDERS E-MAIL: utpbooks@utpress.utoronto.ca

Every effort has been made to contact copyright holders; in the event of an error or omission,
please notify the publisher.

The University of Toronto Press acknowledges the financial support for its publishing activities of
the Government of Canada through the Canada Book Fund.

CONTENTS

ILLUSTRATIONS

ACKNOWLEDGEMENTS

Karen and I met while teaching a methods course in anthropology at York University. Our love of the discipline is what led us to finally write this book. We consider ourselves to be anthropologists who proudly work "at home" with a singular focus on culture in North America. A special thanks to all the undergraduate students who helped us better understand how to teach anthropological methods, and how to make this defining characteristic of the discipline accessible and valuable to others. It is our hope that this book will provide the tools for understanding others' cultures and subcultures in a world that is so diverse. We have tailored this book to North American students' projects, but we think that it might also be useful to anthropologists living and teaching in other places as well.

The relationships we developed with our contributors over the past few years are very important to us and to the integrity of this book. Not surprisingly, the group of North American anthropologists, Canadian and American, featured in this book are generous individuals who are devoted to cultural anthropology and its development as a discipline. They are all keenly aware that, as a discipline, cultural anthropology attempts to remain current while relying and focusing on century-old foundations in terms of theory and method. Their reflections on fieldwork experiences provide a holistic view of what cultural anthropologists do, think about, and strive to achieve. Each vignette was carefully crafted by our contributors with the aim of inspiring a new generation of cultural anthropologists, as well as others interested in qualitative methods. What they have decided to share are personal descriptions of what it is really like to be "out in the field." Thank you!

We would also like to thank the team of production managers, editors, and others at the University of Toronto for their timely work and pleasant communication. In particular, we would like to thank Anne Brackenbury, who is an amazing editor. Without Anne's help, this book would not have been as clear, concise, and comprehensive as it is. Thanks, Anne! Also, a special thanks to the reviewers who helped us hone the details of the book over the past few years. Although we will never know who you are, we hope you see your carefully crafted and constructive criticisms in the text.

INTRODUCTION

As an anthropology student, you have likely encountered many troubling, romanticized stereotypes about the discipline. Karen McGarry remembers once giving her incoming freshman students an exercise that asked them to write down the first five words that came to mind when they heard the term "anthropology." She then made a word cloud that highlighted many of their common stereotypes about the discipline:

FIGURE 0.1: Word cloud generated on the first day of class by first-year anthropology students in response to the question, "What do you think anthropology is?" Karen McGarry, September 2015.

Many of you have undoubtedly challenged people's misconceptions of anthropology as the study of the "exotic" or of "dinosaurs." However, such essentialist public perceptions of the discipline are difficult to change in the face of sensationalist discoveries reported by *National Geographic* or *Discovery Channel*, which typically privilege archaeology over other disciplines. Similarly, the mainstream media tends to foreground visual representations of "exotic" peoples and locales, while sensationalist images of Otherness are frequently perpetuated in popular films, such as the *Indiana Jones* series.

Many of you have probably also had to justify your choice of anthropology as a major to your parents or other family members. In an environment where metrics and financial outcomes increasingly dictate notions of individual "success," anthropology has been hailed as a poor choice of major for an undergraduate. In 2012, anthropology was positioned first in a ranked list of the ten worst college majors by *Forbes* magazine. Ranked on the basis of postgraduation incomes and unemployment rates, anthropology, it seems, is stereotyped as an interesting yet impractical major. Within the context of an increasingly neoliberal educational environment with corporatizing tendencies, universities are often expected to teach their "consumers" practical skills for long-term employment. Whether or not your professors support such trends, we are faced with an important question: Where does this leave anthropology? Long imagined (erroneously) as a strictly "academic" discipline that caters to the esoteric research interests of people with PhDs, anthropology, even sociocultural anthropology, can seem lacking in practical applicability. Do sociocultural anthropology and, particularly, **ethnographic methods** and **ethnography** have any relevance today? The point here is that, if the general public (including your potential employers) position anthropology as the study of far away, exotic "Others" (including dinosaurs!) and as irrelevant to seemingly "modern" concerns, then what is the relevance of sociocultural anthropology—and particularly its focus upon qualitative, ethnographic methods—in today's job market? Why study anthropology, and why or how is it increasingly important in an era when quantitative, **big data** tends to be promoted and favored within many government and corporate sectors as a form of solutions-oriented and problem-based research?

With liberal arts education under increasing scrutiny for its perceived lack of relevance and utility in today's job market, we hope to highlight how and why the methods and **methodologies** used by sociocultural anthropologists increasingly "matter" in helping to address a variety of research questions, "real life" issues, and social and cultural problems. Throughout this book, we seek to de-exoticize anthropology, its methods, and its methodologies, and to highlight how you, as a student of anthropology, can conduct meaningful and relevant qualitative, ethnographic research within a variety of academic and nonacademic settings within North America.

Why Ethnography and Why Now?

In 2008, Chris Anderson, the editor in chief of *Wired* magazine, argued that the growing availability of big data, made possible through the increasing surveillance of public Internet searches (as evidenced by projects such as *Google Flu)*, will render qualitative research obsolete. The sheer enormity of data concerning people's lives, cultural beliefs, and social perspectives that is at the disposal of social scientists negates the need for other forms of data collection and interpretation. Within this context, what is ethnography's purpose, and is it still relevant? Indeed, many anthropologists express concerns about the ever-increasing reliance on big data to solve or even understand social problems (e.g., Boellstorff and Maurer 2014; Collins 2014; MacPhail 2015). Nevertheless, Theresa MacPhail (2015) makes a compelling case for a synergy of quantitative "big data" with ethnographic qualitative research. In the midst of doing ethnographic fieldwork at the US Centers for Disease Control and Prevention (CDC) in 2009, she witnessed researchers' panicked responses to the H1N1 influenza pandemic and their attempts to "make sense" of the big data at their disposal. As she argues,

> They [the researchers] spent hours scanning a vast ocean of online data for the latest lab reports, accurate case counts, clinical information on hospital cases, and whether or not patient samples had tested positive for influenza and had been typed as H1. Those initial numbers and reports hadn't told them much. The data that was floating around was also missing contextual information that would help the CDC's analysts to make better sense of the information they already had. What they still needed was on-the-ground knowledge and human interpretations of the information already available, not simply more data.

Qualitative research thus provides necessary contextual information (via individual stories and narratives of personalized experiences) to help investigators interpret quantitative data. Contrary to the many popular assumptions, the term "big data" does not mean "raw" data, in the sense that all data constitute temporally, spatially, and culturally constructed knowledge. As Boellstorff (2013) argues, "there is no Archimedean point of pure data outside conceptual worlds." It is within this context that ethnographic methods can contribute to our understanding of big data. Writing for the blog *Ethnography Matters*, Tricia Wang (2013) appropriates Clifford Geertz's notion of "thick description" to argue that ethnographic methods not only provide a context for understanding big data but also add a rich, textured, and descriptive explanatory paradigm for the varied meanings of human behavior. In addition, ethnography can help capture the diversity of human experiences that mere statistics cannot provide. As Wang (2013) articulates, "Big data reveals insights with a particular range of data points, while thick data reveals the social context of and connections between data points. Big data delivers numbers; thick data delivers stories. Big data relies on machine learning; thick data relies on human learning."

Given the potential contributions of ethnographic methods to the study of human behaviors, anthropologists are increasingly aware of the need to encourage their students to think about how a specifically ethnographic perspective can be employed both inside and outside of academia to help understand or even "solve" tangible social problems. Anthropologists, for instance, are in growing demand within corporate sectors in such fields as marketing and advertising (e.g., McCracken 2011), within health services, and in a variety of governmental and nongovernmental contexts. It is thus imperative for undergraduate students to gain tangible experience in ethnographic fieldwork methods and methodologies. Given growing university pressures and mandates to increase experiential and/or "active" educational opportunities for students (Kolb and Kolb 2005), anthropological fieldwork methods courses will likely see increased growth. The benefit is that students will be equipped to utilize these methods within their varied nonacademic places of employment.

Indeed, many large corporations now hire anthropologists. For example, Intel Corporation, founded in 1968 in California, is now a multinational corporation whose engineers invent computer processors, microchips, cellular phones, and products for other large corporations such as Apple. In 1998, Intel hired anthropologist Genevieve Bell to explore consumer demands and trends of the future (see Singer 2014). Her work was deemed so successful that Intel expanded its team of social scientists (many of whom are anthropologists) to over 100 individuals who travel around the world to examine how people use various technologies at home and at work. Key here is the idea that different cultural groups have different perceptions of the value of various technologies, and different technological needs.

Ultimately, then, ethnographic methods "matter" within both academic and nonacademic settings, yet Tim Ingold (2014) argues that it is necessary to further uproot the discipline from its academic stronghold and to make anthropology count within a wider public sphere by reimagining what constitutes "ethnographicness" (383). Ingold states that anthropology's narrow definition of what counts as "ethnographic" (a study conducted during official fieldwork sojourns of specific periods) is causing the discipline to descend into a state of irrelevancy and that it is necessary to rethink how ethnography can and should be conducted in a variety of contemporary contexts. He asks, for example, why it is that everyday encounters and conversations or routinized events are never imagined as "ethnographic."

Ethnography, he argues, is best understood as an open-ended, nonlinear process of education that oftentimes results in unexpected interpersonal engagements and insights. Methods such as participant observation "are contingent on the circumstances and advance toward no end. They rather tread ways of carrying on and of being carried, of living life with others—humans and non-humans all—that is cognizant of the past, attuned to the conditions of the present and speculatively open to the possibilities of the future" (Ingold 2014, 390). With this in mind, then, we must examine why *anthropological* ethnography still matters. In an environment where related disciplines like sociology increasingly claim to make use of similar research methods and where the term "ethnographic" is often used as a synonym for "qualitative research," what makes ethnographic fieldwork, traditionally viewed as an anthropological "rite of passage" and a hallmark of sociocultural anthropology, unique?

Ethnography Matters!

Anthropologist Kirin Narayan (2014) argues that *anthropological* ethnography helps foster the development of a socially responsible citizenship as well as build several essential traits within an increasingly multicultural and cosmopolitan world. She attests that ethnography should be valued:

> For the discipline of paying attention; for learning from others; for becoming more responsibly aware of inequalities; for better understanding the social forces causing suffering and how people might somehow find hope; and most generally, for being perpetually pulled beyond the limits of one's own taken-for-granted world. (Narayan 2014, para. 2)

Fieldwork positions anthropologists to understand the sociohistorical roots of various forms of social inequality, and its consequences. Because anthropologists advocate for understanding cultural perspectives from the viewpoints of those that they study, they are well equipped to explore local and global interconnections and how various structural forces perpetuate inequalities. For example, anthropologists are specialists in understanding the nuanced ways in which different societies adapt and respond to various forms of internal and external change, such as warfare or political conflict, colonialism, or other factors. Because societies are understood as dynamic and constantly in flux, anthropological fieldwork seeks detailed and historical analyses of cultural perceptions of various phenomena predicated upon

thick description. One example, for instance, is **globalization**. Although globalization was often viewed as a culturally divisive phenomenon, it has become, among other things, an important lens through which notions of cultural change and appropriation can be understood through the use of thick description and through integrating the perspectives of multiple actors. Globalization is now perceived by many anthropologists as a justification for ethnography, as it can capture the detailed, complicated, and localized effects of globalization on various communities. In other words, globalization does not have the same effect everywhere. It was often assumed, for instance, that globalization would lead to increasing cross-cultural homogeneity within societies, or increasing sameness. This has been referred to as Americanization, McDonaldization, or Disneyfication, among other terms. In other words, the idea was that "local culture" (e.g., local cuisine, language, clothing, worldview) would dissipate and eventually be subsumed by trade liberalization and the global circulation of mainstream American media, as well as of mass-produced commodities. However, ethnographic fieldwork has explored how cultures respond to the forces of globalization and has demonstrated that people often resist globalization or syncretize it with their own culture. In some societies, we see a surge in ethnic, religious, or national identifications in response to the perceived threat of globalization and the perceived hegemony of Western—and particularly American—economics and secularism. Thomas Hylland Eriksen (2015), in response to the Paris attacks by ISIS in 2015, argues that anthropology is essential in challenging us/them dichotomies and pervasive stereotypes about the supposed dangers of Islam. He argues that to understand how ISIS rose to power, we need to position it within a larger geopolitical framework of social and economic inequality, as well as regional politics and cultural differences (such as gender segregation and regional population growth). He argues that most Western discourses of ISIS, which dismiss the group as a dangerous religious fringe cult, fail to address the larger economic and political issues that have contributed to its rise to power (Eriksen 2015). In many ways, then, ethnographic approaches, with their focus upon cultural complexity and global-local interrelations, among other factors, have allowed us to understand, with a great degree of nuance and complexity, how cultures change and adapt to new situations.

Doing Anthropology "At Home"

Next to dinosaurs, one of the long-standing stereotypes and misconceptions about anthropology is that the discipline is still exclusively concerned with fieldwork and research among non-Western peoples and places. At the turn of the twentieth century, anthropology distinguished itself as a discipline that focused upon the study of "Others," and those Others were typically non-Western and located in faraway and seemingly "exotic" places. As Gupta and Ferguson (1997, 36) explain, there existed a "hierarchy of purity" with respect to field sites, with a strong disdain for "local" fieldwork, and an emphasis upon the "exotic" as more authentically anthropological. For North American sociocultural anthropologists, this criterion of Otherness was often fulfilled through a focus upon fieldwork among various Indigenous peoples of the Americas. As discussed in Chapter 1, Franz Boas and his many students, for instance, embarked upon several research projects to document the cultures and traditions of Indigenous peoples. By the mid-twentieth century, however, some anthropologists had departed from this trend to study peoples and places closer to "home" in both a geographical and cultural sense. Hortense Powdermaker (1950), for instance, studied Hollywood culture, conducting interviews and participant observation among directors and film executives. By the 1970s, Laura Nader (1972) encouraged anthropologists to study "up," or to conduct fieldwork among individuals occupying positions of power and authority, often within their own cultural contexts. This trend, combined with other factors, contributed to a growing acceptance of doing anthropology "at home." For example, according to Munthali (2001), processes of decolonization, increasing student enrollments at universities, and decreased funding opportunities have led many Western anthropologists to study within their own cultural contexts. These days, you are just as likely to see an anthropologist conducting fieldwork on urban planning in Chicago as you are to find an anthropologist studying rituals in Papua New Guinea.

The fieldwork that many of you will embark upon will most likely be conducted at "home" in North American contexts (or even online). It is important to recognize that your "local" fieldwork is just as important anthropologically as fieldwork conducted in faraway places. Many of you will make important contributions to pertinent research issues or questions that are of importance to many people within your own communities. As we articulate throughout this text, community-based engagement and collaboration have become important and expected aspects of fieldwork methods and ethics. And increasingly, various community organizations are recognizing the important contributions that anthropologists can make to people's lives. At the university of one of the editors of this text, for instance, a community engagement or outreach department accepts requests for research assistance from nonprofit organizations such as homeless shelters, immigrant outreach centers, and charitable organizations, among others. Anthropology students are often recruited to conduct qualitative research to help address various "problems." Recently, for example, a call went out to request assistance in helping to address the cultural, emotional, linguistic, and physical challenges that many new Syrian immigrants to the Toronto area are experiencing. Anthropology students help conduct interviews and participant observation among immigrant communities and devise practical solutions to help people transition into Canadian society. In the process, the students receive university credits for independent study research.

The fieldwork that you do "at home" matters. In addition to the growing awareness of the usefulness of anthropological methods in the corporate sector, as discussed previously, many other organizations are beginning to recognize that anthropological research can help build stronger, more sustainable relationships among people, particularly within cosmopolitan and culturally diverse communities. A newly developing field of "transcultural nursing," for instance, posits that nurses benefit from learning intensively about the various cultural practices and beliefs of their patients and that anthropological training helps nurses provide more culturally relevant care for them (Maier-Lorentz 2008). Similarly, with the resurgence of racialized tension and violence in parts of the United States between the police and African-American populations, there has been much public discussion about contracting anthropologists to study these issues and train police in anthropological methods and issues. In a blog post, Jen Simpson (2014) argues that at least three benefits can be derived from connecting anthropologists and police departments:

1. Anthropologists can help police leaders better understand their departments and personnel and identify opportunities to offer better police services to communities.
2. Anthropologists can help police leaders translate policing to the public and bridge ethical considerations in the implementation of crime prevention policies.
3. By understanding police culture, police leaders can create policy and practices that highlight the spirit of service in policing and emphasize legitimacy, transparency and public confidence.

In particular, it is the qualitative, ethnographic *methods* employed by anthropologists—long-term research, in-depth interviews, the establishment of rapport with informants, and participant observation, among other approaches—that differentiate the discipline from other social science disciplines, such as psychology, which typically use more expedient methods (e.g., surveys). Anthropologists aim to understand *why* people behave the way that they do and how such behaviors are shaped by culture.

Getting Ready for Fieldwork and Reading This Text

Ultimately, our goal is to prepare you for your first fieldwork experiences. The remaining chapters draw upon examples from fieldwork conducted in American and Canadian contexts. Throughout, we are mindful that many of you will be expected to conduct short fieldwork projects within your classes. Given the constraints of ethics approval committees, combined with the logistics of financial and time restrictions, most of you (if you are not away at an ethnographic field school) will probably be conducting your fieldwork "at home" or even online. Most likely, you will conduct interviews or participant observation in your own language and in a somewhat familiar setting. Some of you will work in rural areas, while others will conduct research with various communities of people in places such as Los Angeles or Montreal. The chapters in this text seek to approximate the different realities and fieldwork situations that you might face. Over the years, our experience teaching undergraduate methods classes has taught us that many of the ethnographic examples used in various texts emphasize sensationalistic events or ethical issues (violence, murder, drug warfare, humanitarian crises), which function to exoticize and "Other" already marginalized groups of people (even if that is not what the anthropologist intends). Each of the remaining chapters contains an original vignette highlighting the fieldwork experiences of a North American anthropologist who conducts research in locations and on issues that you may face. Many of the questions they address are academic (e.g., Chapter 2), while others are applied or practical concerns (Chapter 7). These vignettes function to highlight how anthropological issues, questions, and methods are used in corporate, medical, or other settings. Many contributors also emphasize the increasingly important nature of collaborative research, in which the anthropologist works closely with informants to ensure that the research questions asked, as well as the representations of people that are produced in ethnographies, films, or other media, are meaningful to informants. Increasingly, many anthropologists view collaboration as an ethical responsibility, and they involve their informants very closely in all stages of the research and writing process.

Throughout this text, we stress how it is possible to carry out ethnographic fieldwork in multiple locales throughout North America and on multiple issues. At the same time, however, one's choice of a fieldwork "site" is imbued with important political considerations, including an assessment of the power relations between you and your interlocutors as well as a consideration of ethical issues. Should ethnographers, for instance, be able to create field sites wherever, whenever, and with whom they please? In the late nineteenth or early twentieth centuries, few anthropologists were concerned with such issues, and they rarely sought the permission of those they "studied." These days, however, this position is untenable within the framework of the decolonizing methodologies advocated in Chapter 1, for example. It is therefore important, when thinking about working with a particular group of people, not only to obtain informed consent but also to think critically about the possible outcomes of your research and about how your project or research question may affect (both positively and negatively) your interlocutors. Moreover, how are the particular written or visual representations that you cultivate perceived by those with whom you work? Finally, we hope to get you thinking about how and why particular fieldwork "sites" may be easier to access immediately while others might take time. How, for instance, does your positionality in terms of age, gender, ethnicity, race, sexuality (among other factors) contribute to your ability to access particular people? Moreover, are there some field sites that should be off-limits to anthropologists? These concerns of ethics, positionality, informed consent, and anthropology's legacy of colonialism are addressed within various chapters of this text. Ultimately, it is important to think about the politics of your research and to ask yourself how and why you select particular groups of people to work with—and how the research and writing process affects them.

To help guide your reading of this text, we have included several pedagogical features to encourage you to think critically about what you have read and to make connections between individual chapter content and the ethnographic vignettes. For example, every chapter's vignette ends with a section called "Making Connections," which consists of a series of questions that encourage you to connect the broader theoretical or methodological points in the chapter with various examples highlighted in the ethnographic vignettes. Each chapter's vignette has been carefully selected to provide a "real world," relatable example of issues discussed throughout the chapter. The end of each chapter also contains sections called "Try This" and "Possible Projects." The "Try This" section lists a variety of relatively short activities that your professor might assign (some in class and some out of class) to help you put various methods or ideas to practical use. The "Possible Projects" section consists of examples of larger, term-length projects emphasizing a particular method or issue discussed throughout the chapter. Keep in mind, however, that none of these activities should be attempted without permission of and consultation with your professor or instructor. You'll need ethics clearance for some of these activities or projects (see Chapter 4), and your instructor will provide guidance on these ethical requirements.

This text is divided into four sections. Part I, "Origins and Basics," consists of four chapters. Chapter 1 explores the origin and development of sociocultural anthropological fieldwork in North America. It addresses some of the unique qualities, research emphases, and historical trajectories of North

American anthropological fieldwork, and it introduces students to the contributions of key anthropologists such as Franz Boas. Throughout, it highlights the relationship between anthropology and colonialism and examines the long-standing North American research emphasis upon North American Indigenous peoples. This chapter's vignette, by Niki Thorne, represents an attempt at decolonizing anthropology, whereby the traditional (and asymmetrical) power relationships between anthropologists and their interlocutors are critically examined and challenged. In Chapter 2, we consider one of the discipline's key ethnographic methods, participant observation. Throughout, this chapter examines different types of participant observation and how it has changed over time to consider new field "sites"—for example, virtual worlds. George Gmelch's vignette on his fieldwork among minor and major league baseball players draws attention to the importance of considerations such as identity and positionality in fieldwork processes. In contrast, Chapter 3 looks at issues surrounding fieldwork ethics and the politics of fieldwork. In other words, what are your responsibilities to your informants? What is informed consent? In her vignette, Jen Shannon discusses the ethical obligations and challenges of conducting fieldwork among Indigenous peoples of North America. Given the long and deleterious history of colonialism and the negative, often exploitative, interactions with anthropologists that many Indigenous peoples have faced, Shannon explores what an "ethical" form of anthropological engagement looks like. Throughout her vignette, she stresses the importance of collaborating with and involving Indigenous groups at all levels of anthropological research. Finally, Chapter 4 provides you with information on conducting interviews and covers topics such as how to approach people and develop rapport, how to develop questions, and how to conduct different types of interviews. This chapter's vignette is by Dianna Shandy, who conducted fieldwork among Nuer immigrants in Minnesota. Throughout, we learn how she set up interviews, established a sense of trust with her informants, engaged in interviews, and developed her research questions.

Part II, "Notes, Data, and Representation," comprises three chapters. This section of the text deals primarily with the "how to" aspects of ethnographic methods. Chapter 5, "How to Create Field Notes," for instance, discusses how, when, where, and why you need to document your ethnographic experiences. In this text, you are provided with information on different types of field notes and schooled in the importance of taking detailed notes, whether you do this by hand or electronically. Though the individual wishes of your informants and the research context are important factors to respect when writing your notes, it is important to remember that your field notes function not only as mnemonic aids for the inevitable process of "writing up" your work but as a marker of critical issues, topics, and perspectives delineated by your informants.

In this chapter's vignette, Elizabeth Greenspan discusses her fieldwork on memorials and processes of memorialization by visitors to the former World Trade Center site in the aftermath of 9/11. Particular attention is devoted to a practical discussion of what she documented in her field notes and how she went about creating her notes. Chapter 6 focuses on the analysis of your data. Once your fieldwork is complete, you will find that you have a plethora of field notes, audio and video recordings, and transcripts. Inevitably, only a portion of this data will be "used" within the context of your final project or essay. But how do you sort through your data and filter out the "extraneous"? This chapter teaches you one method to sort your data through the use of different types of coding. This process will enable you to use your data effectively and efficiently in a way that sheds light on your original research question. Karen McGarry wrote the vignette and discusses how she sorted and analyzed her ethnographic data on Canadian figure skaters. The final chapter in this section, Chapter 7, focuses on "writing up" research. Particular attention is paid to the ethics and practice of representing your informants, as well as to the importance of situating your work within the context of existing anthropological literature and previous research conducted on your topic. Anthropologist Kathryn Dudley discusses her fieldwork among artisanal guitar makers in the United States. Adopting a reflexive approach, she explores the issue of who is representing whom within the practice and writing of fieldwork experiences. In many ways, the anthropologist, within the context of fieldwork, becomes akin to a new student of a cultural experience. This very idea challenges long-standing assumptions about the anthropologist as "expert." If such a role reversal takes place, then what impact does this have for the practice of writing and representation?

Part III, called "Shifting Field Sites," comprises two chapters, both of which document shifting developments within the discipline: the growing importance of applied approaches and of the expansion of applied field "sites" in anthropology, on the one hand, and the importance of discussing and recognizing one's positionality, on the other. Chapter 8 focuses upon a discussion of the different contexts within which applied anthropologists work. Caura Wood, an anthropologist who is also an executive at an oil company in Calgary, Alberta, explores how she negotiated entry into her fieldwork in the oil industry—and how she developed rapport with her informants. Chapter 9 examines the growing importance of critically examining the relationship between identity and fieldwork. In other words, how do informants' perceptions of an anthropologist's race, class, nationality, ethnicity, gender, sexuality, or other factors impact the fieldwork experience? Moreover, what factors (e.g., grant money) impose limitations on fieldwork projects? This chapter's vignette is by Jean Briggs. Briggs's excerpt from her ethnography, *Never in Anger: Portrait of an*

Eskimo Family (1970), highlights how her individual personality and emotions played a role in her forming relationships with informants. Her work is one of the first autoethnographic accounts written by an anthropologist, and represents a move away from the supposed objectivity of previous, modernist forms of writing within the discipline.

Many anthropologists incorporate visual technologies into their research methods, as photographs, film, or digital forms of media are meaningful and increasingly prevalent ways in which we interact with the world. The final section of this text, Part IV, titled "Visual Aids," consists of three chapters that deal with some of these issues. Chapter 10 focuses on a method called "photo-elicitation," which consists of the practice of looking at and discussing digital or hard copies of photographs with informants to elicit memories of past events and experiences. Lynda Mannik's vignette explores issues of memory, emotion, and collaboration among Estonian refugees who came to Canada from Sweden on the SS *Walnut* in 1948, and it provides an example of how and why the addition of photographs into interviewing can help people remember past events, current identities, and hopes for the future. Chapter 11, in contrast, focuses on the history and use of ethnographic film within anthropology. Jennifer Cool's vignette traces her research among new suburban homeowners in California to examine how and why they are motivated to pursue the "American Dream" of homeownership. Throughout, she documents how she approached and interviewed informants and the various processes and challenges involved in creating an anthropological film. Finally, Chapter 12 is a coauthored collaboration by François Dengah and his undergraduate students. He documents his and his students' experiences playing the online game *Guild Wars 2*; he includes discussions concerning issues of accessibility, obtaining informed consent, and conducting online participant observation and interviews.

Ultimately, we hope that this text provides you with tangible advice and accessible examples of ethnographic fieldwork to get you started on your own fieldwork. Although every fieldwork situation will be unique, we address many of the ethical and logistical challenges that you may face, and we highlight how anthropology "at home" matters.

PART I

Origins and Basics

CHAPTER 1

THE ORIGINS AND DEVELOPMENT OF SOCIOCULTURAL ANTHROPOLOGICAL FIELDWORK IN NORTH AMERICA

Introduction

Chances are, as an anthropology student enrolled in a methods class, you are looking at the title of this chapter and thinking, "Ugh. Why do we have to know *this*?" Given the current pedagogical shift toward privileging tangible, practical, and hands-on experiential forms of education in an apparent effort to increase one's employability, many students might view the study of anthropological history as a waste of time. But all academic disciplines have their own origin stories, or narratives, of how and why the discipline developed. These narratives are critical for understanding the ideas posited by many of anthropology's early twentieth-century thinkers, which continue to form the theoretical and methodological basis of the discipline. Debates in contemporary cultural anthropology ranged from adopting or dismissing ideas espoused by pioneer theorists such as Franz Boas or Margaret Mead. So to understand where the discipline is headed, we need a sense of historical context. Given that this text focuses extensively upon North American examples of fieldwork, we also should address what (if anything) makes North American anthropological traditions unique.

Throughout this chapter, we document the transition from "armchair" anthropology to "modern" fieldwork methods as espoused by anthropologists such as Franz Boas, with a specific focus on the development of fieldwork in North American contexts. We also examine some of the distinctive features of "North American" anthropology. For example, many anthropologists (e.g., Darnell and Valentine 1999; Harrison and Darnell 2006; Stocking 1983) have argued that one of the defining features of early fieldwork in North America is its emphasis upon fieldwork among Indigenous communities. Thus, it is important to contextualize and think critically about the legacy of this trend. To what extent, for instance, was Boas's notion of "salvage anthropology" (unintentionally) ethnocentric? Did these early anthropologists help or hinder Indigenous peoples? Furthermore, in what ways were Indigenous peoples "Othered" by anthropologists?

In addition, this chapter examines the changing nature of fieldwork in North America since the 1970s. We explore decolonizing trends within the discipline and how the "reflexive turn" has encouraged anthropologists to be aware of their own positionality, which in turn shines a light on how social hierarchies, power differentials, and people's perceptions of identities (e.g., gender, sexuality, race, class) impact the fieldwork experience in terms of ethics, representation and writing, and fieldwork engagements. Within this context, we examine these and similar questions: Can we think of the process of fieldwork as subjective, as objective, or are these dichotomies problematic? How does fieldwork impact our interactions with others? Furthermore, what is a field "site?" Is it a place, an idea, a cultural construct, or something else?

The Roots of Ethnographic Fieldwork in North America

If you were an anthropologist conducting ethnographic fieldwork in North America at the turn of the twentieth century, what would it have looked like? And how have things changed over the years? It was in the first half of the twentieth century, largely due to the efforts of anthropologists such as Franz Boas (and his many students), that fieldwork became institutionalized into what George Stocking (1983, 7–8) has described as

> a kind of shared archetypical experience that informs, if it does not generate, a system of generalized methodological values or disciplinary ideology: the value placed on fieldwork itself as the basic constituting experience not only of anthropological knowledge but of anthropologists; the value placed on a holistic approach to the cultures (or societies) that are the subject of this form of knowledge; the value placed on the equal valuation of all such entities; and the value placed on their uniquely privileged role in the constitution of anthropological theory.... It has, in short, been the legitimizing basis for anthropology's claim to special cognitive authority.

Fieldwork's unique status as a shared and definitive marker of disciplinary expertise, however, was only solidified within the last century. In the middle to late 1800s and into the early 1900s, armchair anthropology was still the norm (although it existed alongside early fieldwork efforts).

As Kuklick (1997, 53–55) explains, most anthropologists of this period, the clear majority of whom were male, upper or upper middle class, and white, perceived themselves as "gentleman scholars" and as theorists. The physical practice of fieldwork was thus often viewed as beneath them, and they preferred to work from their "armchairs," often using a **comparative approach** to interpret secondary data written by explorers, missionaries, or others who came in direct contact with various Indigenous peoples throughout the world. From this standpoint, they often created theories and generalizations about different societies, with **unilineal evolution** being one example. However, as anthropologists began to leave their armchairs to travel to colonized nations, often as the guests of colonial administrators, they gradually began to abandon their armchair methods in favor of longer and more sustained forms of engagements with their informants. Long-term interactions involving both qualitative (e.g., participant observation, interviews) and quantitative methods gradually became the norm.

In North America, contemporary fieldwork traditions have their origins in a diverse array of anthropological and proto-anthropological traditions (Darnell 2008), including British, French, and German philosophical, scientific, and anthropological paradigms. Even before the professionalization of the discipline between the late 1800s and early 1900s, and the pioneering influence of Franz Boas, several early fieldwork expeditions and projects by amateur anthropologists were aimed at understanding various aspects of Indigenous cultures. Some of these efforts were in the vein of armchair approaches, while others made early attempts to leave their armchairs for the field. Inspired by the modernist and scientific goals of the Enlightenment, much early research sought to record and classify Indigenous cultures. For example, John Pickering (1777–1846), a lawyer and amateur linguist, attempted to document and classify a variety of Indigenous languages. Similarly, Henry Rowe Schoolcraft (1793–1864), a geographer and geologist, recorded Ojibway texts and language. Politician Lewis Cass (1782–1866) designed surveys to map cultural and linguistic diversity among a variety of Indigenous populations (see Darnell 2008). Hinsley (1983) argues that not until the late 1800s was there a sustained effort to record and understand Indigenous peoples. In the 1880s, Frank Hamilton Cushing of the Bureau of American Ethnology (BAE) "pioneered the method of participant-observation in North America" with his fieldwork among the Zuni (Hinsley 1983, 56). The BAE stressed "particularistic" anthropology that emphasized the individual histories and nuances of particular cultures rather than cultivating cross-cultural generalizations. In Canada, Diamond Jenness (1886–1969) made several expeditions to study Inuit culture, documenting their way of life. Perhaps the most famous of these early amateur anthropologists, however, was Lewis Henry Morgan

(1818–81), a lawyer from upper New York State. Influenced not only by the cultural proclivity toward classification that dominated this time but also by the popularity of social evolutionary models of human behavior, Morgan studied and worked among various Iroquoian populations in upper New York State and authored publications such as *Ancient Society* (1877) and *The League of the Ho-dé-no-sau-nee, or Iroquois* (1851). His goal, however, was to employ a comparative method to sort and classify different types of societies along an evolutionary scale of progress, called unilineal evolution.

It is important to note that, while many early scholars developed friendships and rapport among the Indigenous peoples they worked with, as Morgan did, they were also very much a by-product of their time. Morgan, for example, was writing from the perspective of a white, colonial, upper-class man who ethnocentrically positioned capitalism and technology as markers of success and achievement. In *Ancient Society* (1877), for instance, he argued that all societies progress from simple to complex via a series of three unilineal stages: savagery, barbarism, and civilization. The movement from one stage to another, according to Morgan, was marked by changes in technology. "Savagery" was the stage of hunting and gathering societies that had few material possessions while "barbarism" was marked by the development of agriculture. Finally, "civilized" societies, positioned at the apex of a ladder of progress, possessed art, advanced technologies, and science.

Obviously, unilineal evolution is no longer considered a valid or productive way of thinking about various societies and notions of change over time. It has, however, had a significant legacy. Throughout this period, it was common, and expected, for anthropologists to conduct fieldwork among "Others"—a category usually imagined to consist of Indigenous peoples or other socially marginalized groups. Think for a moment, however, about the interpersonal and cultural dynamics that are implicated in these types of unequal power relationships. In the fieldwork of the late nineteenth and early to middle twentieth centuries, strict dichotomies between subject and object were apparent, and informants had little, if any, say in research design, implementation, or outcomes. This long history of ethically problematic work among Indigenous peoples is documented in a separate section below.

At the same time that Morgan was conducting his research, John Wesley Powell became the head of the BAE in 1879. This organization represented an early effort to professionalize the discipline. Much of the fieldwork conducted under the BAE was aimed (as was most fieldwork at the time) at Indigenous peoples. Hinsley (1983) argues that it was not until the late 1800s with the development of the BAE that there was a *sustained* and collective effort to record and understand Indigenous peoples through fieldwork.

In the 1880s, Cushing "pioneered the method of participant-observation in North America" (Hinsley 1983, 56) with his fieldwork among the Zuni. And, as Darnell (2008, 39) argues, John Powell

> was able to amass a database for understanding the American Indian by eliciting information from (usually unpaid) amateurs who were in contact with Indians, supplementing their labors with fieldwork by his permanent staff. The Bureau was the first American institution to assemble a team of paid anthropological researchers.

Although the BAE in conjunction with early collaborative efforts between museums and universities (e.g., the Peabody Museum and Harvard) represented clusters of professional anthropological work (Darnell 2008), it was not until the advent of Franz Boas that a distinctly "Americanist" tradition developed (Darnell 2008; Harrison and Darnell 2006; Hinsley 1983).

Indeed, as Regna Darnell (2008, 41) articulates, it was the German-born American anthropologist, Franz Boas, who embodied a distinctly North American tradition of anthropology. As she argues, "Boas was able to build on the fieldwork, the mapping exercises, the increasingly rigorous standards for research and reporting, the development of publication outlets and scientific studies, and the idea of anthropology as a professional science." (Darnell 2008, 41). He rejected evolutionary approaches, and through his fieldwork, he stressed the need for more intimate and personal relationships with informants through extended and repeated field trips to various locations (Darnell 2008). Instead of constructing generalizations about societies, Boas stressed the need for **historical particularism**—the idea that each society has its own unique history, so it is important during fieldwork to understand the overall context of human behaviors and actions. Leibing and McLean (2007, 7) comment upon the distinctiveness of "Boasian" North American traditions by comparing them with dominant British traditions:

> British social anthropology was fashioned as a social science that sought generalizable truth. Anthropologists sorted through their collected data to find regularities and cohesion in the confusion wrought by colonialism, and reported these in finished texts, undisturbed by personal sentiment. By the early part of the 20th century in the United States, however, anthropology had borne a distinctively Boasian appreciation for uniqueness and historical complexity. Drawing from his training in German Romantic idealism and materialism, Boas's science had antipositivist leanings that permitted, even sometimes encouraged, personal reflection in his students.

North American anthropology, then, has historically emphasized the importance of culture and its symbolic manifestations as a primary means of inquiry; the importance of historical particularism; and the importance of recognizing the seemingly subjective elements of the fieldwork experience, as evidenced by the widespread attention afforded to reflexivity, particularly after the 1980s. Boas also stressed the importance of political engagement and advocacy. Over the years, he critiqued scientific racism, classism, and other forms of social inequality, and he challenged the policies of governments and multinational corporations (Darnell 2008).

Over the years, fieldwork and conceptions of what constitutes a field "site" have also diversified and shifted away from the study of small-scale, "bounded" communities. This is due, in part, to the increasing recognition that no society is static or untouched by external forces, such as colonialism. Also partially responsible for this change is the advent of globalization, as well as its attendant effects: the development of online communities; the displacement of peoples via war, immigration, or other factors; and the proliferation of diasporic communities in North America.

North American Anthropology and Indigenous Peoples

As discussed, much early twentieth-century fieldwork among North American Indigenous peoples was conducted under the guidance of Franz Boas and his students. Boas felt that the combined forces of colonialism and acculturation, among other factors, were leading to rapid cultural changes among Indigenous groups. Indigenous peoples, he argued, ran the risk of "dying out" as they became increasingly Westernized and urbanized. Government initiatives that sought to assimilate Indigenous youth—for example, the residential school system in Canada—led to a loss of language, cultural heritage, and historical memory. Boas thus advocated for fieldwork aimed at **salvage ethnography**. He and his students felt that there was an urgent need to conduct fieldwork among Indigenous peoples and to collect songs, stories, personal histories, material artifacts, and other tangible items to document and preserve Indigenous cultural practices and beliefs for future generations— before they "disappeared" (see Gruber 1970). Though Boas undoubtedly had good intentions, his conception of salvage fieldwork can be critiqued for its colonial sensibilities and paternalistic underpinnings. In many ways, salvage anthropology is predicated upon the idea that Indigenous cultures are (and should be) static, authentic, and timeless. It ignores the fact that all cultures change over time in response to various internal and external forces and that there is no such thing as a bounded and "authentic" culture untainted by interactions with other groups of people. Consequently, it is erroneous to assume that Indigenous peoples are disappearing; like other cultural groups, they simply change over time. Nevertheless, as Audra Simpson (2007) attests, the notion that Indigenous peoples are "dying out" has had a legacy within academic analyses of indigeneity as well as within government policy. This idea has often resulted in positioning or representing (either intentionally or unintentionally) Indigenous peoples as somehow backward or static, thereby reinforcing Eurocentric colonial ideas about these peoples.

In 1969, the Indigenous author and activist Vine Deloria (1988) drew attention to the ways in which anthropological research among Indigenous communities was often informed by such colonial practices and ideas. Inspired by Indigenous critiques of anthropological research, as well as by the "postmodern turn" in the discipline, many anthropologists have sought to critique the methods and modes of representation of their anthropological predecessors. In the last decade, there have been many critiques of early fieldwork efforts among Indigenous peoples (e.g., Denzin et al. 2008). Over the years, cultural anthropologists have either explicitly or implicitly treated Indigenous peoples as laboratory subjects, and scholars have pointed out the detrimental links between some forms of fieldwork and colonialism:

> Sadly, qualitative research in many, if not all, of its forms (observation, participation, interviewing, ethnography) serves as a metaphor for colonial knowledge, for power, and for truth. The metaphor works this way: Research, quantitative and qualitative, is scientific. Research provides the foundation for reports about and representations of the other. In the colonial context, research becomes an objective way of representing the dark-skinned other to the White world. Colonizing nations relied on the human disciplines, especially sociology and anthropology, as well as their field note-taking journaling observers, to produce knowledge about strange and foreign worlds. This close involvement with the colonial project contributed, in significant ways, to qualitative research's long and anguished history, to its becoming a dirty word. (Denzin et al. 2008, 4)

The acknowledgment of the discipline's colonial heritage and legacy, which has filtered into contemporary fieldwork, has contributed to the proliferation of **decolonizing** efforts. Linda Tuhiwai Smith (2005) argues that decolonizing research involves "the unmasking and deconstruction of imperialism, and its aspect of colonialism, in its old and new formations alongside a search for sovereignty; for reclamation of knowledge, language, and culture; and for the social transformation of the colonial relations between the native and the settler" (88).

In other words, from an anthropological perspective, decolonization involves thinking critically about how processes of colonialism inform our methods and methodologies. This may include an examination of power differentials between researchers and informants, colonial notions of authority and the privileged positionality historically afforded to the ethnographer, and other factors. As we discuss in Chapter 7 on "Writing Up," the vocabulary and images that we select as anthropologists when we write ethnographies can have a sustained political or economic impact on the lives of those we work with. It is thus important to think critically about how our research impacts Indigenous (and other) groups. It also involves being culturally sensitive to the needs and desires of Indigenous communities.

In terms of fieldwork and research methods, the decolonization of research may take the form of collaborative efforts at fieldwork, research, and writing. In Chapter 3's vignette, for instance, Jen Shannon discusses her work with the Mandan Hidatsa Arikara Nation of North Dakota. Her university museum possessed material culture deemed sacred to them, and Shannon was interested in conducting research on the acquisition and eventual repatriation of some of these items. What she discovered was that her research questions and methods (which ultimately entailed the production of a documentary film on the life of the missionary who donated approximately 400 items to her museum) was conceived of in collaboration with the Mandan Hidatsa Arikara. Though she imagined that they might have been angry or resentful toward Reverend Case, the missionary who worked among their ancestors and donated their sacred items to a museum, she found they wanted to learn more about him, and they requested that a film be produced about his life. In this way, both her fieldwork and the dissemination of her results were cocreated and negotiated phenomena.

In other cases, collaborative ethnography can take the form of activist-oriented research, as discussed by Niki Thorne in this chapter's vignette. Throughout, Thorne outlines her personal experiences of growing up near a Mi'kmaq reserve in Nova Scotia. Despite the fact that many of her close friends lived on the reserve and, in some cases, had attended residential schools, she was never aware of Canada's long history of colonialism and exploitation of First Nations peoples. Engaged, activist anthropology became, as she puts it, "deeply personal" for her. In this vignette, she outlines the types of activism that she became involved in, and she also discusses how, at times, she needed to step back from taking an activist role at the request of Indigenous elders.

VIGNETTE

Niki Thorne is a doctoral student in social anthropology at York University in Toronto. Her research focuses upon decolonizing theories and methodologies within the context of research among First Nations peoples, and, more recently, within the Ontario school curriculum.

FIGURE 1.1: Portrait of Niki Thorne, 2017. Photograph by Niki Thorne.

UNSETTLING SOLIDARITY: COMPLICATING DECOLONIZING METHODOLOGIES AND RETURNING TO THE EDGE OF THE WOODS

In 2006, hundreds of angry, mostly white townspeople gathered weekly to rally in opposition to the Six Nations reclamation of *kanonhstaton* ("the protected place"), also known as Douglas Creek Estates, in Caledonia, Ontario. Video footage shows local non-Native teenagers chanting "Burn, Natives, Burn," while warming their hands over barrels of fire to ward off the winter chill. One placard read, "Where is John Wayne When You Need Him?" while another proclaimed, "OKA STRIKE ONE. IPPERWASH STRIKE TWO. GAME OVER!!!" Some sang the Canadian national anthem, and many waved Canadian flags (see Figures 1.2 and 1.3).

Throughout the reclamation of *kanonhstaton*, clan mothers at Six Nations cautioned Indigenous land defenders to go about things in a good way, to be of good mind and good heart even when faced with racist backlash. Solidarity activists of settler descent were welcome to join land defenders and to stand in support of Six Nations—so long as

FIGURE 1.2: Outside the first meeting of the Caledonia "Militia," June 23, 2006. Photograph by Tyler Shipley.

FIGURE 1.3: Protest against the formation of the Caledonia "Militia," Cayuga, June 23, 2006. Photograph by Tyler Shipley.

we followed Indigenous leadership from a place of peace, respect, and friendship. On several occasions, solidarity activist groups in which I was involved took a dominant role in organizing in response to anti-Native backlash under a banner of decolonizing intentions. Over time, however, through a myriad of moments and experiences, it became clear that outsiders were often reproducing and upholding patriarchal patterns of power despite decolonizing intentions. Eventually, our network of activists from across southern Ontario was asked to leave Six Nations. We were asked by a small group of women, including two elders, to go back to the edge of the woods, to continue learning from a distance, to work on our own self-reflection, and to wait for an invitation before reengaging in further solidarity attempts.

Here, I recount some of my experiences of unsettling, including going back to the edge of the woods, as well as the years of lessons that preceded and the reflections that followed. These experiences have deepened and complicated my understanding of decolonizing methodologies, and have led to more questions: When do decolonizing efforts become recolonizing, upholding (neo)colonial relations of power? What does this mean for decolonizing methodologies in anthropology? What is distinct about the project of decolonization as opposed to other critical and transformative projects? Anthropological research that takes decolonization seriously must necessarily be unsettling. It must interrogate desires for collaboration as well as desires to do research with Indigenous people.

Research is inherently political, shaped by the past, present, and future, as well as by sociocultural and historical factors (see Dunbar 2008). It is therefore necessary to consider how I am inextricably implicated in settler colonialism. My ancestry is primarily white, Anglo-settler, from a lower-class family on the east coast of Canada with a history of trauma, abuse, and addictions. My body is read by others as white, female, and of a higher class than I actually come from. About six or seven formative years of my childhood took place growing up on a Mi'kmaq reserve in Nova Scotia, where I lived with my mother, her partner, and his kids. I took the bus each day from Indian Brook to school in Shubenacadie, but it was not until about ten years after moving away to southern Ontario, while attending a second-year university lecture, that I learned about the Shubenacadie residential school. Only then did I realize that the people I loved, the people who raised me, and my friends' parents, aunties, and uncles must have gone there.

I wondered how it was possible for me to grow up in this place and to never learn the histories of the reserve system, residential schools, or forced assimilation—colonial injustices that shaped the lives of the people I loved and considered family. This realization helped shape my approach to decolonizing methodologies. It positions me ambiguously, not only as an ally from a position of both settler privilege and complicity but also as someone whose family has been deeply hurt by colonialism. My commitment to decolonizing research is thus deeply personal, and it has been shaped by my past.

My research began as an undergraduate independent study analyzing racist and colonial discourses in news and activist video coverage of the Six Nations reclamation. It then blossomed into fieldwork involving participant observation with solidarity activists and Indigenous land defenders and interviews, as well as research at the Ontario archives, where I pored over old handwritten letters and government reports between colonial Indian agents and ministers of Indian Affairs to locate documentation supporting Six Nations and Tyendinaga land claims. Activist anthropology blended seamlessly and inseparably into solidarity activism for many years, and the years that followed brought insight and substance to my original fieldwork experiences.

My focus was on understanding the historical context leading up to the Six Nations reclamation of *kanonhstaton,* as well as settler-Canadian reactions to Indigenous land defense, including racist backlash. A decade later, I am investigating similar questions, but focusing my analysis on (neo)colonialism and settler Canadians. This refocusing— away from Indigenous ethnography and toward an anthropology of the (neo)colonizers—is largely due to lessons learned from well-intentioned solidarity activism repeatedly gone awry.

I have always conceptualized my research as decolonizing; however, it has taken me years to think through the methodological and conceptual complications to understand what this means. I worked to distinguish my research from traditional (colonizing) anthropological approaches in several ways. I sought to break away from traditions of studying "exotic" others in "exotic" places, favoring accountability, long-term commitment, and promoting social justice "at home." Following traditions in activist anthropology, I sought to support Indigenous land defenders by working with solidarity activists and participating in research that could be useful to the resolution of ongoing land claims. By analyzing racist backlash in response to Indigenous land defense, I attempted to make these racist discourses less commonsensical. Why were neo-Nazis present at the "March for Freedom" organized by settler-Canadians in opposition to the Six Nations land reclamation? Why did people in the neighboring town put so much emphasis on Canadianness through national anthems and flag waving, alongside signs and chants that basically called for the eradication of Six Nations people (e.g., "Where Is John Wayne When You Need Him?"; "GAME OVER!!!"; "Burn, Natives, Burn")?

It took time—years—for the untamed bits of fieldwork data to co-alesce from an overwhelming mountain of information into some semblance of comprehensibility. I can only reflect on those initial fieldwork experiences from where I am now, and in terms of the learning that came later. My current understanding of complications regarding Indigenous ethnography, decolonization, and solidarity is perhaps best summed up by the experience of being asked to go back to the edge of the woods.

The concept of doing things in a good way came up repeatedly over a decade, through the organization of marches, rallies, celebrations, and blockades. For years, I'd heard clan mothers admonishing Indigenous land defenders and solidarity activists alike to be of good mind when approaching contentious situations related to land defense and even racist backlash. If we're unable to do so, then it is important to step back until we can reengage appropriately. We were cautioned about engaging with angry townspeople and outside agitators from a place of anger, ego, or impatience. My understanding of what it means to be of good mind and good heart comes from my experiences with friends, allies, and clan mothers at Six Nations, and years of solidarity activism has deepened my understanding of this teaching, especially in times of complication, disagreement, and contention. This concept reemerged throughout my PhD, when I had the opportunity to read more deeply about what it means to do research in a good way and to reflect on the experiences and the knowledge shared with me by friends, land defenders, and elders at Six Nations. Doing things in a good way means being calm, not allowing one's self to lose control or get angry, even in response to racist backlash and settler intrusion. It is also connected with motive and involves deep self-reflection (see Weber-Pillwax 2003; Wilson 2008). I understand being of good mind to be a guiding ethical principle, deeper than cerebral analysis and involving attention to feelings, intuition, and sensations within the body—listening to oneself in a holistic manner and consciously refusing to disconnect the mind from the heart, thinking from feeling (c.f. Meyer 2008).

Conversations about doing research, or going about solidarity activism in a good way, are ultimately connected with conversations about how colonialism and patriarchy are upheld and unintentionally reproduced through well-intentioned solidarity practices (c.f. Simpson, Nanibush and Williams 2012). Struggles that on the surface are identified as anticolonial or even decolonizing often uphold the same power structures that privilege certain bodies (i.e., cisgendered/male/white) in decision-making over other bodies (Indigenous/women/people of color), leaving us with the paradox of purportedly anticolonial activism and research that ends up, in a sense, recolonizing. This has far-reaching implications.

This was the case, for example, when the solidarity activist groups in which I was involved took a lead role in organizing in response to anti-Native backlash at *kanonhstaton*. With well-intentioned rationale, solidarity activists decided that Six Nations people should not have to deal with racist backlash on the settler side of the Two Row Wampum (a treaty of noninterference). However, by adopting the role of defender, activists often overstepped certain boundaries. Although well intentioned, when primarily white, male-bodied, non-Native supporters took the lead role at the forefront at *kanonhstaton*—speaking over Six Nations women—it represented a small but tangible example of settler bodies engaging in a show of solidarity while neglecting to prioritize the leadership role of Six Nations women. This continued despite repeated critiques over many years, in effect perpetuating (neo)colonial relations of power to the point where settler activists were asked by several women and elders to go back to the edge of the woods. As mentioned previously, activists were asked to continue learning from a distance and to wait for an invitation back to Six Nations territory before reengaging in further attempts at solidarity.

Though it is true that mistakes are a necessary part of learning, it is also true that to learn, one must step back and listen. I went back to the edge of woods and refocused my research more firmly on studying settler colonialism by studying the colonizers, focusing on settler-Canadians. Other, predominately white, male solidarity activists have dismissed these ongoing critiques, continuing their engagement despite contributing toward increasing factionalism in a community to which they do not belong. They were later asked to leave again by another group of Indigenous women.

Despite professed ideals of respect for matriarchal traditions, elders, clan mothers, and women as caretakers of the land, those activists who do not listen repeatedly silence women and clan mothers, who become tokenized and disrespected in spaces of solidarity, spaces that are predominantly controlled and maintained by men and in which white settler men seem to have the most power and control. The language of decolonization has been appropriated in these spaces while many of the power imbalances that come out of histories of colonial control are maintained (Swadener and Mutua 2008; Tuck and Yang 2012). Research that is purportedly anti-oppressive, anticolonial, or decolonizing is often embedded in similar contradictions. Cannella and Manuelito (2008), for example, recognize "the intersection of new oppressive forms of power created even within attempts to decolonize" (47).

The most important thing I learned throughout my fieldwork, and the years that followed, is that sometimes, despite the best of intentions, efforts at decolonization can become recolonizing. Intentions do not excuse the impacts of settler ignorance, no matter how well meaning, and sometimes the most useful thing settler researchers and solidarity activists can do is step back and work on individual learning and self-reflection, refocusing efforts at decolonization in our own communities. If we are to take decolonization seriously, as more than just a metaphor (Tuck and Yang 2012), we must not appropriate the language of decolonization as equivalent to other social justice struggles but rather maintain decolonization as a distinct project. Decolonizing research must align with goals of sovereignty and self-determination, and it must work to further these goals in some way. It must not reproduce (neo)colonial power structures or privilege the voices of white settler activists while brushing aside the cautions and critiques of Indigenous women.

There is decolonizing work to be done in settler communities. For me, this means describing and demystifying techniques of (neo)colonialism among settler-Canadians while I wait and learn at the edge of the woods.

Making Connections

How does Thorne define and conceptualize the concept of "decolonizing anthropology" in relation to her research?

Thorne feels that activism and collaboration are important elements of anthropological practice. In Thorne's vignette, however, many solidarity activists were asked to step back from their work. What factors should an anthropologist consider when determining whether and how they should engage in activist work with interlocutors?

Outline how and why Thorne felt that the well-intentioned goals of the solidarity activists often ended up reinscribing colonial ideals. What might be some ways of avoiding this? In the first half of this chapter, we discussed early anthropological explorations of Indigenous peoples of the Americas. Compare Thorne's work to early efforts. How is her work different?

Try This

Many people think archaeology is the only branch of anthropology, and most know very little about sociocultural anthropology or the methods used by sociocultural anthropologists. For this exercise, you will jot down notes about the basic tenets of cultural anthropology (e.g., the meaning of concepts such as gender or cultural relativism) and its methods and methodologies. Then, meet with three different people informally (family, friends, or acquaintances) who have three different careers; spend five minutes explaining what cultural anthropology is and how cultural anthropologists conduct fieldwork. Finally, ask them to respond concerning whether or not they see any benefits that training in cultural anthropology might have for people in their profession. Did you notice any commonalities about people's perceptions of anthropology?

Possible Projects

1. This research project will lead to an essay that will help you understand foundational anthropological methods and their history. Select an anthropologist who did fieldwork in North America between 1885 and 1950. Some examples might be Franz Boas, Margaret Mead, Diamond Jenness, or Alfred Kroeber, to name just a few. Discuss his or her contributions to anthropological methods or methodologies in North America and any influences (e.g., the people who trained this anthropologist and whether these individuals affected your person's outlook on the discipline). In what ways (if at all) are this anthropologist's ideas still relevant to the field of anthropology? What is her or his legacy with respect to anthropological methods and methodologies?
2. In this chapter's vignette, Niki Thorne focuses upon her use of decolonizing methodologies. Compare and contrast two contemporary ethnographies on Indigenous populations that make use of decolonizing methodologies (see recommended readings below for examples of anthropologists who advocate this approach, but feel free to find your own). Discuss how and why this methodology was used in each context

and how it affected relationships between the researcher and informants or collaborators. In what ways are these methodologies distinct from those employed by anthropologists in the early twentieth century?

Recommended Readings

De Oliveira, Adolfo. 2009. "Introduction: Decolonising Approaches to Indigenous Rights." In *Decolonising Indigenous Rights*, edited by A. de Oliveira, 1–16. New York: Routledge.

Harrison, Faye V., ed. 2010. *Decolonizing Anthropology: Moving Further toward an Anthropology for Liberation*. 3rd ed. Washington, DC: American Anthropological Association. First published in 1991.

Land, Claire. 2015. *Decolonizing Solidarity: Dilemma and Directions for Supporters of Indigenous Struggles*. New York: Zed Books.

Martin-Hill, Dawn. 2008. *Sewatokwa'tshera't: The Dish with One Spoon* [DVD]. [Mohawk Nation] Haudenosaunee Confederacy.

Milley, Kate. 2009. "'Where is John Wayne When You Need Him?': Anti-Native Organizing and the 'Caledonia Crisis.'" *Upping the Anti* 9. http://uppingtheanti.org/journal/article/09-where-is-john-wayne-when-you-need-him/.

Sium, Aman, Chandni Desai, and Eric Ritskes. 2012. "Towards the 'Tangible Unknown': Decolonization and the Indigenous Future." *Decolonization: Indigeneity, Education & Society* 1 (1): i–xiii.

Smith, Linda Tuhiwai. 2006. *Decolonizing Methodologies: Research and Indigenous Peoples*. London and New York: Zed Books, 2006. First published in 1999.

Speed, Shannon. 2006. "At the Crossroads of Human Rights and Anthropology: Toward a Critically Engaged Activist Research." *American Anthropologist* 108 (1): 66–76.

Web Resources

In addition: Refer to a special 2016 edition of *Decolonizing Anthropology* on the online blog, "Savage Minds": https://savageminds.org/series/decolonizing-anthropology/.

CHAPTER 2

PARTICIPANT OBSERVATION

Introduction: "Traditional" versus "Modern" Participant Observation

Many anthropologists argue that **participant observation** is one of the discipline's defining fieldwork methods. In *Argonauts of the Western Pacific*, Bronislaw Malinowski ([1932] 2014) documented his fieldwork experiences among Trobriand Islanders in the South Pacific during World War I. In this ethnography, Malinowski became one of the first anthropologists to advocate for and systematically write about the use and importance of participant observation as a key anthropological method. He defined it as an intensive, long-term engagement (usually a year or more) with one group of people in a singular location. In general, participant observation as defined by Malinowski involved learning the local language, participating in daily tasks, and observing and recording the daily ebb and flow of life. However, Malinowski conducted participant observation in small, rural villages, so for him, it also involved setting up his tent in the middle of a village, participating in and observing daily tasks, and recording Trobriand village life. He proclaimed that this level of integration with villagers was necessary to "grasp the **native's point of view**" (Malinowski [1932] 2014, 25), or adopting what is also sometimes referred to as an *insider's perspective*. In a critique of the variants of **armchair anthropology** and **verandah anthropology** that dominated late nineteenth-century and early twentieth-century anthropology, he emphasized the importance of the experiential component of fieldwork in forming relationships. He deemed this necessary to obtain firsthand knowledge and experience of cultural beliefs and practices. Long-term fieldwork, he argued, was required to develop a sense of rapport with one's interlocutors, to earn their trust, and to effectively "understand" the lives and perspectives of others.

Within the context of the Trobriand Islands circa 1915, it might be considered reasonable for anthropologists to live with the people they study, to stay in one location for a long period, and to participate in as many aspects of culture as possible. Indeed, Malinowski's notion of participant observation is based upon an understanding of the "field" as a distinct geographical place (separate and distinct from "home"), as spatially bounded and contained, and as having a relatively homogeneous population (Gupta and Ferguson 1997). This conception of the "field" would come to dominate anthropological research in the early twentieth century. For example, American anthropologist Hortense Powdermaker (1966) a student of Malinowski's, went on to study actors, directors, and producers in Hollywood. She defined and advocated for participant observation as a form of "mutual communication" that involves "physical proximity of the field worker to the people he studies," a working knowledge of the local language, and the development of a sense of "psychological involvement" (287). She defines the latter as the ability to move readily and freely between different demographics of people, based on class, gender, or other identity markers. At the heart of these more traditional conceptions of participant observation, however, is the notion of the "field" as place.

More contemporary understandings of the "field," however, situate it as a cultural construction of the anthropologist or anthropology student. In other words, we create artificial geographical and ideological boundaries around people, ideas, and places to cultivate our own field sites. Such categories are not fixed or natural; instead, they are the by-product of an academic necessity to delineate a manageable field site for study. In an increasingly globalized world that sees enormous changes in terms of the movements of our interlocutors—as refugees, work migrants, tourists, business travelers, or students, to name a few examples—people cannot be characterized as homogenous and bounded (not that they could in Malinowski's time, either). Many peoples are thus increasingly deterritorialized, and we see new communities emerge via the Internet through the creation of new opportunities for sociality via social media, online gaming, or other forums.

In our increasingly deterritorialized and virtual world, then, how might participant observation look differently if it were conducted in the settings of urban twenty-first century North America? Or what about in virtual worlds? Is it possible to develop "rapport" online? Moreover, is it desirable to replicate Malinowski's ideals of participant observation within field sites such as corporate boardrooms, among sports stars, in online gaming contexts, or with homeless peoples in Chicago? What becomes of Powdermaker's insistence upon "physical proximity" to our interlocutors within the context of an online community?

Changing Notions of Participant Observation

To meet the changing demands of fieldwork sites and research questions, participant observation has evolved over the years as a variable, flexible qualitative method predicated upon experiential knowledge obtained through intensive engagement with a group of people. In essence, it involves "hanging out" with people in various ways to obtain a better understanding of their worldview. Often, it involves participating in and observing a variety of aspects of daily life, depending upon your research question. These can range from the mundane, like helping people wash dishes, to the seemingly unusual or spectacular, like following professional baseball players to their competitive events. Of importance is the fact that there is no "right" way to conduct participant observation. The types of engagements that you have with people will be dependent upon several factors, including the type of research questions you are asking and factors that could include, but are not limited to, the size of the group that you want to explore, whether you are working in a rural or urban context, and the power dynamics between you, the researcher, and your interlocutors.

Participant observation, then, must adapt to meet the changing needs and demographics of our interlocutors, as well as to the diversity of fieldwork sites and contexts. Until about the 1970s, for example, it was far more common for anthropologists to conduct participant observation among disadvantaged or marginalized groups, but anthropologists increasingly **"study up"** (Nader 1972) when conducting participant observation. But working among demographics such as corporate elites often requires the use of a different type of participant observation than the traditional form espoused by Malinowski. Because of the increasing mobility of informants and the advent of new communications technologies like the Internet, many anthropologists engage in a form of participant observation that Hugh Gusterson (1997) calls **polymorphous engagement**. According to him,

> Polymorphous engagement means interacting with informants across a number of dispersed sites, not just in local communities, and sometimes in virtual form; and it means collecting data eclectically from a disparate array of sources in many different ways.... [It also involves] an eclectic mix of other research techniques: formal interviews of the kind often done by journalists and political scientists, extensive reading of newspapers and official documents, and careful attention to popular culture, for example. (Gusterson 1997, 116)

These activities, like reading the news online or in a newspaper every morning, are routine tasks that many of us participate in on a daily basis. Yet we often do so as uncritical participants. However, if you are engaged in polymorphous engagement as a form of participant observation, then you are reading and taking note of newsworthy events with a critical, anthropological lens that involves (among other things) asking questions about the connections between a local, national, or world event and various social, political, religious, or economic patterns and trends. If you are reading about national elections, for instance, you might ask questions such as this one: "What cultural factors contributed to the rise and popularity of the Republican Party in the United States?"

These types of concerns and questions were at the heart of Karen Ho's (2009) polymorphous engagement among Wall Street stockbrokers. Obviously, Ho could not set up a sleeping bag on the couch of a corporate executive at Goldman Sachs. Instead, she drew upon her previous work experience on Wall Street and her existing connections to explore how executives make sense of the notion of financial collapse and how such understandings are mediated through dominant ideas—for example, about the value of individualism and meritocracy, among other factors. In her fieldwork, she conducted interviews and participant observation in a variety of disparate sites: in boardrooms and coffee shops and by reading newspapers and following the stock market. Given the fast pace of life and the expectations regarding socially appropriate business communications on Wall Street, traditional forms of participant observation would not be feasible in this context.

Types of Participant Observation

Acknowledging and perhaps foreshadowing the increasing diversity of field sites and research questions, anthropologist James Spradley (1980, 58–62), identified five "types" of participant observation conducted by anthropologists. Each of these types varies according to the anthropologist's level of engagement (physically and emotionally) with informants. Each variety can be appropriated and adapted to suit the needs of fieldwork questions, people, and places. They are 1) complete participation, 2) active participation, 3) moderate participation, 4) passive participation, and 5) nonparticipation.

Complete participation, according to Spradley (1980), occurs when the anthropologist either becomes or is a part of a particular group of people under study. An example would be George Gmelch's research among American major league baseball players (as discussed in his vignette below). A former minor league ballplayer, Gmelch was often positioned by both himself and his interlocutors as an "insider" within the sport. He came to his research with a background on the ins and outs of training and coaching regimes, the demands of travel, and other factors. As an insider, then, Gmelch already possessed a certain level of knowledge about and status within his fieldwork domain, and gaining rapport among ballplayers, as well as access to them via media accreditation, was somewhat easier than it would have been had he been a complete stranger to baseball.

It should be noted, however, that the insider-outsider dichotomy is not always sharply defined. Many anthropologists, such as Kirin Narayan (1993), point out that this dichotomy is often problematic because our identities are frequently complicated, shifting, overlapping, and heterogeneous. Many people, she claims, are positioned with a "multiplex identity" (Narayan 1993, 673). Thus, the categories of insider or outsider are often unstable in many fieldwork situations. Narayan, an Indian-born and American-educated anthropologist, conducted fieldwork in what she considered to be her home of India, but she found that her informants often did not know how to relate to her. Her multicultural background and geographic mobility defied their traditional understandings of personhood; they could not "fix" her in terms of identity. Was she *really* Indian or American? And what class or caste did she belong to? Ultimately, her status as both insider and outsider was volatile and in flux. Relating this concept back to the notion of complete participation, we see clearly that one's status as a potential "insider" should never be accepted as a given, and, in fact, the anthropologist's positionality will often be perceived differently by different informants across both time and space.

The concept of "active participation" (Spradley 1980) is similar to the notion of complete participant, but, in this case, the anthropologist is not generally perceived by his or her informants as an "insider"; this researcher thus lacks the same level of cultural integration as a complete participant. In this case, the status of the anthropologist as a student of culture is obvious to all parties. Malinowski's research in the Trobriand Islands best fits this model of participant observation. In contrast, the model of "moderate participation" is predicated upon a lesser degree of involvement and interaction with one's informants. It occurs when the anthropologist interacts occasionally with his or her informants, and when greater emphasis is placed upon observation. For example, an anthropologist working in a children's classroom would fall into this category. He or she may wish to examine how a teacher's teaching methods function to gender children, for example. In this case, the researcher would simply watch, observe, record student-teacher interactions, and have minimal contact with the group.

Passive participation involves making observations of events and people, often without their knowledge. Obviously, this method raises ethical issues and should be restricted to large-scale events during which people may remain anonymous. An example might include being a spectator at a large sporting event and observing and writing notes on the actions, words, clothing, and general behavior of sports fans.

A final form of participant observation is called nonparticipation. In this variation of participant observation, anthropologists neither engage directly with the people they are studying nor interact with them. At a surface level, nonparticipation shares many characteristics with armchair anthropology, including reliance upon secondary sources, written texts, and visual data. Although Spradley clearly feels that this approach is inferior to other types of participant observation, it should be noted that much can be learned about people and their worldview by watching popular news broadcasts, surfing relevant Internet sites, or reading popular literature. Much archival research would also fall under this category, and this may be the only method available for historical anthropologists. In other cases, many anthropologists, in fact, incorporate nonparticipation with other methods of participant observation and do not rely exclusively upon a singular model.

Ultimately, it is important to note that hierarchies of value should not necessarily be attached to any of these models for participant observation and that the context of research, the wishes and expectations of one's informants, ethical guidelines, and the research question itself should guide you in your choice of participant observation methods. Furthermore, it is important to understand the politics behind our observations. If an entire class of university students were tasked with conducting participant observation at a bakery, for instance, everyone would return from the "field" with different observations. What you record and notice in your interactions, for instance, will be based upon several factors, including your level of interest in the field site or research question; your gender, age, individual observational skills, and personality; and your interest in and knowledge about food preparation, as well as a variety of other factors. In the end, participant observation is not an objective or replicable phenomenon: it is always filtered through our individual positionalities and perspectives. As a result, our observations are always partial, and we should avoid viewing participant observation as a process rooted in objectivity.

Multisited Observations

In 1995, American anthropologist George Marcus coined the term **multisited fieldwork** to characterize an increasing trend among anthropologists toward issues-based research questions that connect international or global concerns with ethnographic, "local" realities. Some research questions, for instance, require the anthropologist to conduct participant observation in multiple "sites" (defined in both the geographic, spatial sense and ideologically). This research often involves tracking the complicated trajectories and movements of people, objects, or commodities and of conflicts and metaphors, for instance, over time and place and from multiple positionalities (Marcus 1995, 105–13). For example, Karen McGarry (2015), in her study of Canadian high-performance figure skaters, sought to examine the ways in which the global circulation and positive international reception and consumption of skating bodies and representations of skating bodies (on the Internet or via television and other media) was an important means through which a sense of national identity was constructed. This research made it important to track the circulation of the bodies of skating "heroes"—not only within Canada but internationally—and necessitated conducting participant observation at a variety of sites throughout Canada (at training centers and competitions). Also necessary was nonparticipation (watching television broadcasts and doing archival research). McGarry also conducted research outside of Canada, interviewing international journalists and judges. The point here is that this research question necessitated the use of a very different type of participant observation than that espoused by Malinowski. This study emphasizes the importance of movement—the researcher had to not only physically follow informants but also trace the circulation and reception of the bodies of skating celebrities in magazines and other media. In this case, only multisited research enables the anthropologist to begin to understand how localized events are shaped by broader international or global processes. A multisited perspective thus represents a move away from earlier anthropological traditions of treating societies as bounded laboratories that are untouched by external forces and events.

Moving Forward: Integrating Participant Observation into Your Fieldwork

Throughout this chapter, we have highlighted the ways in which participant observation is not predicated upon a "one-fits-all" model. Malinowski's vision of participant observation, for instance, is not universally applicable or relevant. It is therefore important to think critically about how (or if) participant observation can be integrated into your own research project. Below is a list of some of the pertinent questions that you may need to consider when deciding upon what types of participant observation (if any) are applicable to your research:

- Where (geographically or spatially) will your research be conducted?
- How long will you spend doing research?
- Is it necessary to conduct your fieldwork in multiple physical locations? If so, then how does this affect participant observation?
- What level of "immersion" into your interlocutors' lives is feasible, desirable, or viable for your project?
- What should you record when "observing?" If you are participating in an activity, then why did you choose to do so? What do you hope to learn from engaging in this activity?
- Which (if any) of Spradley's "types" of participant observation are viable for your project? Why?

- How do you anticipate that your identity or positionality will affect participant observation?
- Will you incorporate any form of polymorphous engagement?

Remember, participant observation is not an objective or apolitical act, and it is important throughout the research process to consider how your participant observation and fieldwork engagements affect the lives of your informants, and vice versa. Also remember that the process of building relationships and developing rapport, which is often fostered through participant observation, is sometimes fraught with challenges. Some of these challenges are discussed in this chapter's vignette by George Gmelch. Gmelch reflects upon his experiences conducting participant observation among minor and major league American baseball players. Throughout, he discusses and elaborates many of the key concepts outlined throughout this chapter, including the idea of insider-outsider status and the process of developing rapport through participant observation.

VIGNETTE
George Gmelch is a professor of anthropology at San Francisco University. Much of his fieldwork focuses upon the anthropology of sport. He has a special interest in baseball.

FIGURE 2.1: Portrait of George Gmelch, 2016. Photograph courtesy of Joanne Lincoln.

INSIDE PITCH: STUDYING THE CULTURE OF BALLPLAYERS

For many North Americans, sport has become a secular religion. Indeed, the teams we root for, whether the Blue Jays or the Yankees, the Maple Leafs or the Rangers, may reflect a wider identification and sense of imagined community. But that wasn't the reason I chose to study baseball. Baseball had special meaning for me because it was my boyhood ambition, and for four years during the 1960s, it was my career (Detroit Tigers minor leagues). Studying it was a chance for me to understand more about something that had once been a big part of my life and identity before I became an anthropologist.

Looking for a good research topic, I attended a well-known symposium for baseball scholars called "Baseball and American Culture," held at the Baseball Hall of Fame in Cooperstown, New York. After listening to papers about the game and its place in American society, I realized I was out of my league. As an anthropologist devoted to the study of other cultures, I knew comparatively little about historical trends in my own society. It was presumptuous to think I would have something new to add.

But the symposium did point me in a new direction. During the discussion of a paper on professional baseball in Canada, the speaker mentioned to the audience that I had once played in the Québec Provincial League and might be able to shed some light on the topic. Cast in the role of insider, I did have something to contribute to the session, and several participants came up to me with further questions (Figure 2.2).

The advantage of once having been a player helped redefine my inquiry: I would do an *ethnography* of professional baseball. I would seek an insider's perspective and render explicit what is often unseen, or obscure to fans, such as why superstitions and pranks are such a big part of the life.

Long accustomed to doing fieldwork by taking up residence with the people I wished to study and immersing myself in their lives, I wondered how I might do this with ballplayers. Perhaps accompanying teams on road trips was the answer: it would allow me to be in close quarters with players and coaches on the bus, and in hotels, restaurants, and clubhouses. But when I first proposed traveling with the Double A Birmingham Barons—a team co-owned by my college friend, Marty Kuehnert—no one in the parent Chicago White Sox organization would approve my request. Marty discovered that management was concerned about what I might write. As Marty persisted, my bid to shadow the Barons on a road trip passed up and

FIGURE 2.2: George Gmelch playing for the Class A Rocky Mount Leafs in 1967. Photograph courtesy of George Gmelch.

down the organizational chain until it reached the desk of White Sox president Jerry Reinsdorf. He took a chance, and I went on the road with the Barons.

As the Barons bus pulled out of the stadium parking lot on a hot, sticky day in mid-June in 1992—destination Jacksonville, Florida—the manager, Tony Franklin, stood up to introduce me: "I'd like you to meet George Gmelch. He's an anthropologist studying your lives as ball-players. I don't know why anyone would find what you do interesting, but that's his business and he's a whole lot smarter than me [laughter]. Anyway, he was a player in the Tigers organization in the sixties, so he knows his way around. I want you to help him any way you can." The players turned in their seats, craning to get a good look at me. I smiled a lot, trying not to show my nervousness.

In the coming days, there were times when I doubted my abilities to do the research. In my playing days, few players had been to college, and there was wariness about things intellectual. In fact, my teammates had nicknamed me "Moonbeam" because I read books and sometimes visited libraries. Some of that anti-intellectual atmosphere still existed. When I met Jamestown Expos manager Eddie Creech for the first time, and used the term "occupational subculture" in explaining my research, he said, "Whoa, slow down with them big words. You're talking to an uneducated Southern boy." Creech turned out to be bright, articulate, and helpful, but his response made me wonder how his players would react to my scholarly queries, and whether I could even relate to the guys. Would they accept a bearded, graying, middle-aged professor hanging out with them?

However, the ballplayers turned out to be good subjects, and agreeable to being interviewed. Professional baseball needs the media coverage, and therefore baseball management expects its players to cooperate with writers. Players didn't always have a lot to say—some spoke in clichés and, unless prodded, answered questions without giving them fresh thought. In their defense, one manager told me, "It is their reaction to being asked so many incredibly stupid questions by people who just don't have a clue." But since I wasn't asking the usual questions about team performance, managerial decisions, or personalities, after a while I was able to get most players to answer thoughtfully. Although there was some new jargon, such as "the show" for the big leagues or "going yard" for home run or "cheese" for fastball, it didn't take long to get up to speed. Once I got the hang of traveling with minor-league teams and got to know the players better, my insecurity disappeared, and I shed the baggage of my past.

But I wondered if my having once been part of the baseball culture would make it difficult for me to see it clearly. During my last playing season, and already serious about anthropology, I had tried to do some field research, hoping to write a paper about the subculture of professional baseball. But nothing came of it, as my fieldwork failed. I was not only too inexperienced at collecting data and writing daily field notes but also too immersed in the game to see it clearly, to see what was noteworthy. Anthropologists believe that *difference* makes it easier for us to see or grasp the culture of the groups we study. When studying your own group, what you observe often seems like common sense, and you can anguish over the obviousness of everything people are saying.

For me, to study baseball was akin to doing what some call "native anthropology." For the native anthropologist—one who studies his or her own culture—there are losses or handicaps such as those just described, but there are also some benefits. One has privileged access to aspects of local culture, particularly emotive and intimate dimensions, that the foreigner or non-native may never fully understand. Some examples of this in baseball are the anxiety and fear of failing that rookies experience when going to their first spring training and the desperation that one feels during a prolonged slump. One disadvantage of having once been an insider is the expectation that you will understand and be sympathetic to your subjects on certain issues (e.g., in baseball, the unreasonable demands of fans for autographs and the hardships of long road trips). And, as anthropologist Kirsten Hastrup (1995, 158) has pointed out, there is the difficulty of transforming self-evident cultural knowledge into genuine anthropological understanding. However, that nearly three decades had elapsed since I had been part of the baseball world made these issues less of a concern.

Besides, baseball had changed. For starters, it had become very multicultural with the arrival of many Latinos and some Asians. Aspects of baseball's culture, including food, music, and a looser and flamboyant playing style, were showing the new Hispanic influence. Professional baseball in the 1960s had been predominantly a white-American game; by the 1990s, nearly one third of all major leaguers and half of all minor leaguers were foreign born. Martinez, Rodriguez, and Hernandez were now the most common surnames, supplanting Smith, Jones, and Williams. Today, the most common first name in baseball is José, and the most common surname is Ramirez.

Once I learned the ropes, access became easier. I was soon granted press credentials at minor- and major-league ballparks. To obtain a press credential, you have to convince the team's media relations director that your research is worthy, notably that it will have some PR value for the team by highlighting or at least mentioning the team or some of its players. Also, it is important to make clear that you are not a risk, that you know how to behave appropriately in the dugout and clubhouse before the game (e.g., not being intrusive, respecting when players are busy and not available to talk, not taking pictures or asking for an autograph) and in the press box during the game (e.g., not bothering the beat writers and never cheering). Dressing appropriately, in the same fashion as the sportswriters and club officials, is important to blending in. That meant wearing khakis or Dockers and a polo shirt, which I was accustomed to doing anyway. Like the sportswriters, I also carried a small tape recorder and a steno notebook (journalists of all stripes prefer the long and narrow spiral-bound notebook to the more standard 5 × 8 version). Nevertheless, sometimes I would notice a sportswriter looking at my press credential, which is worn around the neck, trying to read my name and affiliation. Sometimes a reporter would ask what I was researching, and that often lead to productive conversations. Though they weren't interested in the same kinds of questions about baseball that I was asking, they had a great deal of knowledge because they were at the ballpark every day, and some traveled with the team as well. Moreover, I found most to be willing to share their knowledge.

I was very insecure when I first began doing interviews with major leaguers, some of them considered to be famous. In my mind, I was not a professor of anthropology but a retired minor-league ballplayer hanging out in major-league clubhouses asking American celebrities to tell me about their lives. As an anthropologist, I could do that, but as a former athlete who had never quite reached the big time, it was more difficult. That problem disappeared as I got to know players better and shed the baggage of my past. But the situation that always made me uneasy was being in confined quarters with a group of players, such as in a corner of the clubhouse, where there was a lot of horseplay and joking. It made the boundary between the in-group of players and me—the outsider—palpable. I did my best to avoid those situations, trying instead to talk to players one on one.

My ballpark fieldwork days began four hours before game time when the first players and coaches trickled in. During "pregame," like all credentialed media, I had access to field, dugout, and clubhouse. There was a lot of time to conduct interviews because players are only occupied with their pregame preparations (e.g., stretching, throwing, batting practice) for about half of the four hours they are at the ballpark before game time. During the game, I watched from the press box and interviewed baseball wives near the family lounge. It wasn't the kind of participant observation I was accustomed to in my earlier fieldwork, but it would have to do.

A lot of anthropological research is serendipitous, as was my decision to include baseball wives and groupies. While interviewing New York Yankee centerfielder Bernie Williams, he kept saying, "Oh, you should really talk to my wife. She would know better than me." After a while I thought, "Well, why not?" The next day I interviewed Waleska Williams, and she was terrific. She introduced me to other Yankee wives, and I wondered why I had not thought earlier of including them. Speaking to baseball wives led me to an interest in groupies, the young, often scantily clad and overly made-up young women who pursue ballplayers and who are a major concern and threat to baseball wives. My attempts to interview groupies, however, got off to a rocky start. At a minor-league game in London, Ontario, I asked the usher if she could introduce me to a few of these young women. Misunderstanding my motives, she returned with a policeman. Groupies became a separate chapter in *Inside Pitch* (Gmelch 2006).

One of the great pleasures of returning to baseball was being back in ballparks. Ballparks are magical places—emerald green fields crisply outlined in chalk, the sweep of the grandstands stacked in tiers, and the silhouette of the light towers with their bright lights against the dark night sky. Phillip Lowry (2009) titled his book *Green Cathedrals* because the more he studied ballparks, the more he thought they resembled places of worship. Ballparks are also exciting for their activity—batting practice, fielders taking infield, fans pleading for autographs, players being interviewed by the media, others sprawled on the grass stretching or playing pepper, groundskeepers watering the deep brown infield dirt or renewing the foul lines with fresh chalk. For me, no research setting will ever match the ballpark.

Another bonus of the research was that it took me back to many of the towns I had played in a generation before—towns in Minnesota, North Carolina, New York, and Québec—and to Tiger Town in Lakeland, Florida, where I went to spring training. Revisiting them and their ballparks with the smell of grass, pine tar, and rosin and the sound of metal spikes clacking on the cement runway leading to the dugout and field brought back many vivid memories. At night, I dreamed that I was playing baseball and hitting better than ever. I was a star. Reconnecting with former teammates and two old girlfriends whom I hadn't seen in 25 years, I rediscovered who I had been in my youth. Our recollections of one another, though a generation old, were unclouded by new, shared experiences.

By the end of my research, I came to believe that my four years in pro ball had been good preparation for the academic career I later pursued, and for life generally. In baseball, athletes learn to get along with people—teammates and coaches—from diverse class, racial, and ethnic backgrounds. Traveling half the season and being at the ballpark for eight hours every day with 24 other guys fosters, more than any other sport, "people skills." By interacting with Latino teammates, I got to use and refine the Spanish that I had learned in Stanford University classrooms. And by playing and living in Québec for two seasons—and dating a monolingual francophone woman— I learned rudimentary French. Both experiences contributed to my decision to change my major to anthropology. Baseball also taught me, as it teaches all players, how to deal with failure, of which there's a great deal in the game—hitless nights, slumps, losing streaks, subpar seasons, injuries, and demotions. In everyday life, whether part of the academic or the business world, people rarely deal with the level of failure that is commonplace in pro ball. Baseball taught me how to deal with pressure (if you don't, you don't last long). And in baseball, I learned that you should develop concentration and focus—and work hard to survive, to stay in the lineup, and to move up to the next level.

Though my research journey occasionally became personal, it was an understanding of the life and culture of baseball that I was after, and that has become a permanent interest. I now teach a course on the anthropology of sport in which baseball is a component, and every now and then, I request a media credential and go back to the ballpark to talk to players to keep up with how things are changing.

Making Connections

Throughout the vignette, Gmelch talks about how he engaged in "studying up." How did this affect the fieldwork process and the methods that he employed?

What were some of the benefits and challenges that Gmelch experienced by being labeled an "insider?"

How would Gmelch's research be different if he had not been a ballplayer himself? How might this different status have affected his fieldwork experiences? What did participant observation look like throughout Gmelch's fieldwork? What forms did it take?

Try This

Observe the environments you move through in one day and the ways you participate in them. Every time you move to a different environment, take five minutes to write down what you observed that is particular to that environment. Some examples would be bus stops, on the bus, in a classroom, in the cafeteria, at a friend's house, in the library, in your room, and at the pub. Compare your observations with those of a colleague in your class. What are some of the similarities and differences in your observations? For example, some people focus more upon what they see, whereas others might comment upon smells or other sensory experiences. The goal here is to encourage you to be more observant about your physical environments and the various activities that take place within them.

Possible Projects

1. You are tasked with recording and commenting upon the actions and attitudes of spectators at a sporting event. Attend a large-scale sports event that attracts many spectators. Observe the behavior of spectators during the game or event and take notes. When you get home, reflect on your notes and discuss how your background and interests affected what you observed and recorded. For example, if you are female, would your observations be different if you were male? How does your age, level of interest in sport, or other factors influence the types of observations that you make? Moreover, what did you leave out?

2. It is important to consider how your informants' perceptions of you as an "insider" or "outsider" affect the types of observations that you make, and the type or level of participant observation that you conduct in the field. For this project, select a topic that interests you—for example, gender in the workplace. Instead of conducting fieldwork with one group of people, however, you will conduct participant observation in two different locations and with two different groups of people. Your first location should be among a demographic that considers you to be an "insider," such as work colleagues, school friends, or family members. Then, conduct participant observation (with people's permission) with a group that would consider you to be an "outsider." Compare and contrast the types of observations and the type of participant observation that you do. What are some of the differences and similarities? What do you think are the main reasons for these differences? Finally, what do these similarities and differences indicate about the process of doing participant observation?

Recommended Readings

DeVita, Philip R. 1998. *The Humbled Anthropologist*. Prospect Heights, IL: Waveland Press.

DeWalt, Kathleen Musante, and Billie R. DeWalt. 2010. *Participant Observation: A Guide for Fieldworkers*. 2nd ed. Walnut Creek, CA: AltaMira.

Fife, Wayne. 2005. *Doing Fieldwork: Ethnographic Methods for Research in Developing Countries and Beyond*. Basingstoke, UK: Palgrave MacMillan. https://doi.org/10.1057/9781403980564.

Gmelch, George. 2006. *Inside Pitch: Life in Professional Baseball*. Lincoln, NE: University of Nebraska Press.

Gmelch, George. 2016. *Playing with Tigers: A Minor League Chronicle of the Sixties*. Lincoln, NE: University of Nebraska Press.

Hume, Lynne, and Jane Mulcock, eds. 2004. *Anthropologists in the Field: Cases in Participant Observation*. New York, NY: Columbia University Press.

Yamaguchi, Tomomi. 2007. "Impartial Observation and Partial Participation: Feminist Ethnography in Politically Charged Japan." *Critical Asian Studies* 39 (4): 583–608. https://doi.org/10.1080/14672710701686059.

CHAPTER 3

ETHICS AND THE POLITICS
OF FIELDWORK

Introduction

Imagine that you have just entered your field site and one of the participants asks you to keep a secret—a secret about an illegal incident. What do you do? Or, on a subtler note, what do you do if someone you are interviewing asks for your advice, or opinion, on an important topic? Perhaps it is an issue that could have long-term implications, such as selling art or artifacts. Do you give your best advice? Having **integrity** and conducting fieldwork and research in an ethical manner are inherently complicated in cultural anthropology because of our focus on cultural relativism. Being ethically minded means that you are concerned with doing what is right and what is moral. **Ethics** are not legal mechanisms: they are based on philosophies, cultural meanings, and practices. Conducting ethical research means that you follow a set of standards in terms of moral values. The problem for cultural anthropologists is that **morals** and values shift and change (sometimes to a greater rather than lesser sense) depending upon your cultural context. For one example, the cultural values of a Canadian anthropologist might not necessarily match up with the cultural meanings and values of the Mexican migrants she is working with. Added to that, morals and values shift and change over time within cultures. This translates on an individualized basis, so what people say and what people actually do can be two very different things. For example, if an interlocutor was asked to explain his family dynamics, he might focus on idealized cultural beliefs and values concerning the complementary roles of husbands and wives, whereas in his day-to-day life he might practice a modified version of this ideal, or even a completely different set of roles that seem amoral in comparison. This is one of the reasons Carolyn Fluehr-Lobban says all research in the twenty-first century should be collaborative in terms of ethical concerns.

Fluehr-Lobban, one of the foremost American scholars on ethics in the social sciences, has been arguing since 1991 that "research that involves research participants/collaborators as partners in the research process ... is 'ethically conscious' research" (2008, 175).[1] She argues for a break from traditional anthropology where informants and research subjects were kept at a distance and examined from an objective scientific position that, in North America, was often attached to colonial ideologies and government funding. Although in contemporary terms there has been a move toward advocating practices that assist in promoting the well-being of those being studied, this focus is still paternalistic by nature, involving research that is planned, executed, and published strictly by anthropologists alone. True **collaborative research** puts people first; it considers them partners in "voluntary, informed, negotiated, open, reciprocal research, based on locating a common ground of mutual interest and benefit between researcher and research populations" (Fluehr-Lobban 2008, 177). This collaboration extends even to the point at which, as Jen Shannon explains below, "they come up with the questions that matter to them." Whether you are willing or able to conduct a purely collaborative research project is another story, but this is the ideal moral stance that should guide you. The language used in revisions of the codes of ethics and on informed consent forms (which we will discuss) is central to making this cultural and ideological shift.

Ethics in Two Nations: History and Practice in the United States and Canada

Following the atrocities of World War II, cultural anthropologists in North America abided by an informal code of ethics based on protecting research participants. A focus on **do no harm** originally stemmed from physically invasive medical research conducted by some anthropologists working under the Nazi regime. The history of a formal **code of ethics** in the United States begins with the creation of a standardized set of rules drawn up by the American Anthropological Society (AAA) in 1971, even though debates ensued at annual AAA meetings as early as 1965 (in Denver) due to Project Camelot.[2] Initial arguments centered on whether anthropologists should give up their right to academic freedom, and, in particular, the effect that review boards would have on ethnographic work because of its spontaneous and relational nature (Jorgensen 1971). During this period, cultural anthropologists and ethnographic researchers, who were advocating for standardized ethics, basically had the same concerns as they do now, including the right to privacy, consent, and confidentiality for research participants. A new code was created in 1996 that emphasized "do no harm" as the basic principle of all four fields. As well, it offered specific language concerning "informed consent" and highlighted the moral responsibility to focus on issues of advocacy (Fluehr-Lobban 1998). The current code, completed in 2012, provides this statement on the extent that "do no harm" applies:

> A primary ethical obligation shared by anthropologists is to do no harm. It is imperative that, before any anthropological work be undertaken — in communities, with non-human primates or other animals, at archaeological and paleoanthropological sites — each researcher think through the possible ways that the research might cause harm. Among the most serious harms that anthropologists should seek to avoid are harm to dignity, and to bodily and material well-being, especially when research is conducted among vulnerable populations. Anthropologists should not only avoid causing direct and immediate harm but also should weigh carefully the potential consequences and inadvertent impacts of their work. (AAA 2012)

In the Canadian context, researchers need to get their proposals sanctioned by a research ethics board (REB) at their university. These boards are similar to the ones in the United States called institutional review boards (IRBs) and consist of faculty members, community members, and administrative staff. Decisions in Canada are guided by the *Tri-Council Policy Statement: Ethical Conduct for Research Involving Humans* (TCPS), which was written in 1998. It is the standard for ethical guidelines across Canada, and although each university has a somewhat different set of rules in terms of applications, all universities follow these guidelines (van den Hoonaard and Connolly 2006).

Having Integrity

As a student, you are aware of the definition of academic integrity, which primarily focuses on the importance of not plagiarizing, of not taking someone else's work and claiming it as your own. But what do anthropologists mean when they talk about the importance of integrity to the research process? First, they are referring to the integrity of the discipline. In cultural anthropology, as in all social sciences, **transparency** concerning your research process is central, human rights and fairness are central, as is not falsifying any data. The integrity of anthropologists means that they are honest with themselves and the people they are working with and that they consistently follow strong moral principles in every phase of their research. Ethical practices are what uphold the integrity of the discipline. Carolyn Fluehr-Lobban (1998) explains that the role of ethics in maintaining integrity throughout all the various stages of the research process begins with the formulation of the research question and focus.

Let's say you have decided to work with a seniors' center in the community you are living in. Before deciding on a specific focus, you need to find out if you can carry out the entire project without compromising ethical standards and, also, if your research underscores some of the primary concerns of the individuals you will be working with. Will it benefit this group of people in any way? If not, then can you reconsider your focus? Initial conversations with your research subjects, other anthropology students, and your professor are good starting points. It would also be important in this case to familiarize yourself with the community's history (of trauma or displacement, for example) and with its future goals. Another important consideration for a professional anthropologist revolves around the requirements of funding agencies and the researcher's commitment to these agencies in terms of gathering certain types of information. As an undergraduate student, you probably do not have this concern, but the relationship between your theoretical emphasis and the mandate your professor has outlined for your project is important. Again, make sure you are not compromising the ethical concerns of the people you are working with when making these choices. And finally, it is important to think ahead and focus on the possible negative impacts your research data might have and what the potential conflicts might be (between you and the community). For example, before finalizing your analysis, you need to ask yourself a few questions. Were you respectful? Did you disclose information that your informants did not consent to have disclosed? Were you open with your informants about the form and content of your final report or paper? In collaborative research, interlocutors would be asked to read over the final report or paper and make comments and adjustments to its content to clarify and confirm its analysis—before the study was made available for public consumption (Fluehr-Lobban 1998). This vetting of the final report is often a good general practice for assuring open dialogue and respect for others' rights concerning how they are represented.

Ethics Forms and Committees

Whether you live in Canada or the United States, you will be required to submit a research proposal to either the REB or the IRB at your university. As we mentioned earlier, these forms are slightly different at each university, but they follow the same nationwide guidelines and basic format. The final application will include a proposal that covers all the details of your chosen methods, theoretical focus, and objectives; a completed consent form; and a statement of ethical issues. The latter will provide a discussion of the possible harms and benefits of your research, your ethical stance on consent, the ways you will ensure confidentiality, how you will store your research data, and how you will disseminate your data. The review board's job is to make sure the language you are using is up to date with current guidelines, that the correct protocols are in place concerning the types of methods you have selected (i.e., structured or unstructured interviews or participant observation), and that the ways you will contact the communities involved follows standard ethical codes. If you adhere to the advice of your professor and other advisers in completing these forms, your project should pass quickly, but sometimes proposals need to be rewritten to comply. IRBs and REBs are the gatekeepers of all qualitative research concerning humans, and these boards do have the final say in terms of how you will proceed.

Getting Informed Consent

As we have discussed above, all qualitative research in anthropology in North America requires the researcher to complete a variety of legal forms that must then be passed by an ethics committee. One of these is an **informed consent** form, which is most commonly used before conducting interviews. However, the ethics concerning informed consent encompasses all aspects of research that begins once you enter your field site. In early ethical guidelines, informed consent was merely implied, but more recently, the forms that are signed clearly outline the basic principles of all ethical research, including the following:

1) That research subjects have enough information about your research project to make an informed decision as to whether they want to participate;
2) that research subjects have the right to withdrawal at any time and;
3) that any risks (no matter how minimal) and benefits of the research project have been clearly discussed.

Because anthropological studies take place over long periods, what participants were consenting to initially can change for a wide variety of reasons. To maintain an atmosphere of mutual respect, you must continually discuss what exactly your research subjects are consenting to and what their participation means in this changing relationship and process.

Compared to other types of scientific research, such as biomedical research, for example, cultural anthropology might be assumed to be inherently low risk.

We meet with people, talk to them, and watch what they do, but at issue is understanding how to protect their personal autonomy—how to protect them and their communities from institutional interference (Fluehr-Lobban 1994). And, as Jen Shannon reminds us, ensuring this sort of protection is still a very important issue for all Indigenous communities in North America. Nevertheless, some situations are not conducive to acquiring written consent. Take, for example, a study during which you are involved in lengthy observations at a children's playground where people are constantly coming and going. Attempting to explain quickly to everyone exactly what your research entails and then asking each person to sign a consent form would take up much of your time, and it would be very disruptive to the observation process. In this case, formal consent would not be required unless you briefly interviewed one of the parents, in which case it would be appropriate to obtain oral consent, perhaps on a voice recorder. Conversely, if you were observing the activities in an emergency department of a hospital, you would need informed consent from hospital officials and from any nurses or patients you interviewed directly, but not from the people whom you were just watching.

Conversations about consent need to revolve around what people need to be informed about because your primary concern is the welfare of the people you are working with. Often interlocutors are confused about what they are consenting to even after you feel that you have been clear in your disclosure. They can be exasperated if they speak a different language than you do or if they are recent immigrants living in North America. They might agree without understanding what they are agreeing to. Another cause of confusion might be that the context and assumptions of the academic world are different than those of the one you are studying. Imagine you told your participants that you planned on publishing your findings in academic journals. You would understand what that meant, but they might be unfamiliar with how available academic articles are online or that your study will include personal quotations (even if pseudonyms are used). They might not be aware of how their personal comments are implicated (formulated?) into published statements about the communities they live in. Therefore, disclosure needs to be open throughout and following the research process. Moreover, participants need to be informed about why you are conducting this research, whom you will be interviewing and working with, what theories you are focusing on (even if they don't understand completely), and where your findings will be disseminated (e.g., conferences, journals, books). Throughout the process, informing others about your work should ultimately enrich your research, as they undoubtedly will inform you in return about some of their concerns and interests.

Shifting Fields: Ethics and the Digital World

We will discuss this topic in more detail in Chapter 12, but, generally speaking, research in digital worlds and on the Internet is inherently more participatory, meaning it is more collaborative and involves complex and shifting sets of participants. For example, the researcher might be involved with other engaged researchers in teamwork one day, community advocacy groups the next, and then individual participants following that. There also might be substantial collaboration among the various groups and individuals involved, collaboration that is unseen by the primary researcher. This increased participation can create more tension in terms of ethical concerns and coordinating practices. Having said that, we think many digital projects offer the opportunity for building ethical relationships between researchers, institutions, and the communities they study. Gubrium and Harper explain that conversations that take place in the digital world often include ethics discussions in which participants have, or take, the opportunity to interrogate the principles of the primary researcher's code. They advocate for initial, formal training of all participants in ethical conduct as it is defined by the universities involved, so participants can contribute more ethically in their relationships with each other throughout the research process (Gubrium and Harper 2013).

There are also shifting concerns about informed consent online. For example, let's say your project revolved around the use of photographs posted on a public website. How would you obtain informed consent to use them in your work? Would you contact the webmaster and the head of the organization and ask both to sign the documents? Or would you consult with each member of the organization who had posted a photo and get permission? Conversely, what about posting photos taken by participants during your research projects. These questions bring to light the limitations of informed consent that have been debated throughout the twentieth and twenty-first centuries. They also speak to what some have described as a "methodological myopia" in terms of digital research in which thinking about what participation means, in terms of ethics, becomes very complicated (Walther 2002, 206; Gubrium and Harper 2013, 49). The same goes for confidentiality and anonymity; private conversations can become very public once they enter the online world. As Fluehr-Lobban (2008) reminds us, true collaboration means putting people first and focusing on the evolving scenarios they are immersed in, which could include new technologies, ideological shifts, or cultural negotiations.

VIGNETTE

Jen Shannon is a museum curator and associate professor of cultural anthropology at the University of Colorado–Boulder. She teaches courses in the Department of Anthropology and in the Museum and Field Studies graduate program in the University of Colorado Museum of Natural History. She was a lead researcher in the curatorial section of the National Museum of the American Indian before earning a PhD in sociocultural anthropology at Cornell University in 2008.

ON BEING A TENTATIVE ANTHROPOLOGIST: COLLABORATIVE ANTHROPOLOGICAL RESEARCH WITH INDIGENOUS PEOPLES IN NORTH AMERICA

In *Indians in Unexpected Places*, Philip Deloria (2004) teaches us about the power of stereotypes that shape our expectations of Native American peoples. These stereotypes include what you may remember from Native Americans in classic Western movies: the images of savage and primitive peoples, the generalizations of feather headdresses and tipis, and the depiction of them as peoples of the past. To see how museums and anthropologists contributed to these stereotypes, one need only consider the undated descriptions and static mannequins dressed in loincloths in older museum exhibits and the emphasis in nineteenth- and early twentieth-century anthropology on recording memories of precontact times while ignoring contemporary life.[3]

As a cultural anthropologist who is also a curator in a museum, I acknowledge and am confronted by this troubled history often. I was trained not only in university but also on the job at the National Museum of the American Indian (NMAI) in Washington, DC. Today, many of us in museum and cultural anthropology are committed to working together with Indigenous peoples in support of self-representation and self-determination and to redress injustices of the past. We are working toward making museums welcoming places to Indigenous perspectives and practices, and toward an anthropology that is directed by Indigenous partners and their priorities. We call this work "decolonizing the museum" and "decolonizing methodologies" (C. Smith 2005; L. Smith 1999, 2006). Below, I show what this looks like in practice, and why I have come to see myself as a "tentative anthropologist."

Foundations of Collaborative Research

The methods of cultural anthropology have changed over time; the current paradigm for research with Indigenous peoples is often referred to as "the collaborative turn." In the past, Indigenous peoples were referred to as "specimens" or seen as "primitives" or scientific objects to be studied. Collaborative anthropology—in which Indigenous peoples participate in setting the goals, methods, and outcomes of research—helps to ensure representations of them are not stereotypical, and it engenders mutual respect. We also value collaboration for epistemological reasons: as anthropologists, we value other ways of knowing the world around us and do not want to continue to privilege only Western ways of knowing Indigenous peoples and their experiences.

Some principles that derive from these commitments and provide the foundation for the collaborative research that I do with Indigenous peoples in North America include recognition of Native peoples' sovereignty and self-determination; codirected research questions, processes, and outcomes; honest and open communication; shared research outcomes in accessible media; reciprocity, or exchange with mutual benefit; and value and respect for other ways of knowing and being in the world.

These ethical and epistemological reasons for collaboration are all well and good. But I want to stress here that it is not just for these (very important) sociohistorical, scholarly, or theoretical reasons that we do collaborative anthropology: relevancy and reciprocity are *righteous demands* by the Native American peoples with whom I have worked in the United States. Here is an example from my work with the Mandan, Hidatsa, and Arikara Nation (MHA) Nation in January 2016, though this kind of exchange has happened many times in the field with different communities. They are wonderful, anxious, and unsettling moments.

We were being interviewed on live radio about our current research project with the community (see Figure 3.1), when three quarters of the way into an hour-long discussion, radio host Prairie Rose Seminole asked this question:

Now both of you [Chris and Jen] have studied anthropology, teach it. So, coming into Indian Country, have you had any push back? Cause we don't typically have good relationships with anthropologists.... So, what's your experience there? How are you kind of mending that historical, uh [pause] history, I guess [laughs]. [Everyone laughs] I can't think of an appropriate polite word to say. But we typically haven't had a good relationship with anthropologists, so how are you moving forward and building bridges and making connections that *strengthen* our story and our history and ... you know, we're still here. So how are we bringing that forward?

I responded that, "for me, that collaborative aspect" was moving the relationship forward. It was "not bringing research questions to the community, but having them come up with the questions that

FIGURE 3.1: Live on air at KMHA Radio with anthropologist and ethnographic filmmaker Chris Hammons, undergraduate Atty Phleger, and Prairie Rose Seminole, host of *The Voice*. Screen capture from Chris Hammons, January 2016. Photograph courtesy of Jen Shannon.

matter to them. And then finding an appropriate, meaningful way to work together to tell those stories."

Collaborative Research with the Mandan Hidatsa Arikara Nation

My relationships with members of the MHA Nation began during a consultation with tribal representatives about sacred items in our university museum collection; our relationship evolved over time into a documentary film project and an interactive community website, a citizen science project, and community-based filmmaking workshop (see Figure 3.2). At each step of the way, we checked in, asking two very basic questions: Is this something you really want (us) to do? How should we proceed?

The MHA Nation is located on the Fort Berthold reservation, near the center of the Bakken shale formation associated with the fracking boom in North Dakota. Since 1851, MHA lands have been reduced from 12 million to fewer than 1 million acres. Contributing to this reduction and to the relocation of 90 percent of the community was the Garrison Dam, completed in 1953 by the US Army Corps of Engineers (Berman 2003; Lawson 2009).

In 2011, tribal representatives Calvin Grinnell and Elgin Crows Breast invited me to meet with a group of elders. The group asked

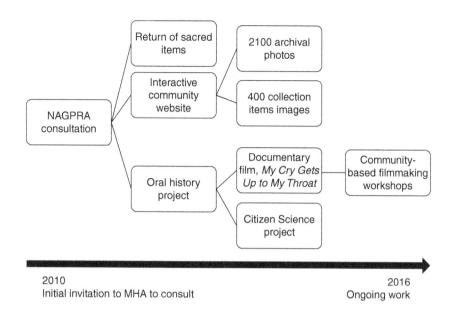

```
                    Return of sacred          2100 archival
                        items                    photos

                      Interactive
                      community               400 collection
     NAGPRA            website                items images
   consultation

                                          Documentary
                                        film, My Cry Gets    Community-
                      Oral history      Up to My Throat      based filmmaking
                        project                             workshops

                                          Citizen Science
                                             project
```

2010   2016
Initial invitation to MHA to consult   Ongoing work

FIGURE 3.2: Evolution of MHA projects over time.

FIGURE 3.3: Preparing sacred items to return home with Calvin Grinnell (MHA Nation). Photographed by Jan Bernstein, June 2014, and shared with permission from tribal representatives Grinnell and Elgin Crows Breast. June 2014. Photograph courtesy of Jen Shannon.

me to conduct an oral history project and make a video documentary about Rev. Case because they wanted to better understand the life and times of a missionary who opposed the dam and, as Elgin put it, "eased their pain" in the "difficult transition."

Each person we interviewed was selected by our community partners, who also helped us develop interview questions. But it was community members' responses to my final question that started to shape the narrative into a cohesive and timely story. In response to the simple question—"Is there anything else you'd like to add?"—almost every person discussed the oil boom. Edwin Benson, concerned, asked people to think "of tomorrow, or the next day, or the next year, year after that—what's going to happen?" (Figure 3.4). Elders were speaking to those community members who were not old enough to know that the contemporary oil boom felt a lot like their experiences during the dam and relocation times. The video was published in 2014 and titled *My Cry Gets Up to My Throat: Reflections on Rev. Case, the Garrison Dam, and the Oil Boom in North Dakota.*

We conducted interviews in 2012 and 2013 and then presented interview clips to participants for them to review and approve, both the clips themselves and the themes we highlighted. We then sequenced

FIGURE 3.4: Visiting Edwin Benson (at left) for an interview at his home. Left to right are Calvin Grinnell, historian Lil Fenn, graduate student Kendall Tallmadge, and the author. Photograph taken by Benson's daughter, May 2013. Photograph courtesy of Jen Shannon.

together the clips and archival images to make a narrative story; the narrator script was edited and approved by tribal historians Calvin Grinnell and Marilyn Hudson. We presented film screenings in several locations on the reservation in 2014 for feedback. It was important to convey that this was an unfinished draft, so the title of the video was "What do you think the title should be?" We received substantive comments and returned again at the end of the year with a final cut (Figure 3.5). All interviewees received copies of their raw, uncut interviews and the final cut of the video. The final cut was also distributed for free on DVD and online.

Throughout this iterative process, we sought consent and participation through methods that go beyond IRB protocols and reading consent scripts to individual participants.[4] Embracing the value of openness, we sought to share what we were doing not just with the interviewees on film but with the community at large. We distributed flyers about community screening events, sent newsletters about our projects to participants, authored articles in the tribal newspaper, were interviewed on the tribal radio, and posted on Facebook to keep community members updated.

At a draft film screening in May 2014, some MHA community members suggested the video be used in schools, and others asked us to make a second video to document the oil boom today. During the final screenings in November 2014, this sentiment was reiterated. The following August we visited the community again to ask two questions:

FIGURE 3.5: Draft film screening after an elders' lunch at the Northern Lights Community Center, November 2014. Photograph courtesy of Jen Shannon.

"Is this what you really want? And how should we go about doing it?" By March of 2016, we developed a plan with MHA community members to conduct community-based filmmaking workshops the following summer to facilitate them telling their own stories about life today. This corresponded with feedback we received that one of the impacts of the oil boom is "negative media" by outsiders. As Juanita Helphrey states in the conclusion to *My Cry Gets Up to My Throat*, "a perspective will be realized, I think, from our point of view—that's the best part."

The success (in terms of community participation and circulation) of the oral history video project led to other projects, such as a citizen science project. Developed in response to community concerns, the citizen science project began with listening sessions with reservation schoolteachers to help create lesson plans to empower students to collect and interpret data about their changing environment. Another important moment of decolonizing in practice for both my team and the Native community members present occurred during one of the teacher workshops in October 2015. A community member interrupted us to demand, "Who owns the data?" Our answer: "You do."

On Being a Tentative Anthropologist

I practice "strong collaboration" in which "explicit attention to the process is part of the project" (Choy et al. 2009, 381); in other words, reflexivity with and among research partners is a part of the collaborative process and its write up (see Shannon 2012, 2014a, 2014b). I also believe that our theory and methods are deeply co-constitutive; how we structure our methods and relations in the field influences the knowledge produced and the theoretical possibilities of our work. Part of that reflexive process has led to my developing a tentative approach to research with and in Indigenous communities.

As we moved into planning the sequel documentary project, I invited ethnographic filmmaker Chris Hammons to be part of our team so that the outcome would be a more professional film than the one I had created with student assistants. I came to characterize and understand myself as a "tentative anthropologist," as I explained to him on our first fieldwork trip together in August 2015. That was definitely how I was feeling during our visit to MHA Nation. He was astonished when I said, as we were driving in the car between meetings, "I don't know if this project will work; until we have support from community members, I am not sure I want to do this...." He kept asking, "What is the film going to be about?" And I would reply, "I don't know!" He came to understand, after several trips and our on-air radio discussion, what it means to codirect our research with community members and why it is important to do so.

As an outcome of our community meetings, our project changed: instead of a sequel documentary, as was originally requested, we developed community-based video workshops to teach tribal members how to make their own films. Through grant funds, we hired two local filmmakers to help facilitate the workshops, and, together, we conducted them in five different segments on the reservation. These short films were distributed through a website and on Facebook.

"Tentative" is defined as experimental, unsure, uncertain—not definite, hesitant. This is the kind of anthropologist I am, based on the history of anthropology and museums and Indigenous peoples, and on my experiences in the field. It means that my work at times feels anxious, and that I have doubts. I sometimes wonder if I should continue. But it also means that when it clicks (and you know when it does!), it feels like we are doing the right thing. To me, success means community partners feel that the outcomes of our work together are appropriate and meaningful to them and that this work "feels right" in its representation of their experience; success means that we do not just have consent but also encouragement and support from the people with whom we work. It feels like we are on a good path, and we are walking it together.

Making Connections

Can you think of ways that you can incorporate the two questions that Jen Shannon asked repeatedly throughout the interviews she conducted: "Is this something you really want (us) to do?" and "How should we proceed?"

If you understand the idea of being a "tentative anthropologist" (according to Shannon's commentary) to mean being "experimental" and "unsure," then how will you apply this idea to your own research to add depth and coherence to your overall project?

How will you make sure that the people you are working with understand what they are consenting to? To make sure they are clear about your intentions, you need to create a set of review questions that follow your explanation of your project.

Write a list of the ways you see yourself as having integrity as a researcher, and then write another list explaining the ways you will demonstrate that integrity during your research project.

Try This

For this exercise, you will be asked to come to class with a comprehensive research question that includes a paragraph about the particulars of your proposed research plan. You will also be willing to participate in a role-play exercise with your fellow students. In groups of three, each of you will present your proposal in a professional manner and provide a handout to the other two students in your group. Your two audience members will pretend to be members of the group or community you are planning on conducting research with. In this capacity, they will ask appropriate questions that reflect their interests, concerns, and rights according to the AAA code of ethics. They will also go over the printed handout to flush out any changes they think should be made. The following week, your group will meet once more to go over any changes that were made to each proposal, to make sure these comply with the desires and perceptions of the communities involved. This exercise functions as a practice session for similar meetings you can plan with the actual groups or communities you are working with.

Possible Projects

1. During the term of your fieldwork, make it a practice to write down any ethical concerns that come up while you are reading through your reflective notes. Most of what you think about will probably not seem important, and most likely much of it will concern relatively minor issues. However, when you are analyzing the bulk of your notes, you may see a trend or consistent commentary about a particular concern. At this point, you still have time to go over these issues with the people you are working with. For example, you might notice during the interview process that many of your interviewees are asking you to explain what a cultural anthropologist actually does. This could indicate that they are unsure of what the results of your research will mean for them and their communities, or perhaps they are concerned about how the results will be disseminated and accepted by the wider public later on.

2. Second, make it a practice throughout your research project to include as many participant-driven questions as you can. Questions that are created by the people you are working with can be central to collaborative research and to in-depth analyses later. For example, Jen Shannon did a thorough job of checking frequently with members of the MHA Nation that she was working with by asking them "Is this something you really want (us) to do?" and "How should we proceed?" Obviously, you will

start with questions you have derived from your comprehensive reading and studies, but make it a practice to let your participants review these questions prior to your asking them and to change them or create new questions that they think are more appropriate. At the least, end every interview session by making sure you ask each interlocutor if there is anything that person would like to add, if he has any questions for you, or if she can think of any questions you should have asked or that you should ask the next person you talk with. This small step will improve the collaborative nature of your research project.

Recommended Readings

AAA (American Anthropological Association). 2012 "Statement on Ethics." *AAA Ethics Blog*. http://ethics.americananthro.org/category/statement.

Brettell, Caroline. 1993. *When They Read What We Write: The Politics of Ethnography*. Westport, CT: Bergin & Garvey.

Fluehr-Lobban, Carolyn. 1991. *Ethics and the Profession of Anthropology: Dialogue for a New Era*. Philadelphia, PA: University of Philadelphia Press.

Fluehr-Lobban, Carolyn. 2003. "Ethics and Anthropology, 1890–2000: A Review of Issues and Principles." In *Ethics and the Profession of Anthropology: Dialogue for Ethically Conscious Practice*, 1–28. 2nd ed. Walnut Creek, CA: AltaMira Press.

Glass, Kathleen Cranley, and Joseph Kaufert. "Research Ethics Review and Aboriginal Community Values: Can the Two Be Reconciled?" *Journal of Empirical Research on Human Research Ethics* 2 (2): 25–49.

Lassiter, Luke E. 2005. *The Chicago Guide to Collaborative Ethnography*. Chicago, IL: University of Chicago Press.

Lonetree, Amy. 2012. *Decolonizing Museums: Representing Native America in National and Tribal Museums*. Chapel Hill, NC: University of North Carolina Press.

Marshall, Patricia. 2003. "Human Subjects Protections, Institutional Review Boards and Cultural Anthropological Research." *Anthropological Quarterly* 76 (2): 269–85.

Plattner, Stuart. 2004. "Human Subjects Protection and Anthropology." *Anthropology News* 45 (2): 5–6.

Smith, Linda Tuhiwai. 1999. *Decolonizing Methodologies: Research and Indigenous Peoples*. New York, NY: St. Martin's Press.

Notes

1   Carolyn Fluehr-Lobban first begins talking about this in 1991 (see *Ethics and the Profession of Anthropology: Dialogue for a New Era*. Philadelphia, PA: University of Philadelphia Press).

2   Project Camelot, a counterinsurgency study in 1964 that involved the US Army, was responsible for hiring anthropologists (among other academics) to analyze certain countries (in particular, Latin America) with the goal of enhancing the government's ability to influence social processes and social orders. For an in-depth discussion see Mark Solovey (2001) "Project Camelot and the 1960s Epistemological Revolution: Rethinking the Politics-Patronage-Social Science Nexus." *Social Studies of Science* 31 (2): 171–206.

3   There is a famous, satirical critique of anthropologists worth reading by Indigenous author Vine Deloria, Jr. (Standing Rock Sioux) in his 1969 book *Custer Died for Your Sins: An Indian Manifesto*. See Chapter 4, "Anthropologists and Other Friends." Some Indigenous peoples have critiqued anthropologists and research in general for extracting information from Indigenous communities and providing no benefit to them, nor even copies of the research; for publishing ceremonial knowledge that is not appropriate to share with the general public; for digging up burials to study them and place them in museums; and for conducting salvage anthropology. This last critique stems from the sort of anthropology done from the mid-nineteenth century to the mid-twentieth century; anthropologists assumed that Indigenous peoples would disappear due to genocide or ethnocide—namely, assimilation—so they gathered up and archived as much knowledge and as many artifacts as possible in the name of preservation. Of course, Indigenous peoples in North America did not die off, and they have since helped shape more ethical research practices, particularly in the field of anthropology.

4   An IRB, or institutional review board, is the department on a university campus that reviews a student or professor's research plan when research involves people. If you are in a discipline that collects data about people, then you must submit your research to the IRB for approval. This oversight originally started with biomedical experiments but is now applied to any research with human subjects, including anthropology. Also referred to as the "human subjects protocol," this ethical review is designed to maintain ethical practice and ensure the protection of human subjects in research.

CHAPTER 4

CONNECTING WITH OTHERS: INTERVIEWING, CONVERSATIONS, AND LIFE HISTORIES

Introduction

Many would say that we are living in an interview society. We are interviewed or see others being interviewed in a multitude of venues. One example would be celebrity talk shows on which interviewers such as Anderson Cooper, Oprah Winfrey, Jon Stewart, and even Jerry Springer interview movie stars and ordinary people to make us feel as if we know them on a personal level (Briggs 2007). The interview process in media venues has also become a form of therapy, both medical and emotional. Take Dr. Phil, for example. On his show very private experiences are aired and discussed on national television in the style of a personal confessional, intended to lead those being interviewed toward an authentic revelation and life-altering experience (Atkinson and Silverman 1997). Other, more everyday interview venues would include doctor's offices, hospitals, online opinion polls, and job interviews.

Anthropologists have been practicing various forms of the interview process since the mid-1800s. The following comments were published in 1874 by the British Association for the Advancement of Science, and they refer to the relationship between an anthropologist and "Native" interviewees.

> It is almost impossible to make a savage in the lower stages of culture understand *why* the questions are asked, and from the limited range of his vocabulary or ideas it is often nearly as difficult to put the question before him in such a way that he can comprehended it.
> The result often is that from timidity, or the desire to please, or from weariness of the questioning, he will give an answer that he thinks will satisfy the inquirer. (Quoted in Skinner 2012, 25; see also Read [1874] 1892, 87–88)

Interview styles and the theories surrounding their use have shifted and changed over time, and obviously contemporary anthropologists would never assume a staunch, ethnocentric position of authority as suggested above. These days, the focus is on the participatory nature of interviewing and on how interviewers and interviewees build relationships and cocreate narratives. According to Kvale (1996), the interview is literally an *inter view* or exchange of views between two people, and not a one-way conversation.

In cultural anthropology, the value of the texts that are produced from oral interviews lies in their ability to let others voice their beliefs, opinions, perspectives, and memories—to tell their stories. Interviews can become part of a research project in two ways. First, they can be a way of gaining in-depth information in a "positivist vein"; the information gained, in other words, is viewed primarily as objective data. An example of an interview question yielding objective data might be, "Can you tell me the ages, genders, and current careers of all of your siblings?" This question can allow for the sharing of intimate details of an individual's lives that are articulated through cultural meanings. Interviews can be one way of exposing others' perspectives and ideas "of democratizing in a broad sense" (Wodak as seen in Briggs 2007, 573). Second, the ideal aim is centered on helping people connect their feelings and memories with their real-life circumstances by telling stories. This follows in the "interpretivist tradition"; interviews are less structured and are used in conjunction with other methods, such as participant observation, in an attempt to understand meaningfulness broadly speaking. In this way, active and engaged listening is as important as reflecting on the authority assumed as an interviewer.

How to Approach People

Choosing your interview participants is a very important component of the process and can take time in terms of gaining access and permission. If you are involved in a long-term research project, generally you will have already spent many hours practicing participant observation with the group of people you are working with, and you have gotten to know many of them on an intimate level. In this case, whom you choose to ask about interviews will generally be based on the **rapport** you have gained. You could, for example, ask those you know best and feel most comfortable with first. Once word gets around that your interviewees have had a positive experience, then others will agree more easily and will often contact you to ask to be interviewed.

If your research project is based on interview sessions only, then you will need to find people in the communities you are working with. For example, if you were working with recent Syrian refugees at a local church, you might send out fliers, post notices on the bulletin boards, or make presentations at church meetings. Anthropologists have also been known to simply place ads in newspapers or online, asking for potential participants to contact them. Once you find a few interviewees, you can then work through word of mouth to contact others. This is called the **snowball method**. It works like this: contact is made with one or two key informants, and then you ask them for a list of people that they think might be interested in being interviewed. If you follow this protocol at the end of each interview, your list of new names keeps growing exponentially—it snowballs (Russell 2006). Dianna Shandy used this method in her work and talks about how snowball sampling can allow for networking in a large city. In this instance, she welcomed the diversity of ethnic contacts that was gleaned from developing multiple snowball samples, starting from multiple entry points, because doing so meant her final list of interviewees mimicked larger populations from other cultures and ethnicities that lived in the same urban setting. For smaller projects, such as the ones you will be conducting, the single snowball method is best because it allows for networking within a small demographic, which helps you stay focused on your topic. If the network you create becomes too diluted, it can be problematic, though. For example, you planned on talking to single mothers living within the poverty line, and you end up with the names of their friends of friends who are more wealthy and not single; deciding not to interview some members of your newly created network might create hard feelings within the wider group.

When? Where to Meet?

Contact well in advance the people you are planning on interviewing and decide on a place and time to meet. Make sure from the onset that they are very clear about what will transpire (e.g., how long the interview will be, what types of questions you will discuss, whether you will use recording devices). Scheduling is usually dependent on what is convenient for the interviewees, as most have busy schedules. Timing can affect an individual's mood and therefore the type of conversations that will take place. Also, make sure you pick a place that is quiet and comfortable for both of you. The noise level is obviously very important if you are using a recording device or if you want to create a flow in the conversation. Interviews generally last between one and three hours, with some running even longer, so you want to make sure you will not be distracted for this length of time. It is also important to remember that types of places can color the types of things people talk about. For example, if your research project is focused on a certain business, your participants might want to meet with you in their offices because it is more convenient. They may feel free talking about certain information in this location and not as comfortable talking about other types of information in close proximity to colleagues and their boss. In this case, it might be better to meet in a more neutral space. Also, if, for example, you are planning on talking about an emotional topic, or a topic that has the potential to be emotional, it might make more sense to meet in someone's home rather than in a busy coffee shop. Ultimately, it often boils down to what it most comfortable for the interviewee. Talking with you should not make interviewees feel nervous or uncomfortable for any reason.

How to Develop Questions

There are three things to think about when writing and organizing your questions:

1) What types of questions you will ask and why?
2) What order should they be in?
3) How should they be worded?

Language is very important in terms of making interviewees feel comfortable and in encouraging conversation. Question order is important for gaining rapport and for maintaining the flow of the conversation, which allows for deeper thinking and continuity. For example, if you were asking questions about someone's political beliefs, it would be best to start with more neutral questions about their lifestyle, background, or career. Sensitive questions or questions that you feel might reveal emotions or controversy should be asked in the middle of an interview or toward the end, so the interviewee has time to feel relaxed and not threatened in any way. Nonjudgmental wording is also critical in this instance. Questions that presume something about the interview should be avoided, and these are the types of questions that participants will avoid (Leech 2002).

An interview can be built on a variety of types of questions and each has its own specific purpose. Generally, anthropologists talk about **open-ended questions** versus **closed questions** and direct questions versus indirect questions. Because there is a focus placed on thinking like an ethnographer, opened-ended questions are usually the most popular, especially in starting off an interview. Opened-ended questions may be focused on a certain topic but are designed to leave the answer open—to let the interviewee decide how she or he would like to answer. James Spradley coined the term

"Grand Tour questions" to describe questions that impose few boundaries but rather allow participants to talk about, or give a spoken tour of, a topic (1979, 88–89). He argues that this is one of the best ways to learn about cultural practices, meanings, and themes that are important to the person being interviewed. One easy example would be, "Tell me about your family life."

Closed questions are designed with the opposite intention, to gain specific answers or pieces of information that are important to your research project. Direct questions often happen spontaneously during an interview, as a way to clarify something that was said. For example, after a lengthy conversation about childcare, an interviewer might ask, "What are the ages of the children and how does this impact your daily schedule?" An indirect question is less interrogative and might be worded this way: "I was just wondering if the ages of your children affected your daily schedule in any way?" These types of questions require a less obligatory response. Anthropologists try not to use leading questions that put words into an interviewee's mouth or assume a correct answer because doing so can damage the rapport you have created. A good example of a leading question is one that starts with "Most people"— such as, "Most people like to shop in supermarkets as opposed to outdoor markets. Do you prefer to shop in supermarkets?" These types of questions suggest that there is a right answer.

The Structure of Interviews

In basic terms, interview styles range from informal to formal; the terms used in cultural anthropology are **unstructured interviews** and **structured interviews**. At one end of the scale are informal interviews. As Russell (2006) suggests, in some ways we all conduct informal interviewing throughout our daily lives when we ask questions and talk to people we meet. One example might be a conversation you start up with a stranger in the dentists' office, where you talk randomly about your lives while you wait. For an anthropologist, informal interviewing might take place during participant observation or while the researcher is casually taking part in a community event. This informal interview involves a very different type of talking than would happen in an unstructured, semi-structured, or structured interview because, once you meet with another person with the intention of conducting an interview, at the least, there is a shared understanding that your meeting is purposeful.

The structure of an interview follows from the type of information required. Ethnographers commonly choose to engage in unstructured interviews because they allow people to express themselves more freely. This type of interview, similar to the Grand Tour question, gives control to the interviewee. You can still use a set of questions, but they are all open ended and the interviewee is given free rein to talk for as long as he or she wishes about each topic, and to express personal opinions and emotions. Structured interviews are similar to a survey: the questions are very specific, the interviewer sticks to a script, and the interviewees are not allowed to change the topic. In this case, you would generally have more questions and each would necessitate less time to answer. They are designed for projects that required standardized data. Generally speaking, most anthropologists work within a semi-structured model, using both styles to their advantage but usually beginning with an unstructured atmosphere and interjecting more structured questions when specific information is needed.

Handwritten Notes versus Audio Recordings

Whether or not you decide to use a voice recorder or just take notes during your interviews will depend on the amount of detailed information you need, how many interviews you are undertaking, and the potential effects on your participants. Some people feel more comfortable with one method or the other, but not both. Some people do not mind being recorded; others hate it. Very small digital voice recorders can be hidden under something close by after you have started, such as a few papers. That way, the interviewees know they are being recorded but forget about it as time passes. This allows them to feel comfortable and focused on your conversation as opposed to the lights of the recorder. One tip for organizing your recordings is to tape comments before each interview and to include the time, date, place, and interviewee's name. After the interview, it is also a good idea to tape some quick reflections on the experience from your point of view, noting body language, changes in speech, facial expressions, or anything else unique or significant. Also, make sure to check your batteries before you start. There is nothing worse than imagining you have recorded a few hours of conversation only to realize later that your recorder was not working. Transcribe each interview shortly afterwards, so you do not forget details, body language, and the overall experience. Without a doubt, computers can speed up some aspects of the interview process. For example, some researchers contact interviewees through email. Computers can also assist in recording and organizing data as well as in transcribing field notes and interviews. However, conducting interviews while taking notes on your laptop is generally frowned upon. Many people feel intimidated by someone sitting in front of them writing handwritten notes about what they are saying, and typing on a laptop exacerbates this feeling and can create a technological wedge that destroys intimacy and may enhance the feeling of being objectified.

Life Histories Are Different

The first **life history** interviews were collected by anthropologists in the early 1900s and focused on the autobiographies of First Nations North American chiefs. Its popularity as a method has shifted over time, depending on the theoretical imperatives in the social sciences concerning the acquisition, or definition, of definitive data (Goodson 2001). Life history interviews differ from standard interviews in that you are asking someone to narrate her or his life. In this way, the narration becomes more of a performance that is linked closely with identity and influenced by the ambiguous nature of memory. Life history interviews are very open, often having no structure other than a few questions or prompts throughout. Your primary responsibility is to listen actively, which we will elaborate on later. Therefore, it is more appropriate in this instance to jot down a few notes during the interview about certain things you might like to clarify later. Also, you both need to be clear about where you left off in the life history narrative so that subsequent interviews can continue in a consistent manner. It can take numerous interviews to complete a full life history. In contemporary anthropology, a reliance on the importance of linear, chronological narratives has been replaced by an interest in how people perform their identities and how they express multiple subjectivities. Remember, life narratives often require several meetings and many hours of transcribing. It takes approximately six hours to transcribe every hour of recorded oral narrative.

Focus Groups or Group Interviewing

Focus group interviewing is a very popular method used by marketing, media, and health researchers. It is less popular in cultural anthropology, but it does provide certain types of information that can add to your research study. Professional marketing researchers conduct focus groups with small groups of strangers (2–12) to glean in-depth data and a range of opinions and responses to a certain product. Most often in anthropology, the members of the group know each other and the anthropologist, and their conversation is a follow-up to previous meetings or interviews. Finding a time and place that suits everyone is sometimes difficult, but once a focus group interview is organized, the actual meeting is conducted in a manner similar to that of a standard interview, except that when the anthropologist asks a question, all interviewees respond, which leads to spin-off conversations among group members. For this reason, group interviews are more difficult to mediate and transcribe. Lynda Mannik conducted small group sessions of three to four people who knew each other and who had already been interviewed separately. Her purpose was to explore their opinions and perspectives on a museum display that depicted their experiences as refugees in 1948. The focus group interview was beneficial for her study, in comparative terms, because they had all talked about the photographs taken during this experience in private, individual sessions, and then, as a group, they talked about how the same photographs were used in the museum's public display.

The Qualities of a Good Interview

In our current "interview society," we have come to think of the interview as a natural way to reveal the truth, and we tend to view the truth in an objective manner and to think that it can be gleaned by listening to what other people say. Cultural anthropologists have a very different way of thinking about this practice, and this difference is one of the hurdles for novice interviewers. For anthropologists, the focus is on **dialogic anthropology**. In other words, anthropologists view the production of knowledge as always taking place within an interaction, so meaning is relational. It is the interactive, human communication that takes place during an interview that is seen to provide the most important information, which is why these dialogues are considered to be "meaning-making occasions" (Holstein and Gubrium 1995, 4; Skinner 2012). Of course, as a researcher, you are responsible for choosing a topic, finding people to talk to, writing up the questions, and conducting a professional interview, but it is what happens during the interview between you and the interviewee that should be the meat of your analysis. You are the creator of the interview itself, but then you must let go and see yourself as an equal partner in the process. Norman Denzin asks us to think about interviews as reflexive exercises and as performative. As he says, "Interviews are part of the dialogic conversation that connects all of us"; therefore, he reminds us, words matter and affect people (Denzin 2001, 24). This is what makes interviews ethnographic: they are a part of participant observation, not outside of it, and they are collaborative (Skinner 2012).

Be Aware of Everything

Ethnographic-styled interviews are so much more than just face-to-face conversations. As a competent researcher, you obviously need to be paying attention to what people are saying, but you also must consider how they say it (which is often more important), their facial expression, body language, physical movements, and any other sensory information related to the interview, such as outside noise or movement that might be distracting your interviewee. In the vignette below, Dianna Shandy talks about noticing the books that her interviewees brought with them and how important these books became in her conversations with the people she interviewed. You also need to be self-conscious about your own input, your own self-expression, both physically and verbally. This sounds like a daunting task and definitely takes practice. Martin Forsey (2010) uses the term **"engaged listening"** to describe the intention of an ethnographic researcher, for whom listening is as important as observing and the interviewer "listens deeply" to understand the "cultural context of individual lives" (561, 567). The visual experience you have as an interviewer is key to understanding the meaning of what your participants are saying. You need to think of yourself as an observer, a participant, and an interviewer all rolled into one.

It Is Good When the Interviewees Get Something Out of It!

An ethical anthropologist always keeps the welfare of the people he or she is talking to in mind, and considers this welfare an important aspect of any research. Ultimately, the goal is to create a project that in some way positively enhances the lives of the people you are working with. When someone asks to interview you, that person is already attesting to the value of your opinions and perspectives, which is very self-affirming. Being interviewed lets people talk about aspects of their lives more openly and often leads to novel and enlightening conversations. The interview as an experience can be therapeutic. Simply listening to someone talk about his or her life is the basis of a therapeutic relationship. Interviewees have also claimed that life history interviews have added meaning to their lives (Mannik 2013). When people from certain demographics are interviewed about important social issues, the resulting analysis and research reports concerning the group's opinions, feelings, and perspectives can offer solutions to problems, policy initiatives, and social change. Interviews can be powerful tools for social change as well.

VIGNETTE

Dianna Shandy is the associate dean of the Institute for Global Citizenship and a professor of anthropology at Macalester College in St. Paul, Minnesota. Her work spans US and international settings, and she has broad research and teaching interests in gender, migration, political conflict and violence, and research methods. Her specific research projects have explored college-educated women negotiating work and family in the United States, African asylum seekers in Ireland, and the South Sudanese and Somali diasporas in Europe, North America, and Africa.

ON THE MOVE: REFLECTIONS ON FIELDWORK WITH THE NUER IN AMERICA

Anthropologists are known for traveling to their field site, often to faraway locales. My work complicates this idea by describing research at home concerning a population that was on the move. I describe the research's inception, making contact, developing relationships, and how my positionality shaped the interviews. I work with the Nuer who are the focus of one of anthropology's most famous case studies. My research illustrates how their lives in the United States intersect with their ethnographic past and the implications this dynamic has for fieldwork.

I first learned about Nuer people living in the United States when I was visiting Minnesota from New York, where I was a graduate student at Columbia University in the 1990s. The man I was visiting (and later married) invited me to his friend's house to participate in what I thought at the time was a rather bizarre practice—an outdoor barbeque, with snow on the ground and temperatures below freezing.

FIGURE 4.1: Portrait of Dianna Shandy, 2009, Minnesota, USA. Photograph by Claire Kayser.

It was there that I noticed, in the pile of newspapers for the fire, a full-page color photojournalistic spread describing Nuer people from southern Sudan as recently resettled refugees living in Minnesota. At the time, I was writing grant applications and preparing to return to Namibia for doctoral research on issues of gender, race, and post-conflict reconstruction. I had lived and taught school in Namibia after completing my undergraduate degree and had subsequently returned to do my master's thesis research there.

All of that changed when I encountered the Nuer. Of course, it wasn't a first encounter. Most anthropologists have been introduced to "the Nuer" at some stage of their training. Sir Edward E. Evans-Pritchard, whom I fondly thought of by his initials EEEP, launched the Nuer people into the global scholarly consciousness with his famous trilogy: *The Nuer: A Description of the Modes of Livelihood of a Nilotic People* (1940), *Kinship and Marriage among the Nuer* (1951), and *Nuer Religion* (1956).

This unsolicited distinction has not translated, however, into any discernible benefit for this iconic people. In the decades since Evans-Pritchard conducted his research in Sudan, the Nuer people who live there have undergone many changes. Ongoing civil war, destruction, and disruption of the most fundamental aspects of life have characterized some of the most tragic shifts. Yet, more often than not, in anthropological discourse, the Nuer persist in the ethnographic present of the 1930s (Shandy 2008). Even as I am writing this, I am aware that I am in some ways perpetuating this dynamic by writing about "Sudan," because in 2011, South Sudan became its own nation and the world's newest country. At the time I began doing this work, however, the Nuer people's home country was still called Sudan—the larger entity from which South Sudan later seceded.

I first made contact with Nuer people by phoning a social service agency and a church listed in the newspaper article. These contacts connected me with several people, including a Nuer man, whom I will call Nyang, who agreed to tutor me in the Nuer language. When I arrived at Nyang's apartment, it was simultaneously very strange and very familiar. It was strange because, quite frankly, telling someone you want to "study" them or the group to which they belong feels odd. People, understandably, wonder why, how, and what your agenda is. Yet, as a transplant to Minnesota, I found Nyang's apartment comfortingly reminiscent of places I had lived in Africa. At this stage, I hadn't changed my plans to return to Namibia, but I wanted to know more about this population which, until that point, most anthropologists associated with Evans-Pritchard's Sudan.

When I started working with Nuer people, I largely tried to ignore EEEP. I was determined not to let his preconceived categories influence me. One of Evans-Pritchard's most notable contributions regarding Nuer people was that they had a "segmentary" system of political organization. If the lineages were going to segment, I wanted to hear it from the Nuer people I interviewed. After all, he was the late Evans-Pritchard. It wasn't like he was around and I could ask his permission to work with "his" people. And, even though the Nuer were a famous group, no one, at that point, had written about them outside of Africa.

Though I didn't label it as such at the time, I developed my questions using an ethnographic method that derives from ethnosemantics (McCurdy et al. 2004): I asked general open-ended questions about people's experiences, letting their responses shape my follow-up questions and my additional probes for examples or stories. I let the people I interviewed lead the conversations and strove to get information on what people *did*, not just their opinions. I found that kind of information much more useful. I took handwritten notes throughout, and I sometimes, with permission, used an audio recorder. Likewise, I was always doing participant observation during most of my interactions, taking time to jot down my notes each day—even if I didn't know whether the information was important or where it all would lead. I typed up most of my notes, and they have, therefore, survived many a move, and are "searchable" in a way they would not be if they were not digitized. Many of the photographs that I took were portrait-like shots that people asked me to take. I also printed and shared copies with them. In hindsight, I wish I had taken more candid shots—not to reproduce for publications but to serve as an aide-mémoire for my own work. Like many anthropologists, I was doing a sort of "discovery" anthropology that wasn't necessarily driven by a hypothesis or a problem I was trying to solve. It is only now, in rereading and reflecting on this experience, that I appreciate how early in the fieldwork process I identified what would later become a central theme in my work: the geographic dispersal of Sudanese, both in the United States and globally, and how they create and maintain relationships across spatial divides. This idea later formed the foundation of my book on this work, *Nuer-American Passages: Globalizing Sudanese Migration*.

I kept meeting with Nyang in his apartment, which the refugee resettlement agency had helped him secure in an impoverished part of town with a high crime rate. In 1995, the *New York Times* dubbed Minneapolis "Murderapolis." I had moved to Minnesota from New York City, so I didn't find the neighborhood that different from places

I knew. Yet, when I look back at my field notes from this time, I did feel some level of unease at first, taking the bus to this neighborhood and walking to Nyang's apartment. I would hold my breath as I entered the building, as the smell of urine in the carpeting in the corridor was overwhelming. The challenges of being a recent immigrant in America crystallized for me when Nyang asked the landlord to replace the filthy carpet in his apartment before his wife and young child joined him: I was dismayed to see the workmen take up the carpet only to unroll and install a used and slightly less filthy version of the same carpet that they were replacing.

One way I made additional contacts was through Nyang and his wife. Their friends would drop by their apartment, and these contacts led to other contacts. I tried to always call ahead before coming, because sometimes Nyang's work schedule shifted. One day I forgot and arrived to find no one home. I had the phone number of another Nuer man I had met the week before who lived nearby. I phoned him, and he invited me over. There, I met another set of people—both those who lived there and others who were visiting. At some point, Nyang changed jobs, making it more difficult to meet. I learned of a Nuer pastor beginning to offer informal Nuer language classes to interested community members and began attending. I also broadened my ties with social service providers, sitting in on meetings and collecting documents. These service provider interactions prompted new questions to ask my Nuer contacts.

I am a mixed-methods researcher. I'm not afraid of numbers, but qualitative research is my strong suit. One issue that qualitative researchers encounter, particularly among refugee populations, is the issue of a "sample." It is difficult to study refugee populations using larger data sets in the United States because refugees are not tracked there. The refugee apparatus makes it difficult to discern that refugees are living in our midst. In the United States, we call this the scatter approach. If the larger population is unknown, drawing a "representative sample" is problematic. Anthropologists can address this problem by being intentional in looking for multiple nodes of contact within the population. One can start with one individual and "snowball" out from there. One can, instead, use several points of entry, developing multiple "snowball" samples. The goal is to keep looking for things you haven't yet heard. If I had "snowballed" out from my tutor, I might have limited my sample to one particular lineage, Sudanese town, Kenyan refugee camp, or only people with higher education levels (an anomaly among early Sudanese refugees). By using multiple nodes,

I diversified the sample—doing life history, ethnographic, and survey interviews with over 700 people.

At this point, influenced by the postmodernism sweeping through academia and a healthy dose of pragmatism, I began to appreciate that learning Nuer in a non-immersive context and visiting people in their apartments wasn't like living in a small village, as I had done in Namibia, or even when I studied for a year in Ivory Coast. I'm not a fan of the term "commuter anthropology" because it implies a sort of less-authentic anthropology. Rather, I was doing "urban anthropology" and both the study population and I were geographically dispersed. I came to appreciate that I was not a chronicler of "the Nuer"—EEEP had already done that. (And I fully expected that Nuer people would be far more effective in telling their own story from their own point of view.) Rather, I was documenting a process of interaction and engagement between Nuer people and the spaces, places, people, and institutions involved in refugee resettlement and integration.

The first time I fully comprehended the power and enduring legacy of EEEP, though, was the time I went on a cross-country journey to visit Nuer people in another state. Bizarrely, we traveled in a 40-foot recreational vehicle.

I was dismayed when people began filing into the RV with jaunty greetings and books tucked under their arms. *"Ehhh, Maale." "Malpon-du." "Eh ... Maale. Jinatin."* Pal had a dog-eared copy of *The Nuer* with its unmistakable gold cover that hadn't changed in decades. Jal had *Nuer Religion*. Buom had a copy of *Nuer Dilemmas*, a book by anthropologist Sharon Hutchinson (1996) about life in Sudan. Although I thought the 50-hour or so round-trip drive to Nashville would be ideal to engage people in informal interviews about many topics, instead, we resembled a literature review on wheels:

> ME: "So, Pal, what was life like for you in Sudan?"
> PAL: "I raised cows. See. . . " gesturing at Evans-Pritchard's *The Nuer.*
> ME: "I see. But, I'm interested in *your* life."
> PAL: "Have you read *Nuer Dilemmas*?"

Fortunately, not all of my conversations with this group rehashed the existing ethnographic literature, particularly when we talked about their lives in the United States. I learned, however, that a people's anthropological past can become entwined with identity in the present. As we traveled through the night, the men stayed up late playing dominoes, shouting, and singing. While they taught me to play, I learned that dominoes were a huge event in the refugee camps in East Africa. People would sign up days in advance to play in tournaments. While playing and chatting, I learned a good deal about what quotidian camp life was like—the deprivations and hardships but also the incredible creativity and resourcefulness of the refugees who lived there. I learned from this experience of playing dominoes the deep value of letting interviews take the shape of conversations and letting the people you are interviewing guide the direction the sharing of information takes.

Making Connections

What would be a good set of open-ended questions that you think will work for your project, according to the ethnographic method that derives from ethnosemantics (McCurdy et al. 2004), research during which participant's responses are allowed to flow naturally?

In what sort of places do you see yourself conducting research? How do these places enhance your research project?

Taking Shandy's lead, how would you describe yourself as a "mixed-method researcher?"

What are some of the strategies you will use to create rapport with the people you are working with? (It is probably best to develop a "Plan A" and a "Plan B" when thinking about this question.)

Possible Projects

1. **Life History Skills**: Over the course of the term, you will be responsible for conducting life history interviews with one family member. This extended set of interviews should follow the specific practices of life history methods: namely, you should focus on listening and encouraging the informant's own story in every way, on emphasizing what he or she thinks is important to tell rather than what you think is important to ask about, and on making sure you remain objective. You will need to spend many hours and multiple sessions with this person, and during this time you will record and then transcribe her or his life story. It is also important to write down any questions you have during the interview, which can be asked at the end. Near the end of the term, you will return the life history to your interviewee and ask for feedback.

2. ***Engaged Listening***: For this project, you will compare individual interviews with a focus group interview, and then you will analyze your experiences and perceptions as an interviewer. Choose one topic (that relates to your research) and write a set of ten questions linked to exploring that topic. Some of the questions should be fairly neutral and some should be more politically motivated. Ask four friends or family members to participate. Plan individual interviews that will last about an hour, and include a set of approximately five of the questions. After transcribing all of these individual interviews, think about and compare them with a focus on "engaged listening," as outlined by Michael Forsey. Next, ask all four participants to meet for a focus group interview. Mediate a discussion with this group that focuses on the other five questions. Take notes during this experience and then write a short paper that compares your experience as an interviewee in these very different types of interviews.

Recommended Readings

Cole, Ardra L., and J. Gary Knowles. 2001. *Lives in Context: The Art of Life History Research*. Walnut Creek, CA: AltaMira Press.

Gibbs, Anita. 1997. "Focus Groups." *Social Research Update* 19: 1–7.

Holstein, James A., and Jaber F. Gubrium. 2001. *Handbook of Interview Research: Context and Method*. London, UK: Sage Publications Inc.

Mintz, Sydney. 1979. "The Anthropological Interview and the Life History." *Oral History Review* 7: 18–26.

Morgan, D. 1988. *Focus Groups as Qualitative Research*. London, UK: Sage Publications Inc.

O'Reilly, Karen. 2005. "Interviews: Asking Questions of Individuals and Groups." In *Ethnographic Methods*, edited by Karen O'Reilly, 72–88. New York, NY: Routledge.

Plummer, Ken. 2001. "The Call of Life Stories in Ethnographic Research." In *Handbook of Ethnography*, edited by Paul Atkinson, Amanda Coffrey, Sara Delamont, John Lofland, and Lynn Lofland, 395–406. London, UK: Sage Publications Inc.

Spradley, James P. 1979. *The Ethnographic Interview*. New York, NY: Holt, Reinhart and Winston.

Thompson, Paul. 1988. *The Voice of the Past*. 2nd ed. Oxford, UK: Oxford University Press.

PART II

Notes, Data, and Representation

CHAPTER 5

HOW TO CREATE FIELD NOTES

It's a symbol of your occupation. A material symbol.
(Anonymous quotation seen in Jackson 1990, 15)

Introduction

After months of planning, writing a proposal, and passing ethics committee requirements, you finally land at your field site. Imagine yourself standing there alone about to begin the research you have been thinking about for weeks or possibly months. What do you do next? Start writing field notes!

Creating **field notes,** whether they are actual handwritten reports, drawings, or photographs, is the cornerstone of collecting qualitative data. Anthropologists write them while they are involved in all other methods, from observation to participant observation to interviews. Surprisingly, very little has been written about the practical side of this process. Scholars have argued that this neglect is due to the highly subjective nature of the content and design of field notes, which are often scribbles in a notebook and poorly executed drawings (most anthropologists are not artists!) that are not deemed worthy of public attention. Field notes also often describe personal feelings and opinions, possibly biases, which may be misinterpreted by outsider readers. Many field notes are undecipherable and only have meaning for their writers because of the personalized shorthand codes they are written in.

Regardless, field notes have always been one of the key characteristic markers of anthropology as a discipline, and of anthropologists as researchers. As Jean Jackson explains, field notes mark anthropology's "pioneering approach to acquiring knowledge," the individualistic approach to discovery and exploration in which good "fieldnotes symbolize what journeying to and returning from the field mean" (1990, 32–33). In many ways, they embody the fieldwork experience and symbolize the relationship between individual anthropologists and the cultures and people they are working with. In the 1980s, Jackson (1990) interviewed over 70 anthropologists to try to figure out how they wrote field notes, how they felt about this method, and what it meant for their research process. She found that her colleagues were fraught with a variety of emotions concerning the process and practice. Many had negative feelings ranging from guilt, disappointment, and confusion; many felt uncomfortable writing things down while in the presence of the people they were working with due to the sense of authority and power this represents; many worried that they were missing important information or revealing too much information about their own personal shortcomings. Conversely, there were some anthropologists who said they loved to read and show their field notes to others and viewed them as invaluable sources of information to which they repeatedly referred. Jackson concluded that the process of writing notes while in the field is central to anthropology as a discipline and to anthropologists' identities. These notes represent translations between cultures and between individuals, and they also represent translations between real, lived experiences, daily life, and academic theses and analysis (Jackson 1990). As created and creative objects, they embody the relationships that are worked out in the field.

When and When Not to Take Field Notes

Since all fieldwork is relational in nature, when and how you take field notes can have implications for how the people you are working with judge you as a professional and as a confidante and, therefore, can affect how they act and what they say. For example, looking down and away from someone when you are in the middle of an intimate conversation can be construed as rude, and the person may stop talking to you. Writing down what someone is saying while that person is in the middle of a thought can be distracting and can also make your speaker feel as though she or he is being analyzed on the spot. Doing ethnographic work often means straddling the divide between creating ethical and authentic relationships and collecting data. Deciding when and how to write field notes depends on the situation and the people involved. If you are in a public place—observing in a crowded sports arena, as one example—taking brief notes is probably quite inconspicuous. Another example might be taking notes on a laptop computer in a crowded coffee shop. However, if you are in a smallish room where personal conversations are clearly audible, it is best to ask for permission to write down what you see and hear before doing so. This way you will avoid issues of trust, awkward situations, and perceptions of yourself as suspicious. If you are told no, and people say they are uncomfortable, then you should wait and take notes after you leave the room.

Deciding when and where not to write in your notebook can be complex. Creating field notes in an overt manner from the onset will allow everyone involved to become accustomed to seeing you doing so. Although taking notes spontaneously at any time may seem awkward at first, eventually you, and the people you are working with, will come to see it as normal. "People often understand that such activities are required of students and, therefore, tolerate and accommodate the needs of researchers, who, they believe, want to faithfully represent what goes on" (Emerson, Fretz, and Shaw 2011, 37). Openly taking notes provides flexibility in terms of when and how, because it is expected and will therefore most likely detract less from activities and conversations. However, overt note-taking can sometimes lead to judgments on the part of your informants in terms of when you do or do not take notes. They may develop expectations about certain topics and ask you why you are not taking notes at certain times or about certain topics that they deem important, and these questions can strain relationships (Emerson, Fretz, and Shaw 2011). Once you become a seasoned ethnographer, you will learn when it is appropriate to take notes openly and when it is not. For example, an argument might break out in the sports arena, and you decide to go outside into the parking lot to jot down some notes because otherwise the individuals involved would be embarrassed or become angry. Strategies for deciding when and how to take field notes will change over time and be dependent on specific situations and the people involved. The environment you are working in, the people you are working with, and your own discretion will dictate your decision.

What to Note

Karen O'Reilly (2005) suggests that you start off by writing down descriptions of your field site(s). What do you see when you first enter it? What is the layout of the area? Then start writing about the daily activities of the people in your field site. Who are they? What do they do on a daily basis? What are their verbal and nonverbal behaviors? How do they interact with each other? Generally speaking, you will tend to write down things related to your topic, thesis, and the theories you are working with, so it is important to try to remain impartial and think of yourself as a recording machine. This means you should also focus on writing down things that seem mundane or unimportant—aspects of the everyday that are routine. At the end of the day, you should go over your initial notes and add in reflections on your experiences and observations as well as links to the theories you are working with. This way you begin to create a more in-depth analysis while your field experience is still fresh in your mind. O'Reilly (2005) reminds us that participant observation is not just hanging out and that, along with writing notes, you should be creating maps, photographs, and other forms of visual depiction for later reference. In this chapter, Elizabeth Greenspan explains how she developed a weekly schedule while doing research at the World Trade Center, a schedule that included 15-minute observation sessions during which she jotted down what she saw and heard. She also found the time to take a series of photographs from each memorial area and to create a written transcript of at least three unstructured interviews she conducted.

Descriptive Notes

For our purposes in this book, we are going to talk about three types of field notes, with the first being "**descriptive notes**," which are sometimes called scribbles or **jottings**. These notes consist of one or two words, short phrases, and questions and are often written in shorthand during field experiences to jog your memory later about what you saw and heard. As we mentioned, these initial notes are often more symbolic and cryptic than readable, and they can be very messy. They are the first notes you will take and form the foundation of later writing. Therefore, it is important to focus on complex descriptions that incorporate as many details about the environment and the people involved as is possible. Sensory details (including kinetic, auditory, and olfactory) should be included, so you will be better able to recreate a feeling for what happened. Also, include descriptions of emotions that you feel and witness. When noticing emotional scenes, try to avoid attaching your presumed motives to other people's expressions of emotion. For example, the expression of anger could be the result of a wide variety of factors, including frustration, fatigue, power struggles, fear, or embarrassment. The taking of descriptive notes has been described as a mindset and not just a writing practice because it entails noting "sharp" and "vivid" descriptions (Emerson, Fretz, and Shaw 2011, 31–33).

Reflective or "Cooked" Notes

James Clifford coined the term "cooked notes" in 1989 when he used cooking as a metaphor to reference the process of reading through your jottings and scribblings, and then elaborating and adding details and reflections in order to create something more sumptuous out of them. Ideally, at the end of every day in the field, an anthropologist sits down for a few hours to reflect and write up (usually type up) the experiences of the day, using initial descriptive notes to jog memory. It is important that the anthropologist does this before losing her or his ability to relive emotions and sensory moments. These **reflective notes**, added to your descriptive notes, become the general data files that you will later code and analyze before writing up your thesis or paper. It is at this stage that you will begin to think more about language choice, the words, and the ways you use words to describe actions, people, and places. The goal is to be specific and creative in choosing language that provides the most colorful picture of your observations while remaining vigilant about your biases and preconceived perspectives. For example, in your initial descriptive shorthand notes you could have written, "Interviewee uncomfortable." When reflecting later on the day, you might have added these details: "During the middle part of the interview, Sam became very fidgety and stopped making eye contact; he actually got up out of his seat at one point and walked around the room for a few seconds." Remember, long after your fieldwork is done, your field notes will remain as archives of your experiences.

The reflection process also helps you think about the subjective aspects of your own writing. For example, if two anthropology students were asked to sit in the same coffee shop for the same period, they would undoubtedly come up with a completely different set of field notes, even though they had similar experiences. What they saw, heard, and then decided to take notes on would depend on their personalities, theoretical focus, perspectives on their particular field site, gender, social status, cultural background, and a host of other things. Postionality plays a very important role in dictating what we write about and how we view an experience. To maintain your integrity as a researcher, you must be critically aware of your own position, choices, and the possible effects of your attitudes and beliefs, as well as of your ethical responsibilities. It is also important to remember that the role you play as a researcher, the simple fact that you are in the coffee shop taking notes, alters that environment and the relationships and events that take place within it.

Diary Style: Why Is It Different?

In some ways, field notes are very similar to journal entries or **diary notes** in that they are subjective representations. As O'Reilly (2005) and others have stated, the distinction between taking field notes and writing a diary can be considered quite artificial, and some ethnographers consistently include very personal reflections alongside other observations. For example, Elizabeth Greenspan mentions that she simply wrote comments about her feelings at the end of every 15-minute observation session at the WTC field site. Nevertheless, there is a long tradition in the discipline, dating back to Bronislaw Malinowski's work, of chronicling personal feelings, reactions, actions, and assessments of daily activities in a separate notebook. A diary or journal might also contain abstract things you might have been thinking about, flashes of insight you had while observing, and commentary that will become part of your final analysis. Keeping a separate journal that focuses only on personal experiences is seen by some as a better way to manage the tension between the objective and subjective elements that are inherent in fieldwork. Diaries can also become a place where the ethnographer works out stressful situations and feelings. For example, Bernard says that a diary can be "a place where you can run and hide when things get tough" (quoted in Madden 2010, 126).

Different Forms Field Notes Take

Handwritten Notes

As we discussed, handwritten field notes or jottings are what anthropologists do while they are involved in observation and participant observation activities. Figure 5.1 shows an example of what these notes might look like, although due to personal, creative, and practical processes, all jottings and scratchings will be different. Ideally, you need to document as much information as you can so that, later on, you remember what you saw, heard, smelled, and experienced.

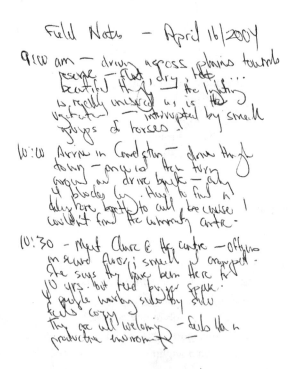

FIGURE 5.1: Mannik field notes, April 16, 2004, Cardston, Alberta. Courtesy of Lynda Mannik.

Transcriptions

Often, anthropologists will use a voice recorder to document formal or informal interviews and reflective commentary of their own at the end of the day or the end of an interview session. Typing up these recordings is the next step in creating data for future analysis, and this process is called transcribing. The finalized documents are called **transcriptions**. Prior to digital technologies, the practice of using a voice recorder was cumbersome, obvious, and much less popular, but contemporary ethnographers often carry a small voice recorder or even just use their digital phones to record comments, thoughts, ideas, and observations. Although making audio recordings is not the same as putting hand to paper, and some considered it to be a less thoughtful approach, recorded narratives can add value to field notes. The drawback is, as we mentioned earlier, that every hour of recorded commentary takes approximately six hours to type up unless you have access to voice-to-text software, which may or may not be appropriate for the project you are working on. Transcripts that will retain their value as research materials because they are clear and contain detailed information need to be formatted properly. Figure 5.2 shows an example of what that formatting looks like.

> **MS Interview, September 2007, Toronto, ON**
>
> *LM: What can you tell me about the photographs that you took on the* Walnut *and afterwards? First, why did you decide to take a camera with you?*
> MS: Oh I had been taking pictures ever since I got myself a camera. When I left home, we didn't have anything really. There were three things that I really wanted, a camera, a fountain pen and a watch, a good watch.
>
> *LM: Did you buy the camera when you got to Sweden?*
> SM: Yes!
>
> *LM: So you always had a passion for photography?*
> SM: Oh yes, I always had a camera with me wherever I went. I used to also do my own printing, so it was kind of a hobby.
>
> *LM: When you were a young boy, how did you see photographs for the first time? Was there someone that you knew who took photographs?*
> SM: I just . . . it started when I was home more or less. I didn't even know anyone who had a camera, but I did see photographs and always thought it would be nice to have a camera. In Sweden I managed to get one. So then anywhere I went I always had my camera. I just more or less couldn't be without the camera. I still do it, but not as much anymore. Things have changed now—you can get small cameras that are much better than the old ones.

FIGURE 5.2: "SS *Walnut* Interview I." Courtesy of Lynda Mannik.

Diagrams and Drawings

Creating comprehensive drawings and diagrams is perhaps the least common practice in the field note-taking process. Often, ethnographers will quickly sketch out a map or draw a chart of an area or event, as is shown in Figure 5.3, but rarely do they focus on just drawing a scene to capture the essence of what they are witnessing. We would argue that this is primarily because many scholars do not consider themselves capable of drawing realistic images and are not trained in the practice of more abstract visual techniques. They would be too uncomfortable, for example, bringing a set of paints to document an event. Michael Taussig (2011) provides an interesting collection of visual notes and commentary on this practice in his recent book *I Swear I Saw This*, which provides many examples of the various forms drawings, found objects, and watercolor paintings can take.

Carol Hendrickson (2008) developed her skills as an ethnographer by creating "**visual field notes**" in a variety of forms, and she reminds us of the power of visual representation. She advocates for the use of this method because 1) people are drawn to you, and they will approach you to talk about your drawings or paintings, which creates a more participatory environment; 2) words, jottings, drawings, maps, and photos can be combined to create a visual collage that enhances records and memory; and 3) a visual record makes it easier to tack back and forth between descriptive observations, reflective thought, and theoretical insights, which adds to a more holistic conceptualization of knowledge production (121–23). One interesting, and somewhat simple technique, is to create a collage and bricolage of items found at the field site. Hendrickson collected local food labels and packages along with other discarded items to represent snippets of everyday social life. Her active engagements with these visual, material items helped her think through local-global connections, media and marketing strategizing, urbanization, gender roles, and the impact of government policy (2008).

Photographs

All anthropologists take photographs while doing fieldwork, some more so than others, and this is a time-honored practice. Photographic records have been considered useful as memory stimulants and as ways to capture environments or spaces. Primarily, they have been thought of as embellishments to textual descriptions. However, they can also be used more succinctly to create visual diaries, not chronological objective accounts of an event per se, but subjective, strictly visual renditions of the experience of fieldwork through the eyes of a researcher. Prosser and Schwartz (1998) explain the difference between a visual record and a visual diary:

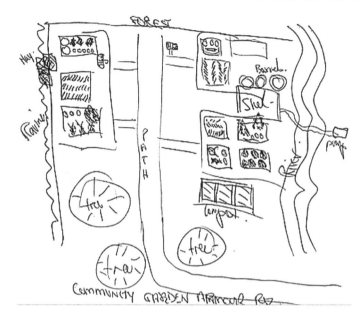

FIGURE 5.3: Community garden at Armour Road. Courtesy of Lynda Mannik.

> [A] diary is a self-reflexive and media literate chronicle of the
> researcher's entry, participation in, and departure from, the field. The
> images generated within this paradigm are acknowledged to be the
> unique result of the interaction of a certain researcher with a specific
> population using a particular medium at a precise moment in space and
> time. (123)

A visual diary would stand on its own as a document that describes what a researcher saw, heard, and felt, and, therefore, it would need to be a creative photographic rendition of highly subjective and personal perceptions and feelings. This method entails becoming very conscious of yourself as a combined witness and participant.

This chapter has presented a basic list of the different ways you can make and take field notes. It has also described how they should look. Every ethnographer will have a varied combination of styles and a different number of notes, photos, and drawings when her or his fieldwork is complete. When you work on your projects, and if it is your first time conducting qualitative fieldwork research, it would be a good idea to at least experiment with all of these forms. That way, you can get a good idea of what works best for you and for the type of research you are doing. Field notes that are abundant in form and content also give you much more in-depth data to work with when you start analyzing and writing.

VIGNETTE

Elizabeth Greenspan is an urban anthropologist and writer. She is the author of Battle for Ground Zero: Inside the Political Struggle to Rebuild the World Trade Center and a senior researcher at Penn-Praxis, the center for applied research and outreach of the University of Pennsylvania's School of Design.

FIELD NOTES, PHOTOS, AND MEMORIES: THE WTC AFTER 9/11

I saw the World Trade Center (WTC) site for the first time in early November 2001, two months after 9/11. Wreckage still filled the 16-acre hole, but by this time, temporary plywood walls marked the site's boundaries to keep all but recovery and cleanup crews out. Like everyone else descending upon the rubble—and there were thousands each day—I spent those first hours circling the walls, trying to find a vantage point from which to see in (Figure 5.4). Adventuresome folks climbed lampposts; I stood in lines to look through ground-level gaps. Like everyone else, I was, first and foremost, an observer. What distinguished me is that I kept coming back. For months, and then years, I spent time at the site every week, observing growing makeshift shrines and disappearing rubble, and writing down all of my observations in a spiral-bound, paperback-sized notebook.

Most of my earliest memories of the World Trade Center site are memories of taking field notes. That first visit is the only time I can remember when I wasn't clutching my notebook, which came to contain every scene and conversation I had. I have one photograph of myself at the site in those early months—a police officer asked me if I wanted him to take my picture, and I couldn't think of a reason to say no—and when I looked back at the picture recently, I wasn't surprised to see the notebook in my left hand.

Before that first visit, I didn't know what I would write down. I was interested in how people collectively make sense of violence through memorials, and I wanted to better understand how cities work. But these were abstract questions, which didn't mean much once I arrived at the site. Instead, I was captivated by what was happening right in front of me—how the crowded mix of tourists, mourners, rescue workers, vendors, television crews, police officers, and regular New Yorkers making their way were redefining this destroyed place.

Doing this research has taught me that creating field notes is partly instinctual; it's about noticing what catches your attention

FIGURE 5.4: Elizabeth Greenspan standing next to St. Paul's Chapel at the WTC site, April 9, 2002. Photographer is unknown. Photograph courtesy of Elizabeth Greenspan.

and recording these details as thoroughly as possible. But it has also taught me that creating field notes is partly systematic. That is, field notes have an order, or at least they should. During that first visit, I quickly knew that my job going forward would be to record the rapid activity occurring around the site. After a second visit a week later, I was shocked at how much had changed—street corners contained more clusters of memorials, the plywood walls sported more graffiti, the lampposts no longer held anyone up (Figure 5.5). It would be impossible to capture every moment of change and evolution, but through systematic observation and notes—a routine—I thought I could capture broad changes, and I did.

A weekly field note often looked like this: Written notes made from 15-minute observation sessions at a series of crowded memorial hubs; a few dozen photographs of each hub; and a written

FIGURE 5.5: Maintained shrine on Greenwich Street, WTC site, February 19, 2002. Courtesy of Elizabeth Greenspan, the photographer.

transcript of three unstructured interviews with people visiting the site. Quite a bit happened over the course of 15 minutes, and capturing the full scope of activity in a particular spot over a 15-minute stretch of time required a startling amount of focus. It was often exhausting. Talking to people—approaching them, telling them about my work, asking them a few questions, frantically scribbling down their words—was even more exhausting. Although it's probably possible to sit and observe for hours, that kind of schedule would have burned me out, and it wouldn't necessarily have revealed more, either.

During my observation sessions, I paid attention to both the people and the space. How many people were passing through? What were they doing (e.g., photographing, reading memorials, looking, making their own notes)? What new memorials or graffiti did I notice? I sat, I watched, I wrote. I also photographed these areas. Photographs are an important part of field notes, but they're also a rather lazy way to record places and people—it's easy to forget, years later, why you had wanted to take a certain picture—so they shouldn't replace written notes (Figure 5.6).

In my interviews, I wanted to learn what people noticed about the site during their visits. I don't know how I decided whom to approach on a given afternoon. It was pure instinct. Over time, I

FIGURE 5.6: Notes and graffiti covering doors, WTC site, February 19, 2002. Photograph courtesy of Elizabeth Greenspan, the photographer.

noticed I was approaching more women than men, and from that point forward made a conscious effort to interview the same number of men and women each month. I developed a standard set of questions, which included why they had come, what stood out to them about the WTC site, what they thought about what they were seeing, and whether they had any opinion about what should (or shouldn't) be rebuilt. Without prompting, all told me where they had been on September 11.

After doing a research session like this, work usually took two to three hours; I'd take a break, and then, while the images and words were still sharp, I'd jot down some reflections. I'd read through my pages of notes and, on the side, in brackets, write down any immediate associations and questions. I'd note possible patterns, previous conversations or observations that came to mind in light of these new bits, and things I wanted to know more about. I'd also make a comment at the end of the field note to record my feelings and takeaway thoughts. What did this particular visit leave me thinking about and wondering? What most caught my attention? What, instinctively, do I think is most interesting?

When I started my research that November, the WTC site's periphery included six large memorial clusters—collections of flowers, teddy bears, flags, banners, and homemade dioramas that kept acquiring new items and, therefore, kept occupying more and more space. One cluster, filling a corner at an entrance into the walled-off recovery work, caught my attention more than the others. The other clusters were messy; but the memorials at this corner were neatly arranged. Despite my weekly visits, I never saw anyone bring a piece of fence or rehang fallen bouquets, but someone was clearly taking care of these memorials. Who? Why? I thought it would be interesting to interview these helpers; maybe they had ideas about why the shrines were important. I was also wanted to document the gradual formalization of memorialization, which these invisible workers were part of. These spontaneous shrines, after all, were the first collective expressions of what 9/11 meant, and they required care and upkeep.

One afternoon, after sitting on the curb and making notes for 15 minutes, I worked up my nerve to talk to the police officer. "Excuse me, do you know who is taking care of these memorials?" I asked. The officer scoffed. "Sorry. Pruning flowers isn't my forte," he said. I shuffled off, confused and sort of embarrassed—it wasn't really a dumb question, was it?—and I returned to my curb, dutifully recording this exchange. Later that afternoon, I noted that the officer's response seemed strange. Shouldn't he know? Does he really pay no attention to what's going on with the memorials? Months later, this brief interaction became central to my analysis. Initially, I had decided to document the memorial clusters because they were interesting. The police officer was singularly unhelpful in this regard (I never did figure out who was taking care of the shrines), but he helped me realize that the memorials, a vibrant part of the most heavily policed, heavily monitored piece of land in the country, were going rather unnoticed by at least one police officer standing a few feet away, and probably by others too. He helped me appreciate a broader trend: the degree to which officials were ignoring the public's memorialization practices at the site.

George Orwell wrote, "To see what is in front of one's nose needs a constant struggle" (1946). He was writing about the sweeping political negotiating and decision-making that most people are rarely privy to but that nonetheless will manifest in our everyday practices and norms. But his words are meaningful at smaller scales too. Even the actions that *do* transpire right in front of us, including the practices and conversations we record in our field notes, can be difficult to see.

I often felt as if truly seeing, and by extension understanding, what was happening at the WTC site was a struggle. So much was happening, so quickly, and I could only observe disconnected moments and scenes. But gradually, my routine helped me overcome my doubts and uncertainty. I worked hard to write notes when I planned to write them *and* to stop when I determined I would stop (after 15 minutes!). I knew that whatever I saw or heard on any given day was partly luck, but I hoped that, by adhering to my routine, even seemingly unique moments—such as the brief conversation with the police officer—would make sense as part of a broader set of patterns. Eventually, they did. Even though I had not originally defined my study as one of the politics of public space, I came to realize over time, though my fieldwork, that I was observing how people claim ownership over space through grassroots practices, such as spontaneous memorialization, and how institutions and private business owners respond.

What's dangerous about the "field note creating routine" is that, inevitably, it becomes too comfortable. It becomes easier to create field notes than to stop and move on to next steps and, ultimately, complete the study. After all, there is always something a little new to see. The WTC site was particularly challenging in this regard. It was always changing, often dramatically. Indeed, in 2016, the site's office towers and train station were still not finished; construction will continue for many more years.

I sensed it was time to stop creating new field notes when each weekly field note started to look more like the ones that had come before. This happened roughly three years after I first visited the site. The site itself still transformed every month, with new infrastructure and fences and temporary memorials. And most of the people I spoke to had never visited Ground Zero before, so our conversations were always, in some way, unique. But, eventually, by 2004, the content of my new notes grew increasingly similar to that of previous notes. People kept delivering the same sets of items, which meant that the walls and memorial clusters gradually felt familiar, and the words I used to describe them were similar too. During interviews, I began to hear repetitions—the same phrases and reactions from different people. At times, I wondered if I wasn't paying enough attention or if I was somehow missing something going on someplace else. In hindsight, I think I was beginning to see what was in front of my nose.

I still have my handwritten field notes, which ultimately filled many notebooks. I have been working from them for over ten years. I wrote a doctoral dissertation and then a book about the rebuilding and memorialization of the WTC site, as well as multiple articles in both academic and popular journals. I kept returning to the site after 2004, but less regularly, and turned to analyzing my notes. Like the field note process, the coding process emerged somewhat organically. The themes and notes in brackets and in the comments at the end of each field note helped me develop a coding system. I was often tired or distracted by the time I was making these first-pass evaluations, but they were more revealing and insightful than I appreciated at the time. It's important to protect time for free writing and thinking during your fieldwork, but it's also important not to spend *too* much time reflecting, lest field notes turn into a diary—no one, alas, is really going to care how you felt. If there's anything I wish I had done differently, it is to have recorded my interviews with a handheld recorder, so that I could hear people's voices and the uncertainty or excitement or sadness or anger they felt. These sounds, and other people's feelings, are the kinds of detail you forget, but they are also what make places feel more alive, more real, to everyone reading your work years later.

Making Connections

What factors are involved in decisions that you make about when (the timing) and where (the places) you will conduct your fieldwork?

What types of field notes will you choose to create from the repertoire mentioned in this chapter (e.g., visual, handwritten, voice recorded)?

According to Elizabeth Greenspan, it is often what you do not pay full attention to, or do not notice at first, that holds valuable research information. How do you plan on making sure that you notice mundane or seemingly unimportant aspects of your fieldwork and field notes?

Try This

Sit and just watch. Spend an hour just sitting on a street corner and writing down everything you see, hear, smell, and notice. Think about these questions. Whom did you see? What were they doing? How were they interacting? What sound and smells were noticeable? What did you expect to see that wasn't there? Two days later, read over your notes and then write "cooked" notes, reflections on your experience from memory after you have had time to gain some distance. Try to be as objective as possible but also to focus on your inner feelings and perspectives.

Possible Projects

1. Over the course of a term, practice diversity in the forms that your field notes take. This exercise will also allow you to follow Greenspan's example and develop discipline in terms of thinking "outside the box," being less biased, and being more visually creative. For the first week, go to your field site (for the hours you would normally go) and just write down brief shorthand comments or "jottings." Each evening spend at least two hours elaborating and clarifying those notes on your computer, creating more formalized text-based narratives. During the second week, go to your field site (for the hours you would normally go) and just draw what you see, hear, and smell. Following Hendrickson's suggestions, you can produce collages, maps, more realistic drawings, or various other forms of visual recordings. For those of you who do not consider yourself to be artistic in any way, this may seem like a daunting task, but remember that the visual imagery you create is private (for your eyes only), and we guarantee you will feel more comfortable as the week goes on. And finally, on the third week, bring your camera along to your field site and just take photos. This week will be focused on creating a photo diary, so every evening, you should spend at least two hours editing and organizing your photos (possibly adding captions), so they create a daily, photographic journal of your experiences. Later, these individual practices can be synchronized and become part of your scheduled weekly activities that allow you to experience your field site in a more comprehensive manner.

2. Select a field site with a fellow classmate. The site should be a relatively busy public place—for example, a coffee shop, food court, or sporting event. Over the course of a term, conduct participant observation at your site on five separate occasions and at different times of the day for approximately one hour at a time. Although you will both attend the event or be present at the field site together, you and your partner should refrain from having any interaction with one another. Take descriptive notes at your field site, and, each evening, spend some time writing these notes up as reflective notes. At the end of your fieldwork, meet with your partner, and exchange your descriptive and reflective notes. Discuss the similarities and differences in your notes. How can you account for the differences, and what might these differences mean? If you were to each elaborate upon this experience and develop it into a larger project, what themes or issues would you focus on?

Recommended Readings

Goodall Jr., H.L. 2000. *Writing the New Ethnography*. Lanham, MD: AltaMira Press.

Greenspan, Elizabeth. 2013. *Battle for Ground Zero: Inside the Political Struggle to Rebuild the World Trade Center.* New York, NY: Palgrave.

Kouritzin, Sandra. 2002. "'The Half-Baked' Concept of 'Raw' Data in Ethnographic Observation." *Canadian Journal of Education* 27 (1): 119–38.

Malkki, Liisa H. 2007. "Tradition and Improvisation in Ethnographic Field Research." In *Improvising Theory: Process and Temporality in Ethnographic Fieldwork*, edited by Liisa Malkki and Allaine Cerwonka, 162–88. Chicago, IL: University of Chicago Press.

Sanjek, Roger. 1990. *Fieldnotes: The Makings of Anthropology.* Ithaca, NY: Cornell University Press.

Sanjek, Roger, and Susan W. Tratnor. 2016. *E Fieldnotes: The Makings of Anthropology in the Digital World.* Philadelphia, PA: University of Pennsylvania Press.

Van Maanen, John. 2011. *Tales of the Field: On Writing Ethnography*. 2nd ed. Chicago, IL: University of Chicago Press.

Wang, Tricia. 2012. "Writing Live Fieldnotes: Towards a More Open Ethnography." *Ethnography Matters*, August 2. Accessed May 2016. http://ethnographymatters.net/blog/2012/08/02/writing-live-fieldnotes-towards-a-more-open-ethnography/.

Wolfinger, Nicholas H. 2002. "On Writing Fieldnotes: Collection Strategies and Background Expectancies. *Qualitative Research* 2 (1): 85–95.

CHAPTER 6

AFTER FIELDWORK—
ANALYZING DATA

Introduction: What is Analysis?

Simply put, "**analysis**" is the process of interpreting your data. As Karen O'Reilly (2012) writes, "From the mass of data we have collected we want to summarize some points to tell a story about what we have seen and heard" (179). The process of writing this story, however, is not necessarily a simple or linear one. Once you have completed the fieldwork process, you'll probably find that you are feeling somewhat lost in a sea of field notes, transcripts, and perhaps even photographs or other visual material. But do not conflate "analysis" with "description." Your job at this stage is to move beyond a mere description of your experiences to answer questions that start with "how" or "why." How did people come to live as or believe in what they do, and why do they live or believe in this way? This process often requires you to revisit and refine your initial research question. Often, researchers will begin their fieldwork with fairly general sorts of research questions or issues to explore. For example, you might begin by stating that you wish to examine how and why people become interested in playing field hockey. Once you begin your interviews, however, you could notice patterns, similarities, or differences in people's stories and experiences that lead you to refine or narrow your original question. For example, you might observe that several people comment upon a relationship between money and sport. Perhaps people tell you that they got involved because field hockey is a more affordable sport than other options in their community. By the time you get to your analysis, you should clue in that issues of social class are a prominent theme in your data. Thus, you might refine your research question to explore the issue of how social class and identity affect people's decisions to play this sport. This process of oscillating back and forth between the research question, data, and analysis is an "**iterative**" (O'Reilly 2012, 184) analytical process. This refers to a nonlinear means of analyzing your data, in which you are continually thinking about and analyzing data to look for key issues that emerge from the data set itself. Fieldwork, analysis, and writing are thus not necessarily linear processes with clear-cut beginnings and endings.

It is important to note that the analysis of data does not conform to a "one-size-fits-all" model. Each project and fieldwork experience is unique and is shaped by your own idiosyncratic experiences and relationships with informants. At the same time, however, many ethnographers "make sense" of their data through the use of a systematic process called "**coding**." Coding refers to the process of reading through field notes and other data with an eye or ear (if you are reviewing audio recordings) to key themes, issues, and topics that emerge within the context of various discussions. Often, there is an emphasis upon looking for and highlighting the repeated ideas and discussion topics that emerge from conversations. It might be helpful to think about the process of coding as one of selection and reduction. As you sift through your data, you will find key phrases, stories, or words that may provide lucrative information in the sense that they address your research topic directly. By "coding," you are simply flagging or highlighting these key parts of your text for further consideration and analysis. As you read through your field notes or transcripts, write down or type out words or phrases (referred to as "codes") that summarize the themes, topics, or issues that you find in your data. A code is thus a label that summarizes an action, sensation, feeling, or any other ethnographic experience that you document in your data. Your codes can appear as words or phrases in the margins of your transcripts.

Think of the coding process as akin to filing and sorting a pile of paperwork. When writing a large research paper, for instance, many researchers download and save (or print) dozens of academic journal articles that they think *might* be relevant to their topic. After a closer reading of these documents, however, the researcher will consider some articles to be irrelevant and others to be important, but even significant articles can discuss different subtopics or themes related to the main research topic. At this point, to organize our journal articles, we could create "coded" files, and the codes or labels we use will often reflect the different subtopics that we will address in a paper. For an ethnographic project on American women's memories and experiences of being in the workforce in the 1950s, for instance, you might code the files with labels such as "irrelevant articles," "articles on the history of women and work," "articles on feminist theory," "ethnographic research on women and work," and so on. As we'll see, the same kind of labeling occurs, with increasing levels of refinement, during the coding process one uses to organize ethnographic data.

Throughout this chapter, we will discuss how to code your data to draw out important themes and how to organize your data in preparation for the process of "writing up." You will learn to extract key themes and ideas from your interviews, field notes, and other data. These key themes will then help you to focus your written work (as discussed in Chapter 7). In this way, ethnographic research becomes an **inductive** process whereby key issues, debates, and theories emerge directly from the data. We ultimately emphasize that fieldwork and writing are not linear phenomena; rather, both processes are cyclical, as the researcher is continually revisiting and thinking about the data and how what was recorded and collected in the field relates to broader anthropological concerns.

How to Code Data

Once you have completed your fieldwork, you might wonder whether it will be possible to distil all your data into a much shorter project or paper without leaving out important ideas and points. One thing that generally surprises students is that you'll end up using only a fraction of the data that you collect. The analysis process is thus one that is mediated by the idea of selection. Obviously, you will not be able to incorporate all your data into your writing. Some material will be redundant, and much will be off topic and therefore insignificant to your project goals; your job is to sift through your research to identify and select a variety of key themes or issues to focus upon. Think of it like walking along the beach and only picking up a few stones here and there among the millions left by the tide! These issues or key themes may be self-evident to an experienced anthropologist, but undergraduate students usually require some direction and systematic ways of "making sense" of data.

The practice of coding ethnographic data, as Raymond Madden (2010) articulates, is an important one for many researchers, "as the manner in which ethnographers index and code their notes will in part reflect the interrogative frame of their project" (139). Coding involves a repetitive process of reading and rereading your field notes, transcripts of interviews, and other data for key or repetitive terminology, themes, or other ideas. Often, researchers with large data sets will use various sorts of computer software to help with this process. Some of the more popular ones that have been used over the years by anthropologists, for instance, include NVivo, Ethnograph, OneNote, EgoNet and ATLAS.ti. For smaller projects (much like your own), however, researchers can undertake this process without the assistance of software or by using features such as the "search in document" function on Mac computers, for instance, to search your transcribed documents for key terms. Generally speaking, the coding process is divided into three separate yet interrelated types of ethnographic coding: open coding, focused coding, and selective coding. We will discuss each step of this three-step process in turn.

Open Coding

Open coding is the first type of coding that you should use with your data. This type of coding involves a detailed reading of your data, with minute attention to detail on a word-by-word and line-by-line basis. It is often the most time consuming of the three-step coding process. In this step, you will find that you are looking for various themes and making note of them with a code, usually in the margins of your paper. But how do we identify themes? According to Ryan and Bernard (2003), theme identification is one of the most difficult components of the analysis of qualitative research. As they discuss, identifying relevant themes in qualitative data stems from having background knowledge of existing literature on your topic, and a good rule is that "richer literatures produce more themes" (88–89). So, at this point, before you even begin coding, you will need to familiarize yourself (or re-familiarize yourself) with existing anthropological and ethnographic literature on your topic. This does not necessarily mean that you need to do a "close" reading of this literature at this stage (see Chapter 7 on "writing up" for a discussion of how to integrate literature into your work). Simply skim through existing research and ask yourself what issues or key themes other anthropologists (and researchers in related fields) have explored. What are their key findings? You may find that your work converges or diverges from theirs, and these key themes can provide you with a starting point and a baseline for analyzing your own data. Several scholars have offered a myriad of suggestions in the form of lists, questions, charts, and guidelines to help researchers know what to look for, and what to code, during the open coding process (e.g., Charmaz 2006; Gibbs and Taylor 2005; Ryan and Bernard 2003; Strauss and Corbin 1991). These are all based upon the researcher's careful scrutiny of the vocabulary used by informants. Among other things, for instance, the researcher looks for the repetition of concepts so as to analyze larger blocks of text (for the purposes of comparing and contrasting, for example) or to count and assess other linguistic features, such as metaphors. With this in mind, the following list incorporates a variety of traits that you should look for when open coding. Note that this list is certainly not exhaustive, as you may find that you need to code other phenomena that are specific to your ethnographic context:

1. Repetitive words and phrases
2. Facial expressions and actions (What are people doing when they are talking with you or with others? This may include gestures, such as fidgeting or playing with hair, or emotional expressions, such as smiling, crying, or grimacing.)
3. Emotional states of being (Do your informants express any form of heightened emotion surrounding the specific activities, events, or issues that they discuss?)
4. Discussions of events (Events, such as weddings, may be a repetitive feature of conversations surrounding sexual or romantic partnerships, for instance.)
5. The use of what Ryan and Bernard (2003, 91) call "indigenous" categories (This may be understood as context-specific jargon and refers to terminology that is used within a subculture or group of coworkers, for example. In anthropology, we routinely use terms such as "culture," "cultural relativism," or "ethnocentrism." Though these words are not exclusive to anthropology, they certainly have a common and shared meaning among anthropologists and can be classified as "indigenous" categories.)
6. KWIC (key words in context) or an analysis of the specific context in which a key term is used (see Ryan and Bernard 2003, 91)
7. Missing information (For example, are there certain key topics that informants are reticent to discuss or that they openly evade? Ask yourself why people are hesitant to discuss certain topics, as "missing" information may be just as important to analyze as information that is readily apparent.)
8. The use of metaphors and analogies

Keep in mind that the elucidation of themes in the open coding process involves multiple (at least three) read-throughs of your data. On your first read-through, you might want to pay specific attention to vocabulary, or the words used by your informants. It is important to highlight repeated words and "indigenous" categories. Next, you will want to read through to analyze larger sections of text, such as entire paragraphs, so you can explore the context of these key words (KWIC) or metaphors. In what contexts do people discuss certain issues or stories? Finally, read through your data a third time and pay attention to the conversation as a whole. What, if anything, is missing? Use **memoing**, which is noting your observations in the margins of your work or in a column on the right side of the paper. Your memos will consist of more detailed phrases than the more simplistic codes you first wrote in the margins. You might even write questions.

Once you have completed this process, you will find that you have a rather messy set of notes on your transcript. Below is an example of the open coding of a paragraph of transcribed notes from Karen McGarry's notes on participant observation at a skating competition. The names of people have been omitted and replaced with an "X" to protect their privacy. Note that you could just as easily code your data by hand, by printing out your work (or coding handwritten field notes) and using highlighters and pens. However, it might be a good idea to photocopy or scan your handwritten work and make notes on the photocopies or scans when coding, so the original documents are preserved. As you'll see in the following field notes, the initial open coding process can create very messy and confusing looking documents:

JANUARY 14, 2002

Calgary Saddledome, Press conference; 3:15 p.m. **Open Codes**-today was the first p.c. for the pair short programme. Media **Short programme** was called in at 3 p.m. but conference is late; currently 3:15. **Late**-conference organized by Skate Canada, and they seem to use the conference to *promote Canadian* talent. On the Canadian schedule, X Canadian skater is scheduled to speak, **Promoting Canadian** despite the fact that they did not win a medal (the conference is supposed to be for medal winners only, or at least that is what the email that they circulated this morning stated). **Late**-3:25 p.m. had coffee and a horrible tasting pastry with journalist X from X media. He discussed with me why and how he came to cover the games. He is a replacement for X. He was selected because of his long association with hockey, and covering that sport for the network. He admitted **Hockey** that he knows fairly little about figure skating, but he is **Little knowledge of** excited to be here given that Canada has a lot of medal contenders skating; **Canada in figure skating** and he finds figure skaters likeable and **likeable** personable. He also mentioned that he receives good feedback from his viewers, most of whom are women. Many of the **Female fans** fans he writes for, he said, are "diehard" skating fans who tend to **fans** associate the sport with "being Canadian." **Skating as Canadian**-I asked him about the demographics of fans that he meets at Canadian events. He reiterated what the Skate Canada stats indicate – most **fans** fans are female, upper middle class and white. **Demographics – female fans**-He also said that he felt enormous pressure from the television company's sponsors to promote skaters in a particular way **Promote**-sometimes sponsors monitor behaviour by checking in with coaches **Monitor**-X then has to leave to go do some work-around 4:00 p.m. I talk with another journalist, M. She told me about the national association's media conference, where skaters, coaches, etc. mingle for a retreat and skaters and journalists interact. In particular, there are formal sessions at the conference where skaters learn how to act; are taught how to represent themselves to the media. ***Represent*** There are standard responses to questions, and even posture, ***Represent*** gesture, and appearance are policed and monitored. She told me to ***Monitor*** ask to see if I can attend the next event to do participant observation. -our conversation ends when the press conference starts around 4:10 p.m....

As you can see from this short segment above, there are already some repeated codes (e.g., the notion of "monitoring" and controlling skaters' behavior and teaching skaters how to "represent" themselves), and already, even with this small data sample, we have a plethora of codes. Therefore, it will be necessary to read through our transcript a second time, using **focused coding**.

Focused Coding

Focused coding refers to a second type of data coding that is often used by anthropologists and other social scientists. The goal with focused coding is to further refine and reduce the plethora of open codes that you have accumulated in an effort to relate your codes to one another and to identify the key codes for addressing your topic of concern. During focused coding, you read through your data once again and pay attention to groups of repeated open codes. At this stage, you might want to become more analytical and begin exploring the interrelationships among the repeated codes. For instance, if you are exploring people's relationships to their pets and one of your repeated open codes is the notion of "pets as family," then focus specifically upon this concept and start asking questions such as these: Why do they consider pets as family? What types of pets are seen as kin and are any excluded? Do all family members feel this way or are there differences based upon age, gender, or other categories? In what ways are pets like family members? At the end of this process, you could find that you are left with too many key themes. Chances are that you'll have five or more different key themes that you could focus on, which is beyond the scope of a term paper. In this case, you will look through your data yet again to narrow your themes even further.

Selective Coding

Selective coding (also called substantive coding) refers to the final stage of coding and analysis. In this step, you will reread your data to try to determine the key concepts that you will focus upon in your paper. As mentioned previously, you will likely discover several key concepts that you could focus on, but you need to limit your paper to a manageable size. This means excluding data that are irrelevant for your chosen topic. Matthew and Price (2009) describe it as a process of "theoretical generation" in which you ask yourself how theory can be derived from the data you collected and how these data relate to relevant anthropological issues.

In the case of the skating transcript illustrated previously, one key theme that you could engage with in a paper or research project is the notion of crafting representations of people. Though in sports such as figure skating, athletic associations and promoters tend to represent athletes' bodies as "natural," they are anything but. High performance athletes' bodies are akin to finely tuned machines and are the outcome of years of practice, top-level coaching, and monitoring one's nutrition, exercise, and sleep habits, among other things. Bodies are thus carefully crafted and molded to conform to particular athletic and aesthetic norms. In the case of figure skating, the physical appearance and personas of skaters are molded to appear as marketable and "Canadian." So, one key theoretical theme that might emerge in the selective coding process is the relationship between the representation of athletes' bodies in the media and the notion of bodily discipline, as espoused by Foucault (1975, 1990). How and why, for instance, is it important for skaters to appear as "polite" and "disciplined?" Why are their bodies marketed in this way? Rereading the field notes on skating with these questions in mind will help you think more deeply about this theme. If you decided to focus on this issue, then an important aspect of selective coding would be to scan your data to extract ethnographic examples that relate specifically (in this case) to the representation of skaters' bodies.

Ultimately, then, by the end of the selective coding process, you should end up with one or two key themes or issues to focus upon, and, in keeping with an iterative approach, your issues should emerge from your data. In other words, try not to impose themes or issues on your data in an **etic** manner. Let your material speak for itself! Your next step, as discussed in Chapter 7, will be to link your final key theme or themes more intricately with existing anthropological literature and theory.

Codes: Themes that Matter

It is important to note that there is not one "right" way to analyze your data. In fact, multiple people reading the same transcripts or data may come up with several similar and dissimilar codes. The process of analysis is not a completely objective process. In addition to the desires of our informants, our own interests and identities as researchers will help shape what we might consider to be "important" themes during the coding process. It is easy to see this process take shape even within the context of our daily interactions. After a major news event—say, a federal election—many of your friends and colleagues will read or watch the same mainstream mediated news program. Quite often, you will informally chat about what was reported. Even though you all may agree on the key issues that were highlighted, you'll undoubtedly also note differences in opinions as to the major points of the newscast or story. Next time this happens, ask yourself why these differences exist. Could they be the result of differing politics, age, gender, or other factors? Obviously, our positionalities (e.g., age, sexuality, gender, religion, class) play a major role in what we deem to be "important."

The point here is that, although all themes are important, some might "matter" more in terms of your final decision regarding the content of your written work. In keeping with an inductive approach, and recognizing that our informants should be viewed not as objects of study but as collaborators, many anthropologists privilege those themes that matter most to their informants. Increasingly, and to atone for anthropology's colonial past, some anthropologists feel that if a project is not relevant or important to the people we work with, then it isn't a relevant issue to focus upon in an ethnography. Jen Shannon's vignette in Chapter 3, for instance, addresses this issue head on. For some anthropologists, the integration of this kind of an emic approach has become an ethical requirement of the discipline, particularly when working with historically marginalized communities. Though not all anthropologists share this perspective, it is an important issue to consider, particularly if you are working with disadvantaged communities.

Indeed, analyzing data often involves ethical issues. Because analysis necessitates a process of selection, the inclusion or deletion of particular data from analysis is often fraught with politics. In this chapter's vignette, for instance, Karen McGarry discusses how she analyzed her data on figure skaters, with an emphasis on the contentious issue of interpretation (among other things). What happens when your interpretations of experiences differ significantly from those of your informants? Moreover, what if such experiences relate to politicized and potentially inflammatory topics like race and racism?

Securing Your Data

By the time you begin your analysis, you will have amassed a large data set, and it is important that these data are secured and stored properly. As discussed in Chapter 3 (on ethics), one of your responsibilities as a researcher is to protect your informants. Doing so can mean providing pseudonyms for people to protect their identities or changing the names of the places or organizations that would identify where you conducted your research. Another way of protecting your informants (and an expectation of ethics boards) is to secure your data at all stages of the fieldwork, analysis, and writing processes. Your data could include handwritten or digital field notes, research notes, digital or taped recordings, photographs, videos, or any other form of audio, written, or visual recording of your interactions and engagements with informants. Keep in mind that when people consent to participate in your research project, you have an obligation to keep data confidential. Often, people will tell you very personal or emotional stories when providing a life history interview, for instance. So they could feel embarrassed or uncomfortable knowing that this information has been read, heard, or viewed by other people, particularly if their name or other identifying information is attached to an audio or visual recording or a transcript. Your informants put their trust in you, and they often develop a special rapport with you, so it would be a breach of that trust to share (purposefully or inadvertently) your data with family or friends, especially if these data identify the individuals involved.

"Securing your data" thus involves removing any identifying information (e.g., names, dates of birth, addresses) from documents that you store digitally or in filing cabinets. Digital data should be stored in a password-protected file on your computer. Any information identifying individuals should be stored in a separate password-protected file along with the pseudonyms used on all transcripts or field notes. Handwritten documents—for example, written field notes—should also be archived in a locked cabinet that is accessible only by you. Most university ethics boards will request that students keep their data for two years upon completion of their fieldwork (but check about the requirements at your institution). After two years, the data should be destroyed. Digital data can be permanently erased from your computer, and hard copies of any data can be shredded.

VIGNETTE

Karen McGarry is an assistant professor of anthropology at McMaster University. Her research focuses upon the ethnographic study of high-performance sport and sports spectacles as well as educational anthropology.

FIGURE 6.1: Portrait of Karen McGarry, 2016. Photograph by Amy Mcintosh.

THE ETHICS AND POLITICS OF "ANALYZING" FIGURE SKATING

I was never a figure skater, nor did I have any desire to try it; I was tall and not a terribly gifted athlete as a child. I do, however, have many fond memories of being curled up on the couch with my mother on chilly winter afternoons watching it on TV. As somewhat of a "girly" girl, I had a fondness for sequins, cosmetics, frilly costumes, and the drama and glamour of the sport. I never imagined that I would go on to study skating from a more critical perspective as an academic. It wasn't until after I completed my masters in archaeology that I realized that I was sick of digging up stuff—the heat, the bugs, the dirt! It was fun but I wanted to move on. For my PhD, I studied the anthropology of sport. Among other things, nostalgia for childhood experiences led me to explore Canadian figure skating ethnographically. Given that figure skating had long been imagined in Canadian culture (along with hockey) as a particular marker of Canadianness, I ended up examining issues of nationalism and identity construction among figure skaters. I spent 18 months in "the field," and I conceived of my research as both multi-locale and multisited. It was multi-locale as my research was geographically dispersed, and I traveled to six

Canadian training centers to interview 80 individuals. I also conducted participant observation with coaches, journalists, skaters, judges, and others at various Grand Prix competitions, where I was granted media accreditation. This allowed me to sit in on press conferences and to learn how the mass media constructs skating narratives based upon what is said, heard, and seen at events. My work was multisited as I sought to connect these localized events to broader, transnational or global concerns, as well as to understand an issue, such as Canadian nationalism, from multiple perspectives. For example, I was interested in how the circulation of Canadian celebrity skaters in the international media affected their ability to act as "national" symbols of Canadian identity for Canadian skating fans.

Because my fieldwork did not involve a sharp ideological or geographical distinction between "home" and "the field," I imagined the fieldwork, analysis, and writing processes as overlapping phenomena. I even remember writing a draft of the introduction of my dissertation midway through my fieldwork. I was thus continually shifting between the processes of writing, conducting interviews, and thinking. For me, the "analysis" or interpretation of my data involved a tremendous amount of "thinking time." I was thinking about my interviews over coffee, while driving, in the shower, while out for a walk, when opening Christmas presents, and when doing yoga! Intentionally or unintentionally, the process of thinking about my data seemed to take over every waking minute throughout the fieldwork process, as well as during its immediate aftermath. Analysis thus took time, which was necessary for several reasons. First, I had to sort through the sheer enormity of data that I'd collected and think critically about what was "useful" to me. I was somewhat shocked, in fact, to find that I ended up incorporating only a small portion of my data (about ten percent) into my final dissertation. Second, I needed time to understand how to interpret and translate the comments of my informants in an anthropologically coherent and relevant way, and, finally, I had to figure out how to merge their insights with relevant anthropological literature.

For many ethnographers, analysis cannot begin without transcriptions of all data. However, I did not have the time or resources to transcribe the entirety of these data. After an interview, I would re-listen to any audio recordings, and transcribe segments of interviews. I also took notes when re-listening, so I could quickly and efficiently find interview segments based upon pertinent topics of concern to my project. For instance, I would write, "1 minute, 20 second mark: Bryan talks about childhood skating." The fact that I wrote my notes up immediately following an interview helped expedite the note-taking process, as I had fresh, vivid recollections of interview content, and I was able to quickly skip over sections that I perceived to be irrelevant to me.

I was not permitted to take photographs or videos in training centers or during competitions and practices. Given that figure skating is a sport dominated by visual aesthetics, I found it interesting that I was left without any form of primary visual documentation of my experiences. However, while they were being interviewed, people were fond of giving me material things and showing me items such as costumes, medals, or photographs. Objects functioned as mnemonic aids that helped informants remember the sensory details of past events. Their descriptions of competitions were made richer and more detailed the minute that they pulled out their favorite costumes or prized medals. In many instances, their narratives became infused with emotional qualities, such as feelings of trepidation or anxiety leading up to a competition, or, alternatively, with descriptions of their remembrances of the scent of the ice or the hardness or softness of the ice texture (an important consideration for figure skaters) or the sound of the audience.

Objects were also important for skating fans. I attended several museum-based skating exhibitions—for example, "Lace Up," which chronicled the history of skating in Canada. Medals, costumes, videos, and other skating paraphernalia were on display. Here, I had the opportunity to interview figure skating fans and to learn about their connection with and attitudes toward material culture. As in the interviews with skaters, the process of viewing skating memorabilia, such as the famous costume of Olympic gold medalists Jamie Salé and David Pelletier (Figure 6.2), had the effect of generating discussion about Canadian nationalism and pride in the nation (a topic relevant to my work), as well as of eliciting emotions and details about personal experiences that would have been difficult to access via other means.

I mention the role of material culture here because its presence and importance for my informants affected how I analyzed my interviews. I found it impossible to interpret a recording without simultaneously reading my handwritten field notes, which detailed people's physical and emotional reactions to showing me and talking about different forms of objects. It was through their description of objects that the discourses about their experiences became animated with immense detail and sensory attributes. This highlights the importance of considering people's interactions with objects in the analysis process, as these objects can help communicate the oftentimes inaccessible or underestimated sensory components of informants' experiences.

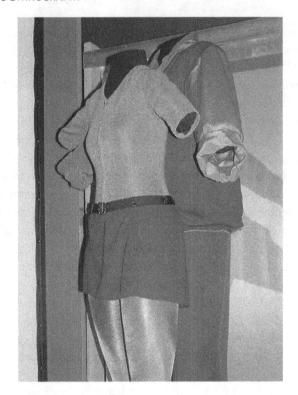

FIGURE 6.2: Skating costume of Jamie Salé and David Pelletier, 2006.
Photograph by Steven M. Blois.

Ultimately, I was left with pages of data from semi-transcribed interviews and numerous books of handwritten field notes from my participant observation. Although never formally schooled in the process of coding, I used various coding principles that I developed on my own to sort and sift through my data. I did not use computer software to analyze my data; I did several visual scans of my field notes and listened to audio recordings with an ear to discussions of key themes. Often, I found that my informants led me to explore issues of concern to them that I never considered at the outset of fieldwork.

During my analysis, I struggled with the fact that interpretation is a politically and ethically complex concept that requires examination at all stages of a project. Who is interpreting what or whom? Moreover, who has the right to make interpretations of data? For instance, I was dealing with sensitive topics such as race and racism because figure skating has historically been a white, upper-class sport in which participation is extremely costly (in terms of travel expenses, coaching and ice time, private clubs, and costumes, for example). This has led to a long-standing culture of sport that is saturated with white privilege.[1] Throughout my fieldwork, I often conducted interviews with elderly white coaches at elite training centers where there existed (from my perspective) a disjuncture between discourse and actual practice. Most people were receptive to my project, and they certainly did not imagine themselves as racist. At the same time, however, nonwhite students were frequently admonished for looking, in the words of one coach, "a little too ethnic." Many coaches were oblivious to this process of "whitening" their skaters' bodies, and an "aesthetic of whiteness" permeated the sport.

Most coaches were adamant that their actual names be used. As one coach said, "It gives your work authenticity and verifiability." My informants knew that I was studying issues of identity within the sport, including race, yet because no one perceived himself or herself as racist, no one viewed any comment as problematic. Given that one of the ethical expectations for anthropological research is to protect one's informants, how can an anthropologist analyze such situations? From an etic (outsider's) perspective, I could certainly explore how such comments converge with the idea that Canadian society is predicated upon hierarchies of race and look at how racism operates in insidious ways at institutional levels. The problem was that many of my informants devoted a substantial amount of their time to my work, and I felt an ethical obligation to protect them. In one instance, I had one elderly coach call my university department after our interview to provide the phone numbers of 15 additional skaters and coaches to consider for my interviews. He then proceeded to call or email me every few months, asking how my research was going. By simply labeling or interpreting coaches' comments and attitudes as "racist," and, worse still, by using their actual names in my work, I felt that would be hurtful to them. At the same time, I felt an obligation to report upon and challenge the pervasive conceptions of race and racism within the sport in order to promote a more inclusive and accepting training environment for students.

There is no easy answer or solution to this dilemma. Ultimately, I decided to incorporate the names of informants into my work selectively. When I discussed issues of race and racism, I often made up pseudonyms for certain coaches, and I decided that my job was not to frame my analysis in terms of an exposé style of writing on racism in the sport. Instead, I addressed the widespread disjuncture between people's ideals of race and multiculturalism and lived realities. To avoid singling out the sport of figure skating as "racist," I also explored how such attitudes operate in other domains of Canadian society. In other words, this type of white privilege was not exclusive to the sport.

A final issue that I considered throughout my "analysis" was derived from repeated questions from informants. When I was granted media accreditation at competitions, I found that I was indistinguishable (from my informants' perspective) from a journalist. One of the questions I most often addressed was, "How is your analysis going to be different from a reporter's?" Given that many journalists were beginning to engage with the interrelationships between national identity and various social issues within sport, I struggled with this question. Many reporters assigned to the media centers of competitions, in fact, had been covering the sport for years and had developed a long-standing rapport with skaters; in this instance, then, the typical argument—that an anthropologist's commitment to long-term fieldwork enabled privileged access to people—fell short. Looking back, I would argue that an awareness of theoretical and social contexts was one of the important and more obvious distinctions between my analysis and that of journalists. Although journalists may also report on racism or other issues within sport, they often fail to connect these issues to broader issues in Canadian society, or to ask this question: "What cultural factors, both inside and outside the sport, have shaped people's beliefs and practices?" An anthropologist's analysis typically links data with theory and translates the thoughts and perspectives of informants into what we might call "anthrospeak." Indeed, one of the biggest challenges for many undergraduate students is learning the academic culture of their discipline, which includes an understanding of theory and how it intersects with various cultural realities. As cultural translators, ethnographers "anthropologize" the experiences of informants, meaning we think critically about how our fieldwork intersects with anthropological themes addressed in the literature. In my case, these themes included notions of race, class, nationalism, and gender, among others. In most cases, this process of translation and analysis is not seamless and is not without ethical or political ramifications for our informants, and for the work we do as anthropologists.

Making Connections

As McGarry discusses, the distinction between "home" and "field" is often blurred in projects that take place in geographically familiar places, like the city you live in. What are some of the consequences of this fuzziness for your analysis? Does it raise any practical difficulties for the analysis process?

In many cases, objects are important items that will be discussed or shown to you during interviews. How are objects significant, and why are they important to consider when you conduct your analysis?

In McGarry's vignette, why was she upset with people thinking that she was a journalist? What is the difference between anthropology and journalism? Given that increasing numbers of nonanthropological scholars and writers integrate an ethnographic approach into their research, what might be some of the things that make *anthropological* analyses distinctive?

Can you think of any other examples that show how an anthropologist's interpretations of events or conversations can differ from those of his or her interlocutors? How would you handle this situation in your own fieldwork?

Try This

Go online and find a newspaper or magazine article with a reader blog, editorial, or comment section. Your article should focus upon a current domestic or international event or news story. Using open, focused, and then selective coding, code the article and any comments as if they were anthropological data derived from your fieldwork. Be as objective as possible, but pay attention to the trends and attitudes of the respondents. What key themes or issues emerge from people's responses to this news story? Can you draw any conclusions from this analysis?

Possible Projects

1. Complete the coding process on your overall project independently, and then select a partner. After each of you has printed out your *uncoded* transcripts (with names, places, and other identifiers blanked out or changed to ensure confidentiality), exchange them. Code each other's data, and when this process is complete, have a conversation with your partner about the similarities and differences in your codes and the themes you uncovered. At the end of your final project or paper, write a three- to four-page report that discusses these similarities and differences. What do these differences indicate about the process of analysis and your positionality in terms of this process? You can include this piece in a section on identity and interpretation in your final project.

2. Use a form of computer coding software (e.g., NVivo, Ethnograph, OneNote, EgoNet, and ATLAS.ti) to code approximately 20 transcribed pages of your interviews or field notes. Then, repeat this process manually. In a short paper, discuss your experiences using this software. How was the process similar or dissimilar to coding manually? Which method did you find more helpful and effective for your research? This conversation adds to reflections on objectivity and could be included in the methods section of your final paper.

Recommended Readings

Altheide, David L. 1987. "Reflections: Ethnographic Content Analysis." *Qualitative Sociology* 10 (1): 65–77.

Bernard, H. Russell. 2011. *Research Methods in Anthropology: Qualitative and Quantitative Approaches.* 5th ed. Walnut Creek, CA: AltaMira Press.

Garner, Roberta M., and Greg M. Scott. 2013. *Doing Qualitative Research: Designs, Methods, and Techniques.* Toronto, ON: Pearson Education.

Glaser, Barney G., and Anselm L. Strauss. 1967. *The Discovery of Grounded Theory: Strategies for Qualitative Research.* Chicago, IL: Aldine Publishing Company.

LeCompte, Margaret D., and Jean J. Schensul. 1999. *Analysing and Interpreting Ethnographic Data.* Walnut Creek, CA: AltaMira Press.

Miles, Matthew B., A. Michael Huberman, and Johnny Saldana. 2013. *Qualitative Data Analysis.* 3rd ed. Thousand Oaks, CA: Sage Publications Inc.

Saldana, Johnny. 2016. *The Coding Manual for Qualitative Researchers.* London, UK: Sage.

Note

1 The notion of "white privilege," popularized by Peggy McIntosh (1989), posits that "white" individuals have certain unearned advantages of privileges over people of color. Moreover, because whiteness is viewed as normative in North America, people considered "white" are unaware of their privileges. White privilege is thus one form of embedded racism that operates in a variety of insidious ways in our society.

CHAPTER 7

WRITING UP AND THE POLITICS OF REPRESENTATION

Writing about People

Which of your five senses would you most miss, if you had to forego one? Chances are your response would be "vision." Western cultures are **ocularcentric**; we are taught that vision is our most important sense, so it is afforded a high value when it comes to discerning what is considered "true." For example, we use phrases like "seeing is believing" or "I have to see it to believe it." Because vision is a primary means by which we experience the world, we often erroneously assume that this primacy of vision will translate readily to our cross-cultural interpretations and representations of data gathered through fieldwork. We tend to view paintings and other forms of art, for instance, primarily for their visual, aesthetic value. In Western cultural traditions, paintings are typically forms of material culture to be looked upon, usually on a wall, in a detached, two-dimensional context. However, in other cultures, visuality is not the primary means through which paintings or other forms of artistic expression are understood or experienced. David Howes and Constance Classen (1991), drawing upon the work of Sam Gill (1979), for instance, discuss how the Navajo make sense of their sand paintings. They argue that knowledge of the Navajo sensorium is necessary before we can understand their varied meanings:

> Photographs of these paintings taken by tourists or art collectors capture the whole of the design from above. The Navajo, however, never see the paintings from that perspective. They situate themselves *within* the painting. When a sand painting is used in a healing ritual, the person to be healed, or "re-created" as the Navajo say, actually sits in the painting. Sand is taken from the bodies of the holy people represented

in the drawing and pressed on the body of the ill person. Thus, while
outside observers see the sand paintings as visual objects, for the
Navajo their tactile dimension is, in fact, more important. (Howes and
Classen 1991, 329)

Their analysis draws attention to the fact that, as anthropologists, we must
be aware that our own worldviews, aesthetics, and sensibilities cannot necessarily be applied to our interpretations of other cultures. In many cases, it
is only through the experience of fieldwork that we learn the complexities
surrounding cross-cultural interpretation and translation.

The process of analyzing and "writing up" one's fieldwork experiences
thus involves an act of translation, or interpretation. In other words, we transform our fieldwork activities, experiences, and interpersonal interactions into
words and images (see, for example, Leavitt 2014; Maranhao and Streck 2003).
In the process, anthropologists are tasked with negotiating how to interpret
and communicate effectively, to diverse audiences, the varied perspectives
and lived experiences of our informants. Though many anthropologists work
in universities and other academic settings, others work for government or
nongovernmental organizations, for museums, or in health-related contexts,
among other fields. Writing for such diverse audiences creates specific challenges.
For example, how does the anthropologist capture the sensory experiences
of fieldwork—of being in another place with different sights, smells, and
sounds—and communicate this experience in another language, which also
expresses cultural difference? Is it possible to translate the experiential, senso-
rial components of fieldwork into written texts? As discussed in Chapters 10
and 11, many anthropologists use film, photography, or other forms of visual
media to communicate and translate their experiences to their varied audiences. However, most anthropologists, especially in academia, rely principally,
if not exclusively, upon discursive texts.

It has only been since the 1980s (with a few exceptions) that anthropologists
have begun to consider the politics of **representation**. Early on, anthropological texts were deemed objective analyses, even though they were closely
implicated in the colonial project of power relations. In 1986, James Clifford
and George Marcus, along with others, drew attention to the complex subjective aspects of ethnography and ethnographic writing to challenge notions
of scientific truths. In the seminal work *Writing Culture*, Clifford and Marcus
(1986) brought forward important redefinitions of anthropology regarding
issues such as who should do fieldwork, how it should be done, what topics
should be studied, and how the results should be represented ethnographically.
Writing Culture became a standard reference point that radically questioned
the cultural anthropological cannon. In this chapter, we examine the politics

of writing and focus on understanding three things: the layers of logic that inform a cultural anthropologist's work, why positionality is central to representation, and the important role that reflexivity plays in every aspect of the research and writing process. This discussion will ultimately highlight how the **dyadic relation** between ethnographers and their subjects has radically changed in the past 30 to 35 years.

Turning Culture into a Text: Interpreting Your Data

As you begin to write up your fieldwork experiences, it is useful to think about the processes of research, analysis, and writing as intertwined and not mutually exclusive. In other words, instead of viewing the research process in a linear manner with a clearly delineated beginning and ending, imagine it as a cyclical process, much like the process of analysis (O'Reilly 2012). The early twentieth century distinction between "field" (the place of research) and "home" (the location of supposedly more detached analysis and writing), as discussed in earlier chapters, is no longer tenable. Given that the field is, for some, not even a distinct geographical place, it makes sense that the realms of research, analysis, and writing overlap. For example, if you are exploring how female professional dancers in a dance studio in Seattle cope with various sources of stress, it is likely that you will return home after an interview and (either consciously or unconsciously) begin the analysis process. Much of your prewriting, in fact, will consist of simply thinking about and reflecting upon your data and on how these data relate to broader anthropological themes or issues. In some cases, the content of your informants' responses may even cause you to alter your research question or line of inquiry. Their responses to your questions might open up new avenues of inquiry, and you could find yourself going back and revising your research question.

Once you have coded your data and selected various themes to focus on in your writing (as discussed in Chapter 6), it will be necessary to engage in library research to help **theorize** your work by incorporating a **literature review** in your project. For example, if gender and women's equality is a key concern for your informants (female dancers in Seattle), and an issue that you would like to focus on in your writing, then you will need to explore and discuss existing anthropological and related literature on gender, gender equality, and women and dance within your demographic, to name just a few topics. It is important to demonstrate in your writing that you have an excellent knowledge of existing research within your field of study. As an undergraduate student, you are generally not expected to conduct original research or present original findings, but you do need to provide the historical and theoretical context of your research. And remember to broaden your research, if necessary. Obviously, if you are studying psychics in West Virginia, chances are there are few (if any) preexisting ethnographic works or academic publications on this specific research focus. As a result, you'll have to broaden your literature review search.

The next step is to turn your attention to your data once again. These data may include your field notes, photographs, and interview recordings, among other things. Your job here is to link your ethnographic data and field experiences with key points derived from existing literature. Ask yourself questions such as these: Do my fieldwork findings support existing research on this issue or topic? Do my data challenge any existing assumptions? What can my project add to existing research? How does existing research relate to my specific experiences? Ultimately, you will need to link your findings and the content of your ethnographic experiences to broader themes or theories. This process involves selection. You may, in fact, be disappointed to learn that you end up using a very small subset of the data that you collect. This is normal, and it does not mean that you collected "bad" data. As Glesne (2010, 226) argues, much of the material you collect will simply end up being "tangential" to the story that you are trying to construct.

Remember to leave sufficient time once your interviews are completed simply to think about your work and how it fits with anthropological literature. Once you sit down to write, be realistic. You should not expect to complete a first draft in one evening; attempting to do so would be a disservice to the hours that you spent in the field. Set reasonable writing goals for yourself; aim to complete a certain number of pages, words, or a defined section of your work each day. As you write, remember to use an active voice as doing so often creates a more direct and engaging form of writing, and in anthropology, it is generally acceptable to use the first person. Though your fieldwork anecdotes should not devolve into an exercise in navel-gazing, remember that you are relating *your* experiences of fieldwork to the reader. So you can expect your writing to be peppered with the selective use of the first person.

According to Madden (2010), most ethnographies, like most forms of academic writing, are comprised of a discussion of the aim or goal of the project, a description of fieldwork experiences, analysis, interpretations, and a conclusion. You do not necessarily need to use the names of these sections as subtitles; just remember that these are the critical components of any ethnography that need to be addressed. As you settle in to write, one of your biggest challenges will be to figure out how to organize and present your results. Glesne (2010) offers a list of some of the more popular approaches for organizing ethnographic data within the context of writing; two of these approaches are explored here. A *thematic approach*, for instance, arranges data by themes or topics, which you can even use as subheadings throughout your paper.

For example, if you are studying how and why people choose to be circus clowns, then you could focus on themes that reflect the issues and topics that came up repeatedly within the context of fieldwork discussions: childhood experiences, feelings of inclusion or exclusion, or other factors. In contrast, some writers chose to organize their papers according to a *zoom lens approach* (Glesne 2010, 229). In this approach, the author oscillates between specificity and more general, abstract, or theoretical concerns. For instance, the author may tell a fieldwork story in great detail and then spend time exploring the varied meanings of it from a theoretical perspective. In this way, the data are continually being explained and linked with theory. When you think through matters of organization, one of the most helpful things that you can do is flip through several different ethnographies and pay close attention to how the writers chose to organize their key ideas. Then ask yourself which approach, or which combination of approaches, might best suit your own fieldwork situation.

Once you have a rough draft of your paper or project, remember that editing is important. Ideally, you should have a complete draft of your paper completed at least one week before the due date. This allows you to begin to conceptualize the writing process as **recursive**. Take advantage of peers, family, classmates, or even university or college writing centers that might be available to you, and obtain feedback about your work. Your reviewer should comment upon organization, grammar, spelling, style, and the thesis statement. If a reviewer has a background in anthropology, then he or she might also be able to provide more detailed feedback on the theory and content of your paper. Upon receiving feedback, think critically and carefully about what aspects of your paper you should change and what can be left alone. This is a selective process. You don't necessarily need to make changes to every component of your paper. Obviously, however, if multiple people comment upon what they perceive to be a "problem" area, then this spot should warrant a detailed evaluation and possibly revision. Also, ensure that you keep on topic. Throughout this process, ensure that every example and every point of discussion always relates back to your research question. Sometimes reading your work out loud helps to ensure that you stay on track.

What Is Representation, and Why Does It Matter when "Writing Up"?

As discussed previously, you will need to think critically about how you represent your informants and your fieldwork experiences. Even the words and phrases that you use to describe your experiences can have long-term consequences for the livelihoods of those you work with. Over the years, anthropology has had its fair share of scandals surrounding representation, ranging from the politics surrounding Napoleon Chagnon's (1968) problematic characterization of the Yanomamo (more commonly called the Yanomami) as "fierce" to Margaret Mead's (1928) claim that all Samoans are peaceful and loving. The problem is that such depictions are **essentialist representations**, meaning that they are predicated upon stereotypes and function to construct gross generalizations about an entire society. In the process, they overlook diversity. If we were to apply such characterizations to our own society in the United States or Canada, for instance, we would quickly see how inaccurate they are. It would sound ridiculous to claim that all Americans are "brash" or that all Canadians are "nice" (both of which are common stereotypes). In the case of the Yanomamo, the American Anthropological Association (AAA 2002) contended that Chagnon's representations of them as "fierce" and violent functioned to cultivate stereotypes of the Yanomamo as uncivilized, backward, and primitive, thus promoting ethnocentrism.

For this reason, representation is often an ethical issue, as discussed in Chapter 3. Indeed, the translation of cultural experiences, worldviews, and beliefs into texts is often fraught with ethical and political implications. When Philippe Bourgois (2002) conducted fieldwork among crack dealers in East Harlem, for instance, he had to consider how to depict his informants, most of whom had committed violent crimes ranging from domestic abuse to rape and murder. Although he did not wish to condone their behavior, he also wanted to challenge mainstream academic "blame the victim" mentalities and show how racism and classism (operating via social structures such as the police, judicial, and educational systems) function to minimize economic and social opportunities for disadvantaged peoples in these communities. Some people find that the only way they can obtain a sense of "respect" is through drug dealing. For Bourgois, the dilemma then becomes (among other things) how to represent his informants. Moreover, what sorts of ethical issues are involved in constructing representations? For example, is it necessary for Bourgois to divulge the content of his graphic conversations about violence and rape? Do these conversations simply reinforce long-standing, negative, and often racist stereotypes about Puerto Ricans in East Harlem? Moreover, how can he protect his informants from the police, who surely want access to his informants' names and contact information and to the details of his intimate conversations? What, ethically, should an anthropologist do?

The dilemma Bourgois faced highlights the fact that, whether anthropologists depict people using language or images, the translation of the experiential aspects of culture involves an act of representation, and anthropologists, as cultural translators, are responsible for crafting particular depictions of their interlocutors. As you write up your fieldwork experiences, then, you'll need to think critically and carefully about the words, phrases, and images that you choose to discuss and represent your informants. Think about the long-term consequences of your representations and about how your informants would view your work. Are you offering a fair depiction of your experiences? Avoid generalizing or sensationalizing your fieldwork, and ensure that you are not representing people in a derogatory manner. Remember that people donated their time to participate in your project, and it is important to treat people fairly and respectfully.

Positionality and Reflexivity

When you are writing up your work, it is also imperative that you consider and discuss your **positionality**. This means that you must take into consideration how your informants perceive you, how this impacts your fieldwork experiences, and, finally, how this informs the practice of writing. This emphasis on positionality, however, was not always an important component of anthropological writing. In the first half of the twentieth century, anthropology was conceptualized as objective, scientific, and replicable. Bronislaw Malinowski and Franz Boas, both of whom would go on to train scores of North American and British anthropologists, were originally trained in mathematics and the natural sciences; they thus viewed field sites as akin to laboratories. In keeping with academic traditions in these fields, early anthropologists often kept "themselves" out of their ethnographies. With the exception of **tropes of entry** (Clifford 1990) into "the field," in which anthropologists documented their trials and experiences of entering into seemingly foreign and exotic places, they rarely discussed their feelings, personal relationships, or experiences in the field. Additionally, this narrative of entry often served to bolster the anthropologist's authoritative, "objective" stance as a distant and scientific observer and left little room for questions about how informants perceived the researcher or other things of a "personal" nature. Malinowski, for instance, kept a famous and separate diary while living among the Trobrianders, in which he documented his personal feelings and experiences. "Scholarly" ethnographies, it seems, were expected to be devoid of discussions about identity, the perceptions of informants, and informants' perceptions of the scholar. In 1964, for instance, Laura Bohannan, in *Return to Laughter*, documented her personal experiences and exploits living among the Tiv in Nigeria. She was so concerned, however, with shattering anthropology's claim to objectivity that she wrote under a pseudonym (Elenore Smith Bowen) and in the format of a novel to reach a wide audience and avoid criticism from anthropologists.

By the 1970s and early 1980s, anthropologists had slowly begun to document in ethnographies their personal experiences and other "subjective" elements of fieldwork. Of the more famous examples, Renato Rosaldo (1980), for instance, explored his ambivalent feelings toward Ilongot headhunting practices, and

Paul Rabinow (1977) discussed the personal relationships that he developed in *Reflections on Fieldwork in Morocco*. These publications, among others, represented a turning point in the ways in which ethnographies are written, as they challenged the long-standing assumption that anthropology was indeed "objective." Since the 1980s, anthropologists have become increasingly aware of the importance of acknowledging their positionality in their writing.

To illustrate why this issue is important, and why fieldwork and the writing process are neither objective nor replicable, let's pretend that your institution has decided to send your entire class to a small village on an island in Micronesia. You are tasked with exploring issues and questions surrounding women's experiences of work and their integration into a wage labor economy. Obviously, you will all have different kinds of interactions with your informants, and they will relate to each of you differently based upon their perceptions of who you are, or your **identity**. For this reason, anthropologists increasingly question how such factors as class, race, ethnicity, gender, age, nationality, and sexuality, among others, impact the types of responses that you obtain from people and the types of relationships that you develop (or if you develop any rapport at all). For instance, such factors as a "generation gap" may play a role in the fieldwork process. It may be easier, in some instances, to relate to people of your own age group. Similarly, in a sex-segregated society that has strict physical and ideological separations between men and women, male researchers will obviously find it difficult to obtain access to women to conduct participant observation and interviews, and vice versa for female researchers. Even personality can impact the fieldwork experience. In a society that expects men to be outgoing within the context of interpersonal relationships, a shy male researcher may be misinterpreted as standoffish or unfriendly. In thinking critically about identity, you must also consider how power affects your relationships in the field. Because, as a discipline, anthropology evolved alongside and as a result of the growth and spread of colonialism, most early anthropologists tended to study groups of people who were marginalized socially, economically, and geographically (see Chapter 1). So does this mean that some people, due to their positionality, are better suited for some fieldwork situations than others? Or, alternatively, that some anthropologists are better able to obtain "the truth?" Fortunately, this is not the case. With the advent of postmodern approaches, it has become the norm to think about our fieldwork experiences as partial ones. In other words, we can only ever obtain **partial perspectives** in the field. Such perspectives are informed by our varied identities and backgrounds. Even though a white, middle-class female may have different field experiences conducting fieldwork at an urban health center in San Diego than a black, upper-class male, neither researcher's perspective can be understood as "right" or "wrong." These perspectives are simply different, and shaped by differing positionalities.

Many of the issues discussed in this chapter, in particular the intersections among representation, writing, and positionality, are explored by Kathryn Dudley in her vignette about her fieldwork among artisanal guitar makers. Her work is especially attuned to power dynamics and notions of authority within the context of fieldwork and writing, and she writes that many of her "challenges revolve around the politics of power and knowledge: who can claim to know what about whom, and how do those claims come to be accepted as the 'truth' about others and ourselves." In other words, we need to destabilize assumptions about academic writing as a form of truth telling and think critically about writing as one form of representation that has historically been predicated upon privileged access to authority: who can speak for whom, and what depictions are constructed? These are all politically charged and ethical issues that you will need to think about as you write up your own work and construct your own representations of your informants and your fieldwork experiences.

VIGNETTE

Kathryn Dudley is a professor of anthropology and American studies at Yale University. Much of her research focuses upon how different groups of Americans (e.g., farmers, artisanal guitar makers) respond to and are influenced by the varied demands and pressures of capitalism.

FIGURE 7.1: Portrait of Kathryn Dudley, 2011. Photograph by Rebekah Butler. Courtesy of Kathryn Dudley.

FIGURE 7.2: George Youngblood reattaching a separated fretboard at the Youngblood Music Workshop, 2007. Photograph by Kathryn Dudley.

THE ETHNOGRAPHIC ENCOUNTER: WHO IS REPRESENTING WHOM?

I was two weeks into a six-month period of fieldwork with George Youngblood, a luthier in Guilford, CT (Figure 7.2). Among guitar aficionados in the Boston–New York City area, Youngblood is recognized as a premier restoration specialist who has been making, selling, and repairing stringed instruments since 1976. On this particular day, I was dressed in the shop apron that Youngblood had given me the week before. It was the apron he usually wore. Putting on an old denim one instead, he had waved aside my demurrals, claiming the suede was "too fancy" for his taste and he only wore it because it had been given to him as a gift. When I tied the apron behind my back, I'd felt the thrill of undergoing a small initiation rite.

The day progressed much as I'd come to expect, with Youngblood explaining the tasks I was to perform and me, with more or less success, trying to accomplish them. I was learning to "set up" guitars, making the minor alterations that enhance an instrument's performance and playability. I had graduated from adjusting a guitar's neck relief and string height to "dressing" its frets by leveling out areas worn down by the pressure of vibrating strings.

As usual, our work was interrupted by visitors and by conversations with Brian Wolfe, Youngblood's business associate who ran the retail end of the shop. We had just finished talking with an unlikely customer: a man in his sixties whose body bore the signs of a lifetime of physical labor and limited economic means. It was unclear what had brought him into a high-end guitar shop, but his scruffy clothes and weathered face marked him as out of place. When he reached out to touch instruments hanging on the wall—acoustic guitars valued at $8,000 to $15,000—Wolfe hovered nearby, ready to avert a catastrophe. The tension in the air was palpable.

Taking the situation in hand, Youngblood invited the man into the workshop and struck up a conversation. What kind of music did he like? How long had he been playing guitar? Out came a halting story of a lifelong passion for hard rock, Gibson Les Pauls, Marshall amplifiers, followed by an unfortunate coda: gradual hearing loss was bringing his music making to an end. I was well aware of Youngblood's capacity to code switch with clientele from different walks of life, but this instance of empathy was particularly moving. The man stood taller, met my eyes with a shy smile, and shook Youngblood's hand gratefully when he left.

Youngblood leaned against the worktable in the center of the room, crossed his arms over his chest, and spoke.

I'm fascinated by the characters that come into this shop. I notice he drove in in a pickup. I wonder if he's a construction worker? Did he deafen himself with a jackhammer or did he play that Marshall stack on ten? What killed his ears? It's sad for a musician to lose his hearing. But he's a character. I like drawing the character out. Brian pretty much dismissed him. But this [shop] is not about business; and it's not about getting stuff done in exchange for the money they give you to do it. It's the whole picture. While he was here talking to us, I feel like you and I had a shared experience of a real character who obviously has come through the years loving the American guitar, albeit the electric version of the thing. I can't help but reflect on the meaning that's been given to his life in all those boring weeks of operating a jackhammer: there are always the guitars back home.

That lutherie was about more than the modest income made doing it was a recurrent theme for Youngblood. His only goal, he often told me, was to earn enough money to meet his basic needs and remain in business. To him, the work itself was the reward, not a means to other ends. But in this moment of affective attunement, something more was present, something in excess of "loving the American guitar" or disdaining capitalist accumulation. It was there in the way the construction worker reached out, hesitantly, for guitars that were beyond his reach economically, knowing, as he must have, that his desire was surveilled. And it was there in Youngblood's insistence that the meaning of this man's life—however degraded by a daily grind of mind-numbing labor—was secured by "the guitars back home." In this shared dreamscape, I sensed, our mutually imbricated desires were magnetized by the promise that intimacy with guitars can bring.

What that promise *was* undoubtedly varied for each of us. But I'll hazard the guess that it had something to do with the skill and knowledge that guitars allowed us to demonstrate, each in our own ways, to our relevant publics. To the extent that we were brought together by a wish to develop and display our respective competencies in this "sphere of practical activity," the guitar promised to capacitate performances of expertise.[1] Not all assertions of expertise are equally valued, however, and this is what gave the episode its pathos and politics. What Youngblood acknowledged in this exchange, I believe, was the imperiled dignity of manual labor in a postindustrial society.[2] By honoring the work of enduring, and endeavoring to transform, a pervasive condition of physical hardship, economic marginality, and diminished national belonging, he extended to our construction worker the respectability that he himself was often denied.

Youngblood concluded his reverie about the "characters" in his shop with an observation—or joke, perhaps—that shifted the epistemological ground beneath my feet. With a bemused expression, he reminded me that he, too, had studied anthropology in college. "For me," he said, gesturing vaguely around the room, "*this* is entertainment; it's not a real job. I'm just hanging out and observing. I'm still an anthropologist, you see, lost in fieldwork. My focus was on cultural evolution and tool use, and tools related to the development of language and communication. I'm still an anthropologist, but I'm posing as a luthier." He paused, pointed at my apron, and gasped, "*You're doing the same thing I've been doing!*"

We laughed, astonished, and apprehended each other anew. A disturbing recognition took shape in my mind, and as my smile faded, I was beset by doubt. *Was* Youngblood doing the "same thing" I was doing? "Of course, not!" the feminist in me retorted, "and it's patronizing of him to presume that he is!" An inner struggle took place as I weighed the truth-value of Youngblood's proposition. The question of who "posed" as whom felt quite real. Was it Youngblood who posed as an anthropologist? His interest in anthropology was genuine, but he had, after all, dropped out of college 30 years ago to become a guitar maker. Or was it I who posed as a luthier? I had, admittedly, indulged in fantasies of "going native" and chucking academia to become a luthier.

This line of thought was cut short when my anthropological training kicked in. Wasn't this "joking behavior"—and my discomfort with it—evidence of a power imbalance in our relationship?[3] In terms of education and income, I could be said to occupy a higher social position than Youngblood did. But that status was dependent on people like him making themselves available for ethnographic study. Without their willingness to be "study-able" subjects, I could not claim to know who or what was worthy of study. Perhaps, in a tension-relieving moment of status inversion, we had switched places, with Youngblood assuming a dominant position and me, in my ill-fitting apron, subjected—and apprenticed—to his world-defining gaze?

As comforting as this interpretation was, I realized that it simply reinscribed, at the level of fieldwork ideology, the very hierarchy of knowledge that he was calling into question. What was up for grabs during our paroxysm of laughter was not *who* was the real anthropologist, but whose form of expertise would prevail—in our work together and in my representation of it—mastery of an artisanal trade or mastery of an academic discipline? For a brief, intoxicating moment, we glimpsed the possibility that the epistemologies of luthiers and anthropologists are, in some vital way, commensurate. Had I embraced this insight despite professional anxieties, I could have appreciated sooner than I did the transformative potential of Youngblood's invitation to upend classical assumptions about how ethnographic knowledge is made.

The flash of mutual recognition I felt that day in Youngblood's shop drew my attention to the uncertainties and uncanniness of the ethnographic encounter—the sensation that something significant is happening even though, or perhaps especially when, its meaning is unclear.[4] It allowed me to experience being "in the field" as an open-ended, intersubjective process in which surprising and unsettling re-alizations can occur. And it has had important implications for how I approach the challenges of writing ethnography. These challenges revolve around the politics of power and knowledge: who can claim to know what about whom and how those claims come to be accepted as the "truth" about others and ourselves. When we represent other people and their ways of life—whether in stories, films, or museum displays—we enter into these political formations whether we want to or not. Whose account of social realities do we present as being the authoritative ones—those of our interlocutors or those of academic theorists with whom we might also be in dialogue? Do we depict our-selves in the scene of fieldwork, including the thoughts and feelings we had during our interactions? And perhaps most important, how do we reconcile our desire to explain what people think, feel, and do with the limits of their understanding as well as our own?

There are no right answers to these questions, but how you think about them shapes the kind of ethnography you do and write. For my part, I strive to maintain a tactical balance between experiential and academic authority, self-awareness and attunement to others, and in-terpretive analysis and consciousness of its limitations. To the extent that ethnography, like life itself, immerses us in a multitude of polyva-lent discourses, our task is to intervene in social and cultural worlds where the mechanisms that link power and knowledge are discon-tinuous and unstable. This means that ethnographers must be alert to the diverse assemblages and ontological possibilities (material and immaterial, human and nonhuman) immanent in every situation, as well as curious about idiomatic expressions and figures of speech. To do this, we must make use of all the interpretive modalities available to us—sensory experience and intuition, self-analysis and reflexivity, active listening and interpersonal empathy, scholarly research and critical theory, and the aesthetic sensibilities of art and literature—to ensure that our representational practices work to interrupt, not re-produce, dominant structures of power and inequality.

If I were to name the most valuable skill that politically and poeti-cally adept ethnographers can develop—in the field as well as in their texts—it would be the ability to recognize and represent the interac-tive process by which we come to understand what matters to others and to ourselves. Knowledge of what constitutes the kind of world that we and our interlocutors wish to live in, separately and together, can never be known in advance of our encounter. Only through at-tentive, painstaking dialogue, within which we risk some of our most dearly held propositions, can we inch toward a common language for talking about the social realities that divide us and the cultural values that bring us together. Only then can we engage in and write about the ethnographic process with the creativity and compassion that George Youngblood extended to a construction worker reaching toward a guitar and questioning his worth in this world.

Making Connections

In her vignette, Dudley marvels at the abilities of George Youngblood to code switch. However, this is an important trait for anthropologists when writing up their fieldwork. How is code switching related to the act of writing?

Dudley discusses the role of power differentials in the writing and translating process. How did the process of thinking about and through power differentials in her fieldwork affect her work?

What does it mean to think about ethnography as an open-ended process? How does this relate to Dudley's experiences?

Try This

This activity takes the form of an imaginary letter that will encourage you to think about your own positionality and why this is important in the fieldwork process. Imagine that you are a cultural anthropologist about to begin interviews with children under the age of consent. Their teacher and parents want to know exactly who you are and why you want to interview these children. Write a letter explaining your "positionality" (i.e., your background in terms of gender, race, age, ethnicity, education, community), your motivations as a cultural anthropologist, and how you will proceed during the interviews. Also explain how the children will be treated and protected during this research process. For specific requirements, go back to Chapter 3 on ethics.

Possible Projects

1. For this project, your professor will pair you with another student. With your partner, decide upon a research question and a demographic of people to work with. Although you may not interview the same people, you should be working within the same "community." Select four people each to interview and use the same interview questions. After you each complete your interviews,

you should both meet to discuss the types of responses that you received and your experiences of the process. Were there any similarities or differences in your findings or with respect to your interactions with informants? Together, write a three-page report that summarizes your collective experiences in relation to how you both self-identified your differences in terms of factors such as race, gender, and personality.

2. Select an area of the world or a group of people that is experiencing war or political conflict with Canada or the United States (e.g., the nuclear bomb testing of North Korea, Russia's occupation of the Ukraine, ISIS terrorist acts around the world) and find at least ten North American visual and textual media articles about this conflict. These can include online or hard copies of various sources, including blogs, mainstream media news reports from outlets such as CNN or CBC, magazines, documentaries, and newspapers. Pay careful attention to the words and images that are used to describe the so-called "enemy." The news media is notorious for creating us–them dichotomies and stereotypes. What sorts of representations are being constructed (through language use) about your society and the "enemy's"? What might be some of the consequences of these representations?

Recommended Readings

Behar, Ruth, and Deborah A. Gordon. 1995. *Women Writing Culture.* Berkeley, CA: University of California Press.

Bouchetoux, Francois. 2014. *Writing Anthropology: A Call for Uninhibited Methods.* New York, NY: Palgrave.

Geertz, Clifford. 1988. *Works and Lives: The Anthropologist as Author.* Stanford, CA: Stanford University Press.

Gordon, Avery. 1997. *Ghostly Matters: Haunting and the Sociological Imagination.* Minneapolis, MN: University of Minnesota Press.

Starn, Orin. 2015. *Writing Culture and the Life of Anthropology.* Durham, NC: Duke University Press.

Stewart, Kathleen. 1996. *A Space on the Side of the Road: Cultural Poetics in an "Other" America.* Princeton, NJ: Princeton University Press.

Waterston, Alisse, and Maria D. Vesperi, eds. 2011. *Anthropology off the Shelf: Anthropologists on Writing.* West Sussex, UK: Wiley-Blackwell.

Wulff, Helena. 2016. *The Anthropologist as Writer: Genres and Context in the Twenty-First Century.* New York, NY: Berghahn Books.

Notes

1 Dominic Boyer's definition of expertise (2008, 39) is a good benchmark. For him, an expert is "an actor who has developed skills in, semiotic-epistemic competence for, and attentional concern with, some sphere of practical activity. By this definition a car mechanic and a street performer are clearly experts in their respective crafts although the qualitative and social dimensions of their expertise are very different (and valued differently) from those of more technocratic (and widely recognized) experts like doctors, lawyers or scientists."

2 This is a theme I have explored in several ethnographic contexts (Dudley 1994, 2000, 2014).

3 The classic reference is Radcliffe-Brown (1940).

4 For ethnographies that examine the haunting uncertainties of fieldwork, see Avery Gordon (1997), Kathleen Stewart (2007), and Lisa Stevenson (2014).

PART III

Shifting Field Sites

CHAPTER 8

APPLIED ANTHROPOLOGY

Introduction

We often represent our anthropology departments at undergraduate recruitment fairs that take place in the fall or spring in university gymnasiums. Attended by potential students and their parents, these fairs are an opportunity to ask faculty, graduate students, and undergraduate representatives about their fieldwork experiences, the academic strengths of the department, coursework, or other phenomena. Here are the two most popular questions that we consistently get: "What is anthropology?" and "What can I do with an anthropology degree?" After educating people about what anthropology is (i.e., we do not study dinosaurs!), we are often tasked with the job of "selling" anthropology to students and their parents. Given the paucity of tenure-track academic jobs, combined with the expense and time commitment involved in obtaining a doctoral degree, many students wonder whether it is, in one student's words, "worth it" to take anthropology or to pursue an academic path leading to a professorship. In other words, what *can* you do with an anthropology degree outside of academia? Moreover, how can you use your ethnographic fieldwork skills in applied situations? Finally, is there a market for these kinds of skills?

This chapter examines how anthropologists are using applied ethnographic methods. **Applied anthropology** (also called "practicing anthropology") functions as a form of "pragmatic engagement" with various communities to help find solutions to various problems (Rylko-Bauer et al. 2006, 178). Rylko-Bauer et al. (2006) maintain that, "if anthropology is truly committed to more than just engaged rhetoric, then praxis and application must play a more central role within the discipline" (178). Stillitoe (2007) argues that there are five ways to envisage applying anthropology. These entail facilitating others' understanding and potential use of externally produced knowledge, using knowledge of local understandings and worldviews to assist with various forms of development, translating cross-cultural knowledge, exploring cultural practices to assist various corporations seeking information on the "market use of knowledge," and "radical ethno-criticism of development" (147–48). Within these contexts, many applied anthropologists work to develop political, educational, corporate, or health policies that produce change. Others work (formally or informally) as activists or advocates for particular causes and on behalf of marginalized groups. In many North American contexts, applied studies have been conducted in a diverse array of contexts to further understand Indigenous knowledge, to highlight problems with the dominant biomedical health care system, to assist corporations with their consumer research, and to address issues surrounding inequalities within urban living, among other things. Many involve specific research design models that emphasize participatory involvement, during which anthropologists and informants mediate, collaborate, and exchange roles.

Increasingly, applied anthropologists can be found working both within academia and in nonacademic sectors. Indeed, Singer (2008) argues that there has been a resurgence of interest in the subfield since about 2007. One of the goals of this chapter, then, is to introduce students to some of the ethical and moral challenges associated with applied work. An important issue we address is the critique that applied anthropology is simply an extension of a colonial mentality whereby applied anthropologists (typically from a first world country and with resources, money, or power) provide help or resources to "fix" the problems of developing nations or marginalized communities without appropriate consultation with local peoples. As we have already seen, however, most contemporary applied anthropologists adopt a collaborative approach when conducting fieldwork, one that enables the interests and perspectives of informants to take center stage. In an applied setting, if an anthropologist is interviewing a group of people while working on behalf of a government organization, he or she often seeks to incorporate and negotiate the varied perspectives and interests at stake. At the same time, however, many people still ask whether the anthropologist's work is in the best interest of informants, especially when the anthropologist is working on behalf of a third party. In other words, is the anthropologist who works for a corporation or a policy arm of the government able to represent adequately the interests and perspectives of his or her informants? Finally, in such situations, who "owns" the data collected by the anthropologist, and does she or he have any control over how data are used by the organization sponsoring the research?

Academic versus Applied Anthropology: Is There a Difference?

Although applied anthropology is often thought to be a recent development in the discipline, it has a long history. According to Birx (2010) the term "applied anthropology" dates to 1906 when a diploma program at Oxford was announced.

Though many early anthropologists would not characterize their work as applied, they nevertheless used their research for practical purposes. Franz Boas, for instance, spoke out against pervasive forms of racism rooted in notions of biological determinism. He submitted two studies to the US Commissioner of Education, arguing that cultural context and processes of enculturation influence children's development. He hoped that his research would have policy implications, specifically with respect to immigration (Nahm and Rinker 2015). Many of Boas's students would go on to conduct applied research. Margaret Mead, for example, studied American soldiers in Britain during World War II and their impact on US–British relations (Nahm and Rinker 2015). Other anthropologists began to work in corporate settings. In the 1930s, anthropologist W. Lloyd Warner worked with Elton Mayo of the Harvard Business School to study issues of morale, fatigue, and productivity at the Hawthorne plant of the Western Electric Company near Chicago (Singer 2008). By 1941, the Society for Applied Anthropology was established in the United States to support policy-oriented, applied forms of fieldwork.

Not all anthropologists, however, were supportive of the growing popularity of applied anthropology. Singer (2008) argues that the attitudes of anthropologists toward applied anthropology could be divided into two camps. The "science as knowledge" school is an outgrowth of anthropology's early collusion with science. Malinowski and others, for instance, imagined anthropology as an objective science and thought that, through the careful application and use of particular methods, fieldwork was replicable. From this perspective, "applied approaches that seek to implement social change violate the notion of cultural relativism and 'data purity,' the idea that data contamination between researcher and subject must be minimized" (Singer 2008, 236). On the other hand, the "science for practical utility" camp argues that science is not objective and that researchers are always informed by cultural biases and subjectivities. Thus, anthropologists should help solve various social problems to improve the lives of others (Singer 2008, 236).

These days, relatively few sociocultural anthropologists would make the claim that the discipline is an objective science. However, many biases and prejudices exist toward applied forms of research, and often distinctions are made between "academic" and "applied" forms of anthropology in North America. As we shall see, however, this distinction is increasingly blurred because many anthropologists who do applied research often also work in academic contexts, and both may use similar (or in some cases, identical) fieldwork methods.

Traditionally speaking, **academic anthropologists** are individuals with PhDs who are employed by universities or academic research institutions. They are usually paid to teach undergraduate and graduate courses, apply for and obtain grant money, conduct original fieldwork and research, perform service work (e.g., serve on university committees), and publish and disseminate their research in the form of conference papers, journal articles, and books. Much academic anthropology is competitive and theoretically engaged and driven, so often the research questions asked by academic anthropologists are motivated by theoretical or other etic concerns. Indeed, one of the long-standing critiques of academic anthropology is that it is out of touch with the needs and interests of the communities these academics work with or that the publications that result from fieldwork experiences are inaccessible for the average person.

Applied anthropologists, on the other hand, have tended to work in more diverse settings. They often have PhDs, and publish their work, and they may or may not be associated with universities or academic institutions. Applied anthropologists have historically been concerned with solving practical problems. As problem solvers, they tend to find employment with corporations and government and nongovernment organizations, among other places. Due to the growing numbers of anthropology graduates, many people seeking employment in anthropology-related fields will likely end up in applied settings. Although some applied anthropologists in nonacademic settings continue to do research and publish their work, others do not.

As many anthropologists attest, hierarchies of value are often applied to different forms of anthropology, with academic anthropology usually garnering greater prestige than applied forms (Rylko-Bauer et al. 2006; see also Bennett 1996; Singer 2008). One of the critiques frequently leveled against applied anthropology is that there is a "decoupling of theory from praxis" (Rylko-Bauer et al. 2006, 178). This critique is particularly severe, given that academic hiring processes have often privileged innovative theoretical approaches. Also, the critique that applied anthropology is atheoretical is predicated upon "vague generalities rather than concrete analysis of specific examples" (Rylko-Bauer et al. 2006, 182). Moreover, it discounts the connections between various valid ways of knowing:

> Usually overlooked in this debate are the basic parallels that exist between domains of theory production and of policy and action. Applied anthropologists use essentially the same epistemological processes except that the referent is different.... Although recommendations within applied reports are rooted in truth uncovered through research, truth qua truth is not the issue; instead, it is effectiveness, formatted in an implied proposition like "If you want to accomplish this, you should do this." If theorizing means positing a

causal link between domains, then application is inherently theoretical. (Rylko-Bauer et al. 2006, 184–85)

Despite any form of disciplinary snobbery toward applied forms of research, applied anthropology is arguably the fastest growing subfield of anthropology (Simonelli and Skinner 2016). With this in mind, what kinds of field sites would applied anthropologists find themselves working in?

Applied Field Sites

The field sites in which applied anthropologists conduct their research are diverse. Two of the more prominent ones are discussed here: medical and corporate contexts. First, large subsets of applied anthropologists find work within health-related contexts, working in hospitals, for government or nongovernment health organizations, such as the WHO (World Health Organization), or for development organizations. One thing that many **medical anthropologists** do is figure out how to introduce biomedical forms of health care in a culturally sensitive manner to eliminate the spread of disease and help people cope with the effects of disease. For instance, during the 2014–15 Ebola outbreak in West Africa, anthropologists were hired by WHO to work with the families and people who had come into contact with an Ebola patient—"to help them readapt to regular life and find the strength to cope with the stigma of Ebola virus disease" (WHO 2015). Anthropologists also worked with local communities to help individuals cope with the loss of loved ones and with the resulting social, emotional, and economic ramifications of such a loss.

Closer to home, anthropologist Caura Wood (see this chapter's vignette) works in a corporate environment for an oil company in Alberta. Anthropologists who work in these settings are "experts" in studying the politics of the region and its industries, and they also possess the necessary cultural background and skills to readily understand local cultural circumstances. Valued for their qualitative fieldwork skills and culturally sensitive approaches to research, applied anthropologists like Wood often work in teams with others who may not necessarily possess the cultural background to effectively communicate and integrate with local communities. Adopting a reflexive approach, Wood highlights in her vignette the subjective nature of interpersonal relationships within the context of fieldwork, as well as the ethical and political ramifications of "studying up" (Nader 1972) within the oil industry.

Like Wood, many other applied anthropologists have found employment in corporate environments. Canadian anthropologist Grant McCracken is arguably one of the most well-known corporate anthropologists. As a consultant, he has been hired by various corporations, including Starbucks, Ikea, Kodak, and Coca-Cola. In many cases, his job is to conduct research with consumers (or potential consumers) of various products to understand how to best market a product to a specific demographic. In his book, *Chief Culture Officer* (2011), he argues that large corporations should hire "chief cultural officers" (CCOs) in the same way that they have chief financial officers (CFOs) or other executives. McCracken also runs a blog about popular cultural trends, called CultureBy, on which he discusses the relationship between consumption and culture, normally drawing upon examples from pop culture. Such research, however, often raises several ethical issues. Should anthropologists work on behalf of large corporations, especially those with histories of labor or worker abuse? What is the social value of such research, if one of the responsibilities of an anthropologist is to protect his or her informants? In addition to working in corporate field sites, many anthropologists work for governments and conduct fieldwork among Indigenous peoples or within military contexts. What are the ethical implications of these sorts of applied settings? These issues are discussed next.

Ethics in Applied Anthropology

As Singer (2008, 326) maintains, "It can fairly be said that applied efforts have resulted in some of the best and some of the worst work carried out in the name of anthropology." Many applied anthropologists have worked tirelessly as advocates for the economic, political, or health-based rights of marginalized groups while others have found themselves working on behalf of organizations with questionable intentions. In some cases, then, applied ethnography raises several ethical concerns. As discussed in Chapter 3, one of the main expectations of anthropologists is to ensure that informants feel a sense of physical and emotional security and confidentiality. Fostering these feelings is especially important to counteract anthropology's long colonial legacy. Indigenous peoples throughout the world, for instance, have historically served as a focus for anthropological fieldwork but have had little or no input into the research questions asked or the final ethnographies that are produced. As discussed in this section (and throughout Chapter 3), one way to counteract this trend is to engage in more participatory, collaborative forms of research with one's informants and to seek their input actively at all stages of the research process. Doing this is often easier to ensure when an anthropologist is the principal investigator and is conducting research through an academic institution or in a setting where there is no expectation that the researcher share or hand over field notes and data. In most academic settings, the researcher has a sense of autonomy over the research process. But what happens when an anthropologist works on behalf of a government organization or a corporation? In such situations, a researcher may not have the same sense of autonomy and control over the collection and use of the data he or she collects.

Lack of autonomy was a major concern in the highly controversial **Human Terrain System**, a project initiated by the US Department of Defense. Between 2007 and 2015, civilian anthropologists with cultural and linguistic expertise in Afghani and Iraqi cultures were hired and embedded with armed soldiers to comprise "human terrain teams." The goal of these teams was to prevent counterinsurgency by visiting local communities and engaging the qualitative research expertise of anthropologists to talk to people about a variety of issues or concerns related to military conflicts. Two of the many ethical concerns raised by this project involved the issues of data ownership and informed consent (see, for example, Forte 2011, 2015). To what extent is it possible to obtain the free and willing participation and consent of participants when anthropologists are traveling with armed soldiers? Moreover, since anthropologists were required to hand data over to the US military, they could not ensure that their research was used to promote the best interests of a community.

Another critique of applied anthropology is that it represents a new form of colonialism with the (usually Western) anthropologist entering a marginalized community to offer paternalistic "solutions" to presumed problems. Some applied anthropologists who have worked in the field of international development (e.g., for development agencies such as the United Nations or for nongovernmental organizations with the aim of "improving" sanitation, education, medical facilities, or other phenomena) have historically come under fire for inadvertently imposing Western-centric notions of "progress" upon societies. Another critique is that they fail to take into consideration local desires and attitudes toward development. In an effort to decolonize the discipline and address these criticisms, many applied anthropologists integrate new forms of **participatory research** methods (discussed next) into their work.

Participatory Research

Participatory research is a method that involves collaborative fieldwork and research that is grounded in a desire to give one's informants a voice and a say in policy development and implementation. In many ways, it works by decentering the authority of the anthropologist at all stages of research. Local communities and informants are invited to participate in research design, implementation, and dissemination. As Jen Shannon's vignette in Chapter 3 demonstrates, collaborative, participatory forms of research are increasingly used within the context of Native American communities, which have felt the colonizing effects of early anthropological research that did little to give back to local communities or to address the needs of Indigenous communities from an Indigenous perspective.

Van Willigen (2002) maintains that this type of collaborative research involves much closer interactions, engagements, and relationships between an anthropologist and his or her informants. It also requires anthropologists to rethink the notion of fieldwork as a linear process of research design, fieldwork, and "writing up." In the case of participatory research, an anthropologist is continually checking in with, or even working with, informants to ensure that their needs and interests are being met. This type of research therefore requires the anthropologist to be flexible in terms of research design and implementation. In some forms of participatory research, the anthropologist works on behalf of a local community and is hired by them. Van Willigen (2002) offers the example of Steven Schensul, who pioneered participatory forms of research when working on behalf of a Latino community in Chicago. In this case, the community hired Schensul for his expertise in report writing and qualitative research skills. Community members dictated the research questions that he was to address and helped him obtain access to various informants for fieldwork purposes. One of the benefits of participatory research methods is that anthropologists can obtain constant feedback from local communities and thus ensure that the needs of these communities are adequately met and represented.

If you were conducting participatory, collaborative research within the context of your own project, what would it entail? How does participatory research affect fieldwork methods and methodologies? First, it is important to note that much participatory research is necessarily **problem-oriented research**, which shifts power (in terms of the ability to devise and generate research questions, for example) away from the researcher and toward community members. Among other things, this focus means that the research questions addressed are aimed at answering highly specific questions generated by host communities. This narrowness is in stark contrast to the much larger scale of early ethnography, which tended to be broad in scope and aimed at understanding a variety of different aspects of a culture (e.g., kinship, gender, politics, economic systems, and material culture). Using a problem-oriented model, an anthropologist could address a specific question such as this: "How can health workers most effectively decrease rates of sexually transmitted infections in this population in a culturally sensitive manner?" To answer this question, the anthropologist must collaborate with community members and health professionals to work with key informants who can be surveyed or interviewed to address issues such as potential cultural barriers to implementing "safer sex" policies or options like condom use.

As discussed, the division between academic and "applied" forms of anthropology is increasingly challenged and destabilized as most researchers position the wishes and goals of their informants above their research interests. This change in purpose has resulted in increasing numbers of participatory, collaborative research projects, as well as in reflexive and frank discussions about the positionality of the anthropologist and the politics surrounding that particular anthropologist's engagements with informants, as discussed below in Caura Wood's vignette about her applied fieldwork in the oil industry.

Ultimately, applied forms of anthropology represent the fastest growing application of the field, and many students will undoubtedly find themselves working in applied settings, both within and outside of academia. So, it is important to consider how the skills you learn within the context of your fieldwork translate into solving everyday problems, even within your own communities. For those of you interested in working in applied settings for your projects, try contacting local community organizations, such as health organizations, recreational or sports organizations, or charities. Quite frequently, they have many questions that they would like to research, but they don't have the money or resources to do so and would welcome your input and expertise!

VIGNETTE

Caura Wood is an anthropologist who has been employed in an applied setting as a corporate secretary and vice president of an oil company in Alberta. Throughout this vignette, she documents her struggles with negotiating identities and processes of "studying up" among her informants. Much of Wood's early fieldwork and employment in this industry was conducted for her doctoral research, but she has since continued to work in this applied setting.

FIGURE 8.1: Photograph of Caura Wood, 2016. Courtesy of Caura Wood.

FIGURE 8.2: Prairie pumpjack, Innisfail, Alberta, July 9, 2016. Photograph by Caura Wood.

SATURATED IN OIL

We were sitting outside on a well-worn porch swing looking out at Mr. and Mrs. Penhold's property, located between Red Deer and Rocky Mountain House, Alberta. They had greeted me with the customary prairie hospitality. A cup of coffee, a homemade muffin, the exchange of pleasantries. We were talking about their experiences with oil and gas companies and surface leases. It was mid-summer, at a time when my job (as VP and corporate secretary for a small oil company) was not that demanding. Directors tended to schedule meetings before June and after August, and investors were known to exit the market or "go quiet" during summer. I had hoped to use this down time to do fieldwork outside the office and to talk to W5 landholders (those with land in the busiest corridor of oil and gas activity in Alberta at the time) about their experiences with the industry. The Penholds were among those I selected because their land sat a few kilometers atop the prolific Cardium formation, which was a sought-after emerging light-oil play. The company I was working for had recently turned its drill bits to Cardium oil too, so I was now trying to "see Cardium" from multiple sites and points of view. I explained my research to them along with the fact that I was an employee of an oil and gas company, which was my access to studying the industry from inside. Mr. Penhold had a long list of grudges against the industry that included noise, odor, disrespect, traffic, pollution, greed, and alleged trespassing. He warned me that he was known to be a "colorful" character and that the industry didn't find him easy to get along with.

I had already explored anthropologically how geologists search for oil and gas. I had interviewed and shadowed some geologists during an internship a few years prior that doubled as a field site. From that experience, I learned that the Western Canadian Sedimentary basin (WCS) underlying Alberta was well studied and mapped. Big data offered by industry software providers such as geoSCOUT™ and AccuMap rendered the history of the basin's geological and log data accessible through a few clicks of a mouse. Drill bits had penetrated the WCS nearly a half a million times over the course of the oil industry's hundred-year history in Alberta, leaving a deep material trace and an archive of subsurface well data. With these database assemblages, geoscientists can navigate a real-virtual basin and discover new sources of hydrocarbons without leaving their desks. I was often surprised by how the subsurface appeared on their screens and how navigation bracketed off all but the economic spaces of petroleum geology. They were searching for signs of "missed pay" or "bypassed pay" from oil and gas reservoirs left behind by a prior era of basin players due to prices or due to the limits of recovery technology. The WCS is not the frontier space of a virgin basin, but the well-traveled space of "salvage accumulation" (see Tsing 2015) where a new round of explorers armed with new techniques and capital are grabbing what was left behind by past corporations.

From my seat on the porch swing, I had a clear view of the Penhold property. Behind me was their home, a doublewide trailer style that sat permanently on the south end of the property facing the farmland to the west. To the northwest end of their land was a favored family site of undeveloped land. Their grandchildren had named it the "mini-forest." Mr. Penhold described the trees as "family friends." He then launched into the reasons he had become so angry with industry. The Penholds were in the middle of a dispute over those very trees. Mr. Penhold had recently been in conversation with a surface Landman who had visited them to obtain a surface lease. At first, the Penholds had been willing to listen because the Landman said the company wanted to work with them to find a suitable site and to determine compensation for the loss of use and disturbances. Mr. Penhold hoped the well would be located away from the house and accessible from an existing property road. He had also hoped to get their main access road paved and a better water line installed, but the company had refused. Worse, the company wanted to drill the well in the middle of the mini-forest, and the compensation being offered was so meager, it had offended the Penholds.

I could see already that this well was going "non-routine," the Alberta Energy Regulator's (AER) term for applications characterized by dispute. "Non-routine" is the landholder equivalent to being the target of a hostile corporate takeover in which the major shareholders (in this case, the government and corporation) vote against management (i.e., the landholder). The odd similarities between these forms of hostility among misaligned stakeholders led me to later refer to drilling permits obtained through "non-routine" applications as "hostile penetrations." Alberta's split title gives the government (in at least 80 percent of the cases) ownership of the subsurface minerals and the right to access those minerals through most surfaces. Consequently, landholders cannot refuse a well but can negotiate, to some extent, their compensation and the particular location of it on their property. I was already attached to the Penholds' mini-forest and shared their indignant response to its devaluation by industry.

Before I left, Mr. Penhold told me he planned to make life difficult for the company, but I never asked who was drilling the well. Shortly after my interview, and to my dismay, I discovered it was the company I was working for. When I sought people to interview, I checked in advance to ensure they were not in a surface lease with my employer, I didn't want any role confusion, and I certainly had no intention of using my role as a corporate actor to extract information from rural landholders. The Penholds seemed clear so I proceeded with my interview. I later found out that because no lease had yet been signed and a well application had not yet been submitted, they didn't appear in my employer's database. I felt sick about it. I immediately called the Penholds and disclosed my conflict of interest. I thought they would be upset; I certainly was. I apologized for my conundrum and hoped they understood that I could no longer engage with their case due to my ethical and legal conflict.

To my surprise, the Penholds encouraged me to continue. "Sounds like you're in an ethical pickle," said Mr. Penhold, "I rather like ethical pickles. You should continue your research." However, because of my management contract, I was in no position to act as their advocate (not that they had asked me to); I did not yet know enough about surface leases to be useful; and, in this case, my role as a researcher was in direct conflict with the terms of my management contract even if their trees had grown on me. I thanked them, and I wished them well. Mr. Penhold promised me a good battle.

On one hand, entering oil and gas in the way that I had, first as an intern and later as an executive employee, had opened a world to me that is privileged and unseen by many. My research objective was to study up (see Nader 1972) and to study the particular performativities of Alberta's oil and gas capitalism, or "petrocapitalism" (Huber 2011). Autoethnography had become my means of writing about the boardrooms and financial transactions I witnessed because most of what I touched was "strictly private and confidential." I could not break confidentiality, but I could use myself as my own informant to describe what I was learning about how oil and gas capitalism was structuring industry, the public, and my own backyard (Wood 2016). I knew this positioning would alienate me from other informants, not because they weren't willing to talk to a corporate actor (they often were and hoped "we" were listening) but because oil and gas contracts create durable, legal, and enforced boundaries. I was now confronting the very relations of power and contestations of value that had no doubt constituted thousands of wells in the province. The barrels of oil equivalent (BOE) of light crude oil and natural gas that flowed from the W5 region of Alberta were all produced through these forms of frictions (see Tsing 2005), and through landscapes made complicit by the rights assigned through split land titles and through settler-colonial relations—not through dialogue and mutual consent.

I also began to see why independent land agents did this work. Face-to-face contact opened parties to their respective humanities—good and bad. Face to face makes it impossible to deny the impacts and effects generated by well sites and by something allegedly as minor as the "removal of scrub trees." Face-to-face encounters, especially when there is trespass, have at times gone very badly, resulting, as in one tragic case, in the murder of a company president by an upset landholder. In another case, the late Weibo Ludwig's acts of alleged "ecoterrorism" and well-site vandalism were followed by the accidental and tragic murder of a teen. Such hostilities emerge through the frictions of production and the contestations over the cordoned-off spaces where oil and gas are extracted from underneath surface owners' land, often against their will (see Nikiforuk 2001, 1999).

What troubled me most during this encounter with the Penholds was my own contaminated positioning (see Stewart 1991). Recognition of this fact is often cause to problematize the failures of objectivity in research and to embrace methods such as autoethnography (see Jones et al. 2013). Indeed, that approach had opened the world of oil and gas finance, deals, and the discursive space of corporate "value creation" to me for anthropological inquiry. Yet that value creation also came through backyards such as the Penholds'. In my attempts to study up, my positioning had alienated me from the very landscapes of extraction I was actively (albeit indirectly) producing as a corporate actor, consumer, and citizen. I felt saturated in oil and in its divisive and dispossessing powers. I also felt more obligated than ever to write about it. I realized that my own contaminated state was not unique. I needed oil to live. I was dependent on it for my research and for my livelihood. It struck me how this is the dirty problem of oil. We all (still) need it to live, and we all (still) barely notice our extreme dependence on it or how it flows from sites of friction underneath the sight lines of society, undergirding social life. That is, until price spikes (or sudden price drops) or acts of dissent shock our economy, our media, our wallet, or our habits—or until climate science and climate change makes denial increasingly uncomfortable.

Mr. Penhold did not disappoint. He was every bit as colorful as he had promised. The vile language used in his letters to the corporation was enough to shake even the most weathered of "oilmen." I smiled deeply when I learned that the Penholds had even written on behalf of their trees and promised a memorable protest should anyone try to remove them. The company I worked for, upon learning that a nearby well targeting the Cardium was uneconomic, took a pass on the Penholds' surface lease. For the time being, the mini-forest lived. But I would never read a balance sheet the same way again. Balance sheets gather up and format the world of oil and gas as line items to be assessed by global financial actors. Those line items and ratios work as indicators of solvency and investability, but they also omit the frictions of production; the matrices of gender, race, and class; and the nonhuman actors (Bear et al. 2015)—all are very present in the production of oil and gas in the field and forest as much as in the office.

Making Connections

What were some of the ethical considerations of Wood's fieldwork experiences that were unique to her roles as both ethnographer and corporate employee?

What did ethnography add to an understanding of oil culture that corporate understandings may miss?

What is a "contaminated" positioning? How did this apply to Wood's context?

What is the value of face-to-face encounters as opposed to mediated interviews such as those conducted over Skype or even by talking on the telephone?

Try This

When attempting to conduct fieldwork and research on a new or unfamiliar topic or cultural group, anthropologists often (inadvertently) impose an etic, or outsider's, perspective. In other words, the research questions that we ask are often driven by esoteric, "outsider" anthropological concerns that may not be deemed important or worthwhile by our informants. Devise a research question about a particular religious or ethnic group that you are interested in but not terribly familiar with. Then, find someone who self-identifies as a member of this group and set a time to discuss your research topic with that person. Ideally, this informant will be a friend, family member, acquaintance, or work colleague. Obtain the person's feedback about your research question. Does she or he feel that your research question uncovers a topic that is worth investigating? What would your informant change (if anything) about it?

Possible Projects

1. Talk to your anthropology professor to see if you can participate in a departmental "needs assessment" about first-year anthropology. Often, anthropology departments would like to obtain feedback from first-year students regarding their positive or negative experiences of first-year courses, their perceptions of anthropology, and their future academic plans. Such research helps inform the content of future courses and other aspects of anthropology curriculum within the department. With the approval of your professor, your job will be to develop a research plan for exploring student perceptions of freshman anthropology classes.

This research may involve interviews, focus groups, or other methods. When you've finished, you will write up your results in a report. Refer to Chapters 3, 4, 5, and 6 for more information on interviewing, research ethics, and analysis.

2. One way to practice your ethnographic research skills is to obtain a volunteer position or internship with a charitable or nongovernmental organization. Send out letters to a variety of organizations in your area that you would be interested in working with. Examples might include a homeless shelter, a community recreational facility, or a charity such as the American Cancer Society. Your job is to find out what specific questions or problems that organization would like investigated. For example, if you are working with a homeless shelter, it might be helpful to conduct interviews with homeless people to find out how the shelter can be improved. Often, organizations would like to have answers to these questions, but they do not have the time or money to conduct such research. Once you have settled on a field site, devise a research plan and figure out which methods will best help you answer your question. When you are done your analysis, write up a report with recommendations for your organization. Refer to Chapters 3, 4, 5 and 6 for more information on interviewing, research ethics, and analysis. Remember, if you are conducting this research while a university student, you are a representative of that institution and are consequently bound by various legal and ethical restrictions, so it is your responsibility to inform the appropriate university personnel of your plans, seek the necessary permissions, and ensure that all rules for conducting research with human subjects are followed.

Recommended Readings

Chrisman, Noel J., and Thomas W. Maretzki, eds. 1982. *Clinically Applied Anthropology: Anthropologists in Health Care Settings.* London, UK: D. Reidel Publishing Company.

Ervin, Alexander M. 2005. *Applied Anthropology: Tools and Perspectives for Contemporary Practice.* Toronto, ON: Pearson Education.

Gwynne, Margaret Anderson. 2003. *Applied Anthropology: A Career-Oriented Approach.* Boston, MA: Allyn and Bacon.

Hedican, Edward J. 2008. *Applied Anthropology in Canada: Understanding Aboriginal Issues*. 2nd edition. Toronto, ON: University of Toronto Press.

Nahm, Sheena, and Cortney Hughes Rinker, eds. 2016. *Applied Anthropology: Unexpected Spaces, Topics and Methods*. London, UK: Routledge.

Nolan, Riall, ed. 2013. *A Handbook of Practicing Anthropology*. Wiley-Blackwell.

Pelto, Pertii J. 2013. *Applied Ethnography: Guidelines for Field Research*. New York, NY: Routledge.

Web Resources

The Society for Applied Anthropology's website has several useful links to information on, for example, publications, reports, employment opportunities, conferences, and guest speakers: https://www.sfaa.net/.

CHAPTER 9

AUTOETHNOGRAPHY: THE SELF AND OTHER REVISITED

Introduction

Autoethnography as a method comes out of anthropology's insistence on defining itself as a reflexive discipline. Its origins lie in anthropology's "**postmodern crisis**" in the 1980s (Ellis et al. 2011), although some autoethnographic forms of writing precede this development. Autoethnography extends the basic theories related to ethics and the importance of maintaining a reflexive position toward in-depth discussions of personal experience within the context of ethnographic encounters. Simply defined, autoethnography systematically analyzes the personal experiences and emotions of anthropologists to interrogate the methods and theories of the discipline while also adding dimension to the studies of others and others' cultures. Numerous North American anthropologists have taken up the challenge of exposing themselves as "positioned" researchers. In fact, the 2012 annual conference for the Canadian Anthropology Society (CASCA), titled "The Unexpected," targeted this issue head on.

Some autoethnographic texts consider the ways in which academic, neoliberal business models affect the types of research that receive funding and ethical clearance or how state censorship and changing geopolitical landscapes affect research (McMurray 2005; Young and Meneley 2005). Other autoethnographies focus upon reflexive analyses of interpersonal relationships that develop in fieldwork situations or on the emotions and shifting identities of the anthropologist (e.g., Briggs 1970). In this chapter, we problematize the long-standing concept of ethnographic authority (e.g., Clifford 1983), wherein the anthropologist as both fieldworker and writer has traditionally used various techniques to bolster his or her "authority" and ability to speak on behalf of his or her interlocutors. Increasingly, such strategies are critiqued within the discipline as colonial and problematic legacies of early twentieth-century anthropology. These days, most contemporary anthropologists acknowledge that the fieldwork experience, and resulting ethnography, is an interactive and thus collaborative engagement. As such, fieldwork and writing are not "objective," replicable experiences, and one must consider how the fieldwork and writing process is impacted by our interlocutors' perceptions of us. In addition, we need to explore how our emotions influence our relationships in the field and our perceptions of our informants. By speaking openly about the experiential aspects of fieldwork, an autoethnographer challenges the ethnographic authority of the writer, and one's informants can reclaim their important role in the fieldwork process. In addition, it becomes possible to interrogate how our own notions of personhood or the "self" inform our fieldwork practice. For example, how do cultural ideas about the appropriateness of outward displays of emotions impact relationships in other cultural contexts (or do they)? The ethnographer's actions, feelings, and interactions are mediated by his or her own cultural background, worldview, and culturally appropriate ways of being in the world. As a result, we need to evaluate critically not only the "Other," but ourselves as well.

Self versus Others

Within the context of **modernist anthropology**, which drew heavily upon scientific and positivist traditions, there existed a sharp distinction between notions of self and Other. As discussed in Chapter 1, many early anthropologists, such as Franz Boas or Bronislaw Malinowski, were trained in the natural sciences, and they sought to apply the natural scientific principles of replicability and **positivism** to anthropological fieldwork methods and writing. The anthropological "self" was thus positioned as an objective and value-free reporter or descriptor of fieldwork experiences, as an arbiter of "objective" knowledge about the "Other." Within this context, self and Other were mutually exclusive and separate categories. The anthropologist was expected to be detached and disengaged from informants at an emotional level. Indeed, the incorporation of discussions of emotions in "scientific" texts was perceived as an indulgent, subjective form of navel-gazing. Recall that Malinowski, for instance, felt that personal feelings should be omitted even from field notes. Instead, he documented his personal feelings about his informants in a separate diary. Ultimately, then, feelings, positionalities, and other seemingly "subjective" information was simply left out of modernist ethnographies. Generally speaking, it was assumed that with proper fieldwork methods, the ethnographer could maintain a strict separation between the supposedly objective self and the Other and could use this stance to arrive at the "truth" about other cultures.

This legacy of modernism resulted in a long-standing view of the anthropologist as an impartial "privileged witness" (Kuklick 1997) and truth teller.

With the rise of anthropology's "postmodern turn," however, many anthropologists began to challenge the notion of a discrete self and Other as both simplistic and colonial, and three critiques of modernist anthropology emerged that acted as a stimulus for the growth of autoethnographic approaches. First, anthropologists started to view themselves and their informants as coproducers of knowledge and as collaborators. In many ways, this destabilized the privileged position afforded the anthropologist and challenged existing power dynamics between "self" and "Other." Therefore, it would become necessary for anthropologists to interrogate their emotions and discuss issues of identity and interpersonal relationships (among other things) in the field. In a nutshell, anthropologists needed to start writing themselves into their own ethnographies. Second, identities began to be viewed as negotiable and fluid, which challenged the notion of a stable self and Other. Third, anthropologists took a greater interest in issues of **epistemology**, which refers to a critical understanding of the contexts of knowledge production. As a result, anthropologists began exploring the political, economic, or other factors that motivate certain types of research, funding structures, and publications. This epistemological approach included a more reflexive exploration and interrogation of the methods and theories of the discipline itself. Ultimately, reflexivity, emotions, feelings, and details of the interpersonal engagements between ethnographers and informants became increasingly accepted and commonplace components of ethnographies. An autoethnographic tradition began to emerge in anthropology in the late 1970s and early 1980s, oftentimes as a form of resistance to the weaknesses of modernist ethnographic traditions.

Early Pioneers of Autoethnography

Even before the rise of anthropology's postmodern turn in the 1980s, however, many anthropologists, either implicitly or explicitly, sought to critique modernity's long-standing self-Other distinction and the notion of positivism. Early examples include the work of Hortense Powdermaker (1950) and Elenore Smith Bowen (1964), whose real name was Laura Bohannan. As discussed in Chapter 1, however, Bohannan's work, which documented her emotional trials and tribulations of doing fieldwork among the Tiv, was considered outlandish in the 1960s, and it was so "unscientific" that she had to publish her work under a pseudonym and fictionalize her ethnographic account to protect her credibility as an anthropologist.

Another example of an autoethnographic account that drew controversy was Jean Briggs's (1970) *Never in Anger: Portrait of an Eskimo Family.* In 1963–64, Briggs spent 17 months in the Northwest Territories in Canada living with an Utku Eskimo family (now the word "Inuit" and not "Eskimo" is used in Canada). Briggs explored interpersonal familial relationships and the bonds that developed, highlighting the emotional characteristics of familial interactions. Among other things, she discusses her own emotions and how they affected her relationships with informants. Outward expressions of anger, for example, were considered childish to her informants and were frowned upon among adults. Briggs's personal experiences of "being angry" in the field are thus discussed from the perspectives of both herself and her informants. From Briggs's perspective, the emotional elements and interactions between her and her informants played an important role in her ability to learn about her informants and their culture. The publication of her ethnography, however, received many critiques (see Walton 1993), and, circa 1970, it was still considered "unscientific" in many circles.

Briggs's (1970) ethnography was one of several notable ethnographic works that began to emerge in the 1970s and early 1980s that paved the path for the questioning of anthropological authority and positivist traditions within the discipline (see, for instance, Rabinow 1977; Rosaldo 1980). By highlighting how cultural meanings and interpretations are always filtered through the subjective experiences and identities of the ethnographer, autoethnographic approaches gained momentum. Some autoethnographic work was influenced by the writings of Victor Turner (1987) and by his work on the anthropology of experience and performance, as well as by the postmodern critique of the discipline in the 1980s. Turner (1987) stressed that all ethnographic encounters are akin to performances, or collaborative interactions and engagements among people, including anthropologists. This challenges the long-standing **ethnographic authority** afforded to the anthropologist and the assumption that the anthropologist is a neutral observer. After the ethnographies of the 1980s, ethnographic encounters increasingly began to be viewed as collaborative and dialogical experiences, which recognizes that anthropologists' narratives are coproduced through linguistic and even bodily engagements with informants. As Chase (2011) articulates, autoethnographic narratives began to be understood

as socially situated interactive performances—as produced in this setting, for this particular audience, for these particular purposes. A story told to an interviewer in a quiet relaxed setting will likely differ from the "same" story told to a reporter for a television news show, to a private journal that the writer assumes will never be read by others,

> to a roomful of people who have had similar experiences, to a social
> service counselor, or to the same interviewer at a different time. Here,
> researchers emphasize that the narrator's story is flexible, variable, and
> shaped in part by interaction with the audience. (657)

This dialogical approach often necessitates collaboration, the destabiliz-
ing of the anthropologist as an authority or "privileged witness" to culture
(Kuklick 1997), and the development of new and frequently experimental
forms of writing and representation.

This is not to say that all anthropologists have been receptive to autoethnographic approaches. Coffey (1999), for instance, has critiqued such approaches
as exercises in narcissistic navel-gazing. In addition, many anthropologists
adhere to more positivist and modernist traditions and feel that autoethnographic methods and forms of writing are without structure (which is often
the point of autoethnographies) and focus too much upon the attitudes and
feelings of the anthropologist. In other words, the objectivity of modernism
has been replaced with an extreme form of subjectivity. As summarized in
the words of Holt (2003), "Autoethnography has been received with a significant degree of academic suspicion because it contravenes certain qualitative
research traditions. The controversy surrounding autoethnography is in part
related to the problematic exclusive use of the self to produce research" (25).

Autoethnography as Method

Given that it is now commonplace and expected for anthropologists to,
at the very least, acknowledge their positionalities and biases in their
ethnographies, we must also consider how autoethnographic approaches affect
ethnographic methods in the field. It should be noted that the use of an
autoethnographic approach does not necessarily privilege the use of one
fieldwork method or another—say, participant observation over interviews.
In keeping with the dialogical nature of fieldwork experiences, ethnographic
fieldwork, it is important to remember, is contingent upon the relationships that
we develop in the field. Also, because autoethnography grew out of a postmodern
influence on the discipline, its methods share many of postmodernism's concerns
with epistemology. As Richardson and St. Pierre (2005) attest,

> The core of postmodernism is the doubt that any method or theory,
> any discourse or genre, or any tradition or novelty has a universal
> and general claim as the "right" or privileged form of authoritative
> knowledge.... But conventional methods of knowing and telling are

not automatically rejected as false or archaic. Rather, those standard methods are opened to inquiry, new methods are introduced, and then they also are subject to critique. (961)

Given the collaborative nature of knowledge production and the fact that your informants' perceptions of you (and yours of them) play a role in inter-personal interactions and knowledge production, it is helpful to pay attention to such things as gestures, facial expressions, postures, emotions, avoidance or reticence when responding to questions, or even the questions that people may ask you during interviews or participant observation. Indeed, many auto-ethnographic approaches emphasize that we need to pay attention not only to discourse, to what people say, but to their bodies as well (Spry 2001). As Spry articulates, "The autoethnographic text emerges from the researcher's bodily standpoint as she is continually recognizing and interpreting the resi-due traces of culture inscribed upon her hide from interacting with others in context" (2001, 711). Our fieldwork experiences are thus embodied engage-ments, and the lived experiences of our informants can be elucidated not only from interview transcripts but also from an analysis of our bodily engage-ments with them. In addition, each idiosyncratic interaction that you have with your informants will produce different types of knowledge and will be filtered through people's perceptions of you and your identity. People read our bodies as well as our conversations for cues about our positionalities, and this affects the types of information that we have access to.

Contemporary Complexities

Another, more recent aspect of autoethnography is to consider limitations and constraints on knowledge production. In other words, what factors affect the research questions we ask and the types of fieldwork that we conduct? Unencumbered by financial concerns, time constraints, family obligations, iden-tity politics, the challenges of obtaining ethics clearance, or other limitations, many of us as anthropologists or anthropology students dream of our ideal fieldwork projects. The reality of fieldwork, however, is that we all experience a variety of constraints that affect our choice of field sites and research ques-tions. Increasingly, for instance, university ethics boards fear litigation should fieldwork with informants "go wrong." Many universities also worry about researcher safety in areas of the world experiencing war or conflict. There is also a growing amount of literature that addresses the ways in which neolib-eral, corporate-driven policies impact how and what we teach at universities, as well as the kind of knowledge that is disseminated within academia.

Some cultural anthropologists have engaged with an analysis of the politics of academia. Leslie Jermyn (2009), for example, critically explores how a university degree has gradually become perceived as a ticket to middle-class culture and employment. Coupled with this perception, the neoliberal restructuring of North American universities, where metrics, student enrolments, and tuition dollars have become a priority, has changed, and in some cases watered down, university curricula. This change, in turn, directly impacts how anthropologists teach the discipline to their students. More time, for instance, is devoted to teaching basic writing and critical thinking skills, and less time is spent teaching actual content. Jermyn (2009) asks us to think critically about the long-term effects of these neoliberal trends, not only on academia but also on how anthropology is conducted and taught to students. Autoethnography, then, does not simply address critical examinations of the self, or of the self-Other relationships in the field, but also the wider sociopolitical contexts within which the discipline operates.

Writing

In many contexts, the adoption of an autoethnographic approach has necessitated the development of new or experimental genres of ethnographic writing, genres that seek to find innovative ways to represent fieldwork experiences. Autoethnographic writing can thus be described as a genre of representation that marks a departure from, and even a critique of, positivist or colonial writing traditions that have historically sought to bolster the authority of the anthropologist. Some scholars see it as a politicized form of writing that provides agency to historically marginalized populations, the historical "subjects" of anthropological research. Mary Louise Pratt (1992) argues that she employs the term "to refer to instances in which colonized subjects undertake to represent themselves in ways that engage with the colonizer's own terms. If ethnographic texts are a means by which Europeans represent to themselves their (usually subjugated) others, autoethnographic texts are those the others construct in response to or in dialogue with those metropolitan representations" (7). In such cases, autoethnographic texts have deeply political and often anticolonial connotations, and they represent a marked departure from modernist texts. This is the case with the life history approach adopted by Elisabeth Burgos-Debray (1981) in her account of the life of Nobel Peace Prize winner Rigoberta Menchú. To provide a sense of agency to Menchú and fellow Maya peoples exploited at the hands of the Guatemalan state, Burgos-Debray uses a first-person narrative to tell Menchú's story and intimately and vividly traces her life events, such that it almost reads as a novel. By naming and graphically depicting violence, Burgos-Debray hoped to educate her global readership about the atrocities committed during the Guatemalan civil war and to incite action and protest against the government.

In other contexts, anthropologists have experimented with a variety of forms of ethnographic writing to decenter the perceived objectivity or **realism** of modernist ethnographies. Michael Taussig (1997), for instance, has experimented with **magical realism** in his writing. Magical realism is a genre of writing and representation that attempts to challenge modernist forms of representation by, among other things, incorporating elements of fantasy. It challenges the notion that there is a singular "reality" by blurring the lines between "fact" and "fiction." It also, in many contexts, seeks to interweave elements of the belief systems and sensory ways of knowing of various cultures into an anthropologist's written narrative. In Taussig's ethnography, he outlines his experiences of studying state power in Latin America by crafting a fictional nation and quasi-fictional informants, who come to explore and understand issues of colonialism and state power through localized experiences of spirit possession.

A dominant feature of most autoethnographic texts is that they place a specific emphasis upon reflexive descriptions and analyses of fieldwork experiences. The vignette that follows is an excerpt from Jean Briggs's *Never in Anger*. Briggs was one of the first anthropologists to describe, in detail, how her emotions impacted her relationships in the field. In her vignette, she discusses her feelings of loneliness and exclusion, and she describes how she often grew tired or confused by the demands placed upon her in her role as an adopted daughter within her Utku family.

VIGNETTE

Jean L. Briggs was a professor emerita of anthropology at Memorial University in Newfoundland and Labrador, a fellow of the Royal Society of Canada, and a recipient of a Lifetime Achievement Award from the Society for Psychological Anthropology. She has conducted fieldwork among Canadian Inuit, Alaskan Inupiat, and Siberian Yupik cultures and is well known internationally as an early pioneer of autoethnographic and humanistic approaches to fieldwork and writing in cultural anthropology. Her book Inuit Morality Play: The Emotional Education of a Three-Year-Old won the Boyer Prize for Contributions to Psychoanalytic Anthropology from the Society for Psychological Anthropology and the Victor Turner Prize from the Society for Humanistic Anthropology. The reprint below is taken from her famous and groundbreaking ethnography, Never in Anger: Portrait of an Eskimo Family, which is considered a foundational text for students learning about method, methodology, writing, and the Canadian Arctic. Her love of language is ever present in this text.

FIGURE 9.1: Portrait of Jean Briggs, 1970? Photographer is unknown.
Courtesy of Hod Briggs.

EXCERPT FROM *NEVER IN ANGER: PORTRAIT OF AN ESKIMO FAMILY*

The first occasion on which I recall feeling that being a daughter might have its drawbacks was the morning I was awakened at dawn by a light touch on my shoulder and looked up to find Allaq standing beside my bed. "Daughter, your father feels like drinking tea." It was apologetically said, but I seethed inwardly at the disturbance. Though Utku are ordinarily considerate of sleepers—I never saw one waked carelessly or as a prank—nevertheless they do not hold sleep inviolable, and any need, however small, is reason enough to wake a person on whom one has a claim. To me, on the other hand, sleep is sacred. I cherish it, and in those days it was even more precious than usual, protecting me, as it did, for all too short periods, from the vicissitudes of the day: the icy breezes that attacked my fingers and toes, the raw fish, the incomprehensible words, the giggles, and above all, the necessity to hold myself in check. I found it exhausting to play an unfamiliar role all day long, constantly to try to react in ways that would be acceptable to my hosts, instead of in ways that came naturally to me, and constantly to keep alert to cues that would tell me whether or not I had succeeded. I buried myself thankfully in sleep at night and in the morning withdrew myself reluctantly from its shelter. So resentment roughened my voice when I replied to Allaq: "Help yourself!" and caused me to turn over sharply toward the wall and pull the sleeping bag over my head. The tea can was in evidence beside the entrance: Allaq could have helped herself by extending a hand, without even entering the tent, and I testily asked myself why she had not done so. She may have sensed my thought; in any case she answered it: "I could have taken *your* tea by the door," she said, "but I wanted to take the tea that you gave your father last night and that he forgot to take home." Permission granted, she silently filled her palm with tea and withdrew, tying the tent flaps behind her and rearranging the stone barricade that kept the dogs out, considerate acts well calculated to make me repent my abruptness.

By calling me daughter, Allaq had justified waking me. However, there was nothing in her request for tea that distinguished it from requests made by other members of the community for small amounts of my supplies. Neither was there anything different in Allaq's impassive reaction to my snarl. In early October, however, when I moved from my solitary tent into Inuttiaq's qaqmaq, the parental nature of Inuttiaq's and Allaq's relationship with me became much more evident, and the conflict between Inuttiaq's definition of the daughter role and mine began to create problems of a new order. The first such problem was occasioned by the move itself. I had been anticipating the move for a month, but when the time came, I was taken by surprise.

The nightly snow flurries were no longer melting in the morning air, and the inlet had lain silent under ice for several days when I woke one morning in my tent to hear unaccustomed sounds of chopping. Rummaging for the several pairs of wool and duffel socks that always lost themselves in my sleeping bag, where I dried them as I slept, I pulled myself, reluctantly as always, out into the cold air. My boots, hung from the ridgepole, were festooned with feathers of frost, and as I drew them down, prickles of snow showered my neck. Shivering and cursing, I pulled on the frozen boots, and, still in my long johns, crunched across the gravel floor to peer between the entrance flaps. Almost all the men of the three households in our camp were out on the ice of the inlet. The old man Piuvkaq was chopping rectangular

FIGURE 9.2: Jean Briggs in her Inuit parka, 2002. Courtesy of Chris Hammond, the photographer.

blocks, like huge dominoes, out of the ice. A dark oblong of water showed where other blocks had already been cut and removed. Pala was knotting a rope around one of these blocks, while other people stood in readiness to pull. I had not a clue to the meaning of the scene I was witnessing, and when Amaaqtuq, seeing my protruding head, came to pay her morning call, her explanation did not enlighten me: "They are making a qaqmaq." It was only as I saw the walls taking shape, the ice dominoes set up side by side in a circle and mortared with slush, that I realized what a qaqmaq was. "Qaqmaqs are warm," Amaaqtuq told me. "Not in winter but in autumn. They are much pleasanter (*quvia*) than tents. You will see. Are you going to live in a qaqmaq?"

I did not know, in truth, whether I was going to live in a qaqmaq or not; I did not even know whether I wanted to. Warmed and protected as I had felt on the evening, a month earlier, when Inuttiaq, with the offer of a cup of tea, had welcomed me as his daughter, I found my-self filled with trepidation now that the move into Inuttiaq's dwelling was imminent. Could I tolerate the company of others for twenty-four hours a day? In the past month my tent had become a refuge, into which I withdrew every evening after the rest of the camp was in bed, to repair ravages to my spirit with the help of bannock and peanut butter, boiled rice, frozen dates, and Henry James. So reviving were these hours of self-indulgence that I dreaded their loss. I prayed that Inuttiaq would not invite me to join them until he built an iglu in November.

My prayer was not granted. It was Allaq who issued the first invita-tion to join the qaqmaq household. She had brought her sewing to my tent, as she often did in those early days. She was making the body of Saarak's fawn-skin winter suit while Amaaqtuq, at her sister's request, sewed the sleeves, and I, unable to assist in such useful preparations for winter, copied vocabulary notes. From the shore came sounds of qaqmaq construction; Pala's was nearly finished. "In a little while we are going to build a qaqmaq, too," Allaq said. "Would you like to move in with us then?" I hesitated. "I don't know; it's difficult; after a while I'll tell you."

"Eeee." She smiled, and nothing further was said. But soon after she had gone home, Inuttiaq came to visit: "Would you like to move in with us when we build a qaqmaq, or would you rather have a separate one for yourself?"

Again I hesitated; then in my halting Eskimo I tried to explain that I thought it might be difficult to live with others, especially at times when I wanted to work. Inuttiaq, in turn, insisted that I would be cold if I lived alone. The conversation grew increasingly confused, each of us uncertain what the other was trying to say—uncertain, too, how to extricate ourselves from the impasse. Finally, I thought Inuttiaq sug-gested that I sleep in his qaqmaq, for warmth, but that my tent be left standing as a retreat: "If you get tired." I was relieved at this compro-mise, and I accepted it gladly. Unfortunately, either my understand-ing was deficient, or Inuttiaq changed his mind, or both. I still do not understand precisely the chain of events that led to my finding myself four days later ensconced without refuge in Inuttiaq's qaqmaq.

It was when Inuttiaq started to build that I began to wonder wheth-er I had understood alright. He began his qaqmaq, as Piuvkaq did, on the morning after Pala had built and moved into his. All three dwell-ings were to be clustered tightly together, as the tents had been, at the head of the inlet. But Inuttiaq's wall, unlike the other two, for some reason refused to hold properly. When the first block fell, and the second broke at a touch, Inuttiaq decided the ice was still too thin for building. He turned to me as I stood nearby, watching. "I'll go fishing today," he said, "and when the ice is better, I will build another qaqmaq for you (he used the singular pronoun), over there," and he gestured in the direction of my tent, some distance away. I assented, surprised at this development but vastly relieved at the thought that, after all, I should have a home of my own, and yet not be obliged to live in a windy tent.

When Inuttiaq appeared at my tent entrance three mornings later to ask if I planned to come and help with the chinking of "my" qaqmaq, I went with alacrity. The circle that Inuttiaq had drawn on the gravel was large, and when the walls were up, the building was, indeed, larger than either Pala's or Piuvkaq's. Inuttiaq asked me if it would be big enough for me, and when I assented, he sent me back to my tent to stuff my loose belongings into sacks for moving. Curiously, Allaq, over in *her* tent, was also packing. I wondered what for, but only when I saw the goods of Inuttiaq's household being moved into "my" qaqmaq did it dawn on me that "my" qaqmaq was, in fact, "our" qaqmaq. I tried hastily to reconcile myself; this, after all, was the plan to which I had originally agreed. It was when Inuttiaq informed my that my tent was to be used as the qaqmaq's roof, since his tent was not large enough, that dismay overcame me. I tried to control it with the thought that I could set up my double-walled winter tent as a refuge instead; but it was small and dark; it was not the cozily familiar summer tent in which I had been living, and I could not prevent myself from demurring at the sudden loss of the latter. I told Inuttiaq that, although I did have another tent, a warm tent, that I could put up, I would like to use the summer tent, folded up, as a seat therein. It was a ridiculous notion, born of an alarm that must have been completely incomprehensible to Inuttiaq, if he was aware of it at all. He must have recognized the folly of the demand at once, but he handled it with the indirectness characteristic of his people. Pointing out again that his own tent was too small to roof the qaqmaq, he offered to let me use that for a seat instead. Then outdoors, next to the qaqmaq wall, he stacked all the household goods that were not to be used immediately, both his things and mine for which there was no room in the qaqmaq, and he covered the cache with his tent.

What could I do? I was helpless to protest, and the very helplessness made me panic. I looked at the square of gravel that had been my home for more than a month and felt its emptiness unbearable.

I *had* to have a tent. Inuttiaq and Allaq were busy, setting a wooden door into the wall of our qaqmaq, mortaring the frame to the ice block with slush, and chopping away the ice inside the frame to make an entrance. Everyone else in camp was indoors, visiting or drinking tea after the day's work. There was no one to offer assistance when I took my winter tent from the household cache where Inuttiaq had laid it and carried it up to my old gravel patch on the bluff. It was a pyramid tent with four built-in aluminum corner poles attached together at the top. In order to erect the tent, it was necessary to spread these poles as far as possible at the base, and then weigh down the canvas between them with stones. It seemed simple, but I had never tried it before, and a strong breeze, which swelled the canvas, did not help. I struggled with the poles, first on one side, then on another, while the wind continually undid my work.

"What are you doing?" Inuttiaq stood at my side. I tried to explain that if I was tired or wanted to type I would use this tent. "You can write in the qaqmaq," he said; 'the tent will be cold." I tried to explain that this was a different sort of tent and that, heated with a primus stove, it would be warm. "I will write sometimes in the qaqmaq and sometimes here," I said, feebly trying to be pliant. But Inuttiaq, after pulling two of the poles apart for me in a half-gesture of helping, departed without further comment to drink tea in the tent of the newly arrived Qavvik, and left me to struggle by myself. It was the first time since I had been with the Utku that I had been left to cope with a difficult activity by myself. People came and went around the qaqmaqs at the base of the bluff, but no one else came up to inquire what I was doing or whether I needed help. And no criticism could have made me feel more vividly than this disregard of the antisocial nature of my act.

The tent stood there, empty and unused, for two weeks, until we took it down in preparation for moving to the winter camp in Amujat. In those two weeks I had never felt the need of a refuge. I basked in the warm protectiveness of Inuttiaq's household. What solitude I needed I found on the river in the mornings when I went fishing with Inuttiaq or, to my surprise, in the qaqmaq itself, in the afternoons when the room was full of visitors and I retired into myself, lulled and shielded by the flow of quiet, incomprehensible speech. No one ever mentioned the folly of my tent, even when they helped to take it down.

In many ways life in Inuttiaq's household was easier for me than life in my solitary tent had been. For one thing it was no longer necessary for me to play hostess. The fact that I could sit quietly in my corner and let Inuttiaq and Allaq entertain our visitors gave me privacy without the chill of isolation. Then too, Inuttiaq and Allaq did their up-most to make me feel welcome. I felt it in the parental responsibility that they assumed for my welfare, more than ever teaching me how to do things, feeding me, and protecting me from the dangerous ef-fects of my ignorance of the land and climate. I felt it also in the many considerate allowances that they made on my behalf in the ordering of household life, assuring me from the first that, if I wished, I might type, or keep my lamp lit later than theirs at night, or "sometimes" eat kapluna food without offering it to them, "because you are a kapluna." They even said they were lonely when I spent an evening visiting in another qaqmaq. That was the most heartwarming of all.

Making Connections

Briggs is up front about how emotions play a role in the fieldwork process. How did her emotions affect her fieldwork experiences and her relationships with informants?

Describe Briggs's style of writing. What are some characteristics of it, and how does it help convey her feelings and personal experiences?

Briggs discusses her frustrations regarding cultural differences with respect to interpersonal relations and notions of personal space. Why do you think that many anthropologists experience such dilemmas but avoid discussing them?

Try This

Take ten minutes and write down two different research projects or ques-tions that you might be interested in exploring. Then, in small groups, adopt a reflexive approach and discuss how aspects of your own identity, person-ality, or other factors may impact your research project and the relationships that you form with your informants. Do you anticipate that your informants' perceptions of you will help or hinder your fieldwork? Moreover, how will people's perceptions of factors such as gender, age, and class affect your access to them and your rapport with them? To explore this question fully, you will need to do some background research on your cultural (or subcultural) group to understand its members' perceptions and expectations regarding gendered or other forms of interactions among people. Working to understand the cultural aspects of interpersonal interaction is particularly important if you are posi-tioned as an "outsider" to this group.

Possible Projects

1. Upon completion of your fieldwork, code your data and gather together the comments about your personal feelings and emotions that occur in your field notes. Write an autoethnographic section about the role of emotions in fieldwork as part of the introduction to your final paper.

2. In this chapter, we discussed how one dimension of autoethnography is to think not only about identity and emotions but also about the sociopolitical contexts within which we conduct our fieldwork. Think critically about how you chose your field "site" or research question. Why did you select the topic that you did? Were there any constraints on your decision due to the politics of ethics boards, funding, time, language barriers, or other factors? If some of these constraints were eliminated, how would your research question or project be different? You can address these issues in the methods or methodology section of your final project.

Recommended Readings

Alsop, Christiane Kraft. 2002. "Home and Away: Self-Reflexive Auto-/ Ethnography." *FQS—Forum: Qualitative Social Research* 3 (3). http:// www.qualitative-research.net/index.php/fqs/article/view/823/1789.

Goldschmidt, Walter. 1977. "Anthropology and the Coming Crisis: An Autoethnographic Appraisal." *American Anthropologist* 79 (2): 293–308.

Hayano, David. 1979. "Auto-Ethnography: Paradigms, Problems, and Prospects." *Human Organization* 38 (1): 99–104.

Khosravi, Shahram. 2010. "*Illegal" Traveler: An Auto-ethnography of Borders.* London, UK: Palgrave Macmillan.

Rapport, Nigel, and Joanna Overing. 2000. "Auto-anthropology." In *Social and Cultural Anthropology: The Key Concepts*, 18–28. London, UK: Routledge.

Reed-Danahay, Deborah E. 2002. "Sites of Memory: Women's Autoethnographies from Rural France." *Biography* 25 (1): 95–109.

Voloder, Lejla. 2008. "Autoethnographic Challenges: Confronting Self, Field and Home." *The Australian Journal of Anthropology* 19 (1): 27–40.

PART IV

Visual Aids

CHAPTER 10

PHOTO-ELICITATION: COLLABORATION, MEMORY, AND EMOTION

What is Photo-Elicitation?

When was the last time you took a photograph? Did you share your photo with others? If so, how? Did you use Instagram, Facebook, Twitter, email, or more traditional cut-and-paste albums? With whom did you choose to share it, and what kind of a representation of yourself (or your experiences) were you trying to convey? As anthropologists, when our interlocutors take, use, and manipulate images such as photographs, these images often become important expressions of various identities, namely gender, class, race, ethnicity, or national identity, among others. As such, photographs are important considerations for anthropological fieldwork as they are often enmeshed in complicated histories, identities, and relations of power. In many societies, the practice of taking pictures represents an important means of storytelling and of documenting pivotal events in people's lives. Increasingly, with the advent of digital photography, smartphones, and the proliferation of a "selfie" culture, photos of the everyday and the mundane have become ubiquitous. Although the first photographs were taken around 1800, the photograph's meaning and importance have shifted over time and space, and its use and significance are dependent upon changing sociopolitical contexts. Because of these altering circumstances, within the realm of anthropological fieldwork, the practice of taking, observing, and sharing photographs raises many issues that need to be addressed: How and why do people take pictures of particular people or events, and how do processes of photo documentation change over time? Is it ethical for anthropologists to take and circulate photos of their informants? How do we handle situations in which informants become visibly upset by viewing certain images and reliving past events? Finally, how can photographs help people remember the past events and personal histories that we, as anthropologists, seek to document?

In this chapter, we explore **photo-elicitation**, a qualitative research method that can be defined is the practice of talking about photographs while looking at them. We will first explain the history and theory of this method as it has been applied in anthropology. Next, we will focus on how contemporary photo-elicitation projects are designed and approached in a reflexive manner, and we will discuss the different forms these projects can take. And, finally, we will explain the pros and cons of using this method.

Although anthropologists who focus on the use of photographs in research methods oftentimes claim that they are a form of communication that can traverse linguistic and ideological boundaries and stimulate discussions about symbolic meaning, photo-elicitation has not, until recently, become a popular tool for ethnographers. This is partially due to the fact that photographs were originally seen as objective visual representations of "the truth" and not as narratives that can be ambiguously read and are subject to multiple interpretations (Edwards 2001). Since the 1980s, however, Roland Barthes (1984) has brought the more subtle characteristics of photography to the forefront in his theoretical discussions. Photography is now most commonly viewed as a way to bridge the visible with the invisible, as a way to reveal imagined and concrete meanings.

In 1967, Collier and Collier designed an approach to photo interviewing, which they hoped would expand anthropological methodologies. Over time and through a variety of scenarios, they began to see how the use of photographs tempered many difficulties they had experienced in interviewing people from different cultures. They claimed that photographs encouraged interviewees to take the lead, minimized inhibition by performing as a third and neutral party, clarified misunderstandings that arose in verbal questioning due to language barriers and cultural differences, "sharpened memories and gave the interview an immediate character of realistic construction," and, as well, assisted in keeping interviewees focused on the research project (Collier and Collier 1986, 106). Overall, Collier and Collier felt that the introduction of photographs to ethnographic work had the ability to relieve informants of any stress they may be feeling as "subjects of [the] interrogation" because these images created an immediate point of access, a simple, functional reason for contact that, for example, facilitated entrance into an individual's home (1986, 106). The researchers also claim that photographs sharpen and unblock memories, offering a neutral point of focus that brings forward freer, more spontaneous responses (Collier and Collier 1986). Marcus Banks reiterates the usefulness of photographs and elaborates on Collier and Collier's findings by stating that photographs can cause people to remember things they have forgotten and can aid in allowing interviewees to see "things" in a new way (particularly in the case of elderly informants). He also emphasizes that photo interviewing serves to initiate a form of research collaboration, lessening the power differential between informant and investigator. The only problematic aspects, according to Banks, may occur if the interviewee cannot make links between the images presented and the topic of research or the intentions of the researcher (Banks 2001).

The Basics

Photo-elicitation, in basic terms, is the process of looking at photographs with interviewees, either individually or in small groups, to evoke memories, stories, and comments or to initiate a discussion during a semi-structured interview process with the aim of exploring values, perspectives, meanings, and emotions. It involves looking at photographic images that work with "parts of the brain that process visual information" to evoke material that is different from that usually acquired through verbal interviews (Harper 2002, 13). The use of this method can include a variety of sources and types of photographs: contemporary and archival photographs, photos taken by the interviewer, and photographs taken by the participants. The range of subject matter and its connection to the interviewee is also broad. However, methods using photographs that have no obvious link to either the interviewer or the interviewee can be problematic. Theoretically, the intimate dimensions of photographs that visually portray one's own body or close social relationships are thought to elicit core definitions of the self that can easily be linked to society, culture, and history. As Douglas Harper argues, "This work corresponds to postmodern sociology's decentered narrative: of the sociology of the body, and of social studies of emotions" (2002, 14–15).

Sharing and viewing photographs creates an immediate point of access, a simple, functional reason for contact that facilitates a private interview. For example, returning photos to those who haven't seen them is a good reason for making contact. Photographs bridge gaps between researchers and those being researched, and these images become a "third party," a safe medium for talking through. They can assist in crossing cultural and language barriers. Photographic images invite interviewees to take the lead in inquiries, and they allow for joint explorations of topics and memories, pushing interviews past a superficial level (Collier and Collier 1986). The depth and spontaneity of interviewee responses to photographs are important factors for anthropologists, who are trying to gain objective information that is not colored by the pressure to perform for research professionals or conform to their expectations. Photographs also readily sharpen and unblock memories, offering a neutral point of focus that brings forward freer, more spontaneous, responses. Once interviews are underway, photographs can become a direct conversation piece, and they can be a good way to evoke freer conversations about emotions and intimate details. For this reason, they are also considered to be useful for probing the nature of identity in respect to self and community.

In Contemporary Practice

Prior to the 1970s, anthropologists primarily thought of cameras as objective recording devices. It was imagined that photographs and films and voice recordings could capture and represent reality in a more accurate way than oral or written narrative. Visual images of events, people, places, and things were thought to be records of factual or "true" information, a form of objective data. Within this context, film and photography played an important role in documenting the cultural interactions that took place in fieldwork, as well as being cultural forms in their own right. Although photography was viewed as a medium that had the ability to capture the actuality of an event, it often did the opposite, in fact. After the reflexive turn in anthropology (as was discussed in the previous chapter) theories about reflexivity became central to understanding fieldwork methods. In turn, this shifted the focus to thinking about how photographs were being used, circulated, and stored. Indeed, anthropologists began to think about the various ways photography is a conduit between the past and the present, in the same way that memory is. They also began to focus on how personal biases and wider ideological beliefs color all facets of photographic production, often concealing or erasing more than was actually documented.[1] Now, anthropologists are very aware of the power of photography to misrepresent, of the inherently subjective nature of photos, and of the fact that meanings are inscribed on a variety of levels and from a variety of perspectives. As Sarah Pink (2001) put it,

> A reflexive approach to ethnographic photography means researchers are aware of the theories that inform their own photographic practice, of their relationships with their photographic subjects, and if the theories that inform their subjects' approaches to photography. (54)

Pink (2001) was the first to discount the name "photo-elicitation" as misrepresentative of the actual process because it suggests a manipulative form of interviewing method when, in fact, it was originally designed to inspire collaboration, create intimacy, and bridge gaps in authority.

Photographs are also objects that can facilitate performances of new identities. Knowledge is not stored in photographs, but it *is* allotted to them through the various ways photos are read and linked to ideas about memory. Photographs are a product of the intentions, point of view, biases, and knowledge of the photographer. They do not take themselves, but they do offer a valuable and creative tool for the production of identity, which is in effect shaped through a conversation that takes place between individuals "snap-ping" photos, individuals posing in photos, and individuals interpreting photos. Meanings implied through this conversation are adverted and derailed frequently within a multilayered dialogical system. Therefore, photographs provide a space where identities are easily negotiated, a flexible and accessible place that allows for fluent and confident new expressions to emerge. This fact empha-sizes the active, relational nature of photographs as objects that carry visual information and create layers of social meaning. Histories and identities, both personal and official, are created through the entanglements inherent to the life of a photograph, even though the visual content of individual images does not precisely narrate either. For an example, the majority of images in the *Walnut* collection, discussed next, resemble the types of photos generally taken by tourists, both in the ways they are framed and in the ways that the subjects are posed, but the subjects and the photographers were actually refu-gees migrating by boat. When these Estonian refugees of the past were asked to talk about these images 60 years later, many memories about the traumas and the camaraderie inherent to surviving such a journey surfaced. These same photographs have been used in a museum display at Pier 21 in Halifax to depict the history of this voyage—and to link it to an official narrative that supports Canadian nationalism.

During the photo-elicitation process it is also important to pay attention to the various types of memories that are brought forward or that are not brought forward. These types can include sensory memories (i.e., memories other than visual memories) or memories of deep trauma, which can cause an informant to leave the room or look away from the photo. Although this method does, generally speaking, elicit clearer memories and often emotional information, this unblocking of memories can be very intrusive. Sometimes, spontaneous memories of negative or distressing events recalled while look-ing at photographs can be difficult to digest because connections between past experience and present identity cannot be easily made or because the memo-ries are too traumatic. This problem is made obvious in the interview Lynda Mannik conducted with the *Walnut*'s passengers, even though the photographs they were looking at were over 60 years old. Conversely, the visual infor-mation in a photograph can be confusing, causing the viewer to feel unsure or even upset. Therefore, what is not remembered can be just as important as what is remembered.

Barbara Myerhoff (1992) introduced "sensory events" as part of the act of remembering, and she claims that recollections are often triggered by phys-ical movements such as dancing and singing, as well as by tastes, smells, and touch. "The body retains experiences that may be yielded, eventually and indirectly, to the mind" (110). Sensory memories also speak to unconscious bodily experiences, including trauma and nostalgia, and are embodied in objects (including photographs), which in turn have the ability to provoke "the awakening of layered memories" in physical manifestations (Seremetakis 1994, 10–11). Elizabeth Edwards (2005) has specifically made the link between sound, the materiality of photography, and memory. She looks at the ways laughter and tears, body language, hand gesture, and tonal variations occur in stories told about photographs. Instead of just focusing on storytelling, she argues that researchers must also pay attention to "active sensory" responses, or the "heard sounds" that draw the listener, and the storyteller, deeper into social relations (37–38). Mannik, in the vignette in this chapter, explains how smells were spontaneously remembered while informants looked at old photos.

Contemporary anthropologists work collaboratively with participants in a variety of ways. They might use **archival photographs** that they have in their possession or that they found through their research, or they might work with historic photos that are already in the possession of the interlocutors they are working with. They might take current photos of the people they are working with, perhaps posing them in certain ways and in certain places. In this case, often the intention is to create images of so-called "real life," not the ideal-ized views of life that are most often found in family photos, and then talk about these images later. Sometimes, anthropologists prefer to facilitate photo sessions during which the participants take photographs themselves, according to certain themes, places, memories, or feelings. This practice is called "**auto-driving**," meaning that the informant is the subject of the photos and has taken the photographs (Van House 2006, 1464).[2] Sometimes the themes are highly controlled by the researcher; other times they are left up to the prerog-ative of the person being interviewed. In this method, researchers meet with people and explain their project and then ask if informants would be willing to participate by taking photographs that relate to both themselves and the project in some way. Researchers and informants then meet at least one more time to look at and discuss the outcome of the photo shoots. Conversations are focused on the content of the photos, the intentions of the photographers, and their interpretations of the process and results. Autodriving is considered to be highly collaborative, and a good method for achieving desirable reflexive information because it allows for expressive contributions from both parties (Jenkins, Woodward, and Winter 2008).

New digital technologies and social media websites have opened up areas where photo-elicitation as a method can be practiced. Most notable are partic-ipatory digital methods using the sharing of photos online through sites such as Facebook and Flickr. This form of participation puts decisions around prac-tices in the hands of the participants or producers, which, in turn, allows them to adapt and create new methods according to their needs. **Photovoice** as a method has gained popularity through digital technologies partially due to its ability to attract young people, its ability to support community advocacy projects, its ability to develop communication skills, and the democratizing effect it has on research more generally. Photovoice is a unique method because it involves giving research participants cameras and asking them to take photographs in places and of people and events, for example, that they think visually represent certain themes. These themes can be either chosen by the participants themselves or the anthropologist, but usually these choices involve a collaborative process. After taking pictures, participants are asked to talk about their photographs with the researcher with a focus on what they mean to them and why they took them. Aline Gubrium and Krista Harper discuss one interesting example of a project that took place in Hungary within a Roma community; the project focused on poverty and environmental problems. The digital photos they took were circulated and discussed within the community and then presented at a public exhibition attended by government officials, which led to further discussions about policy directives (Gubrium and Harper 2013).

Although photo-elicitation as a method was conceived with a sole focus on photographs as useful visual tools, there are also other types of visual materials that have been used in concert with photographs, or independently, for similar purposes. Some studies start by looking at photographs and then ask participants to express similar ideas about identity, for example, through the creation of works of art, from sculpting to painting to drama. Themes that are drawn out differently from each medium can be then discussed. Photographs printed on a variety of objects, such as postcards or cereal boxes, or in newspapers and advertisements, have been used. Other types of visual materials, such as political cartoons, maps, and drawings, have also been used to elicit emotions and memories.

Film-elicitation is another similar method that can incorporate self-made films or use ready-made films and videos. Watching films and videos with individuals or small groups can be very interesting. A variety of forms can be viewed—from television shows to news clips to Hollywood features. However, there are notable constraints and complexities particular to film-elicitation. One involves the required technologies and space needed for viewing, and another relates to the subtle complexities of fast-paced sound and visual productions. Moving images combined with sound can be difficult for the researcher to control and analyze because of the complexity of variables. As we have talked about, each viewer will see something different in a single photograph, and the subjectivity associated with viewing is compounded when an informant looks at film or video. Repeated viewings or separate viewings of still frames of a film or video can assist in more in-depth conversations.

Pros and Cons, and Ethics

There are always pros and cons to every research method, and we have talked about several already in this chapter, but we will summarize these here for clarity. Asking someone to look at photographs with you does not always inspire a positive reply or an invitation into that person's home for a private interview. Depending on the content of the images, informants may not want to look at these photographs at all, or talk to you at length about them. Oftentimes, photographs do create an atmosphere of intimacy and trust, but if for example, they are images of a questionable or traumatic event, they can also make people feel uncomfortable, and as we stated earlier, those working with you might even leave the room or become very emotional. Looking at photographs has the potential to be more intrusive than verbal questions only. Collier and Collier's focus on the ability of photographs to unblock memories has become common knowledge in many respects. However, if the landmarks, people, or other aspects of the content of the photo are not readily identifiable, then viewers can become confused as well, which in turn can block memories. In this case, the interlocutor may turn to the researcher for advice or information about the image, allotting them a position of authority. This contradicts the notion put forth that, as a method, photo-elicitation always neutralizes the power relations between researcher and informant.

On a more positive note, photo-elicitation can be a very powerful research tool that allows participants to express profound meanings about their experiences and emotions. In some instances, it provides a way for individuals to express the essential nature and the intensity of an experience, which would otherwise be difficult to do using words only. Conversations that take place with photographs allow for a deeper, more collaborative level of communication. This method also allows for the explanation of, and the rare performance of, sensory memories and spontaneous memories that have been kept hidden for a long time. Photographs are powerful triggers for hidden memories and therefore provide a glimpse into what has been forgotten.

There are several ethical concerns that are unique to the use of photographs. Many of these are obvious. Make sure an individual's privacy is considered. This means that photographs should be taken in appropriate places and shown in mutually agreed upon places, with the permission of the photographer and the subjects in the images. Ideas concerning what is appropriate can change according to individual desires, social contexts, and the identity of the photographer. For example, it may not be appropriate for a photographer to take intimate photographs of a private moment between two individuals without asking for their permission. It is usually not considered acceptable to take close-up photographs of children without their parents' consent. Distant shots taken by photographers hidden from public view also need ethical consideration. The second important consideration, in reference to digital images, is that they are very portable and can be used and reused in a variety of formats. Therefore, it is important to make sure all parties are clear about where photographs will be used and who will be viewing them over time. As we are all aware, contemporary digital technologies make it very easy for visual images that were intended only for private use to become very public documents circulating on the Internet. Prior to launching a research project in which informants take photos on their own, you should thoroughly discuss ethical concerns and include all parties involved in this discussion.

Perhaps less obvious is the fact that simply looking at photographs can sometimes elicit a powerful affective response. Social scientists using this method need to be prepared to deal with various types and intensities of emotional responses. For example, it is important to pay attention to your interlocutor's body language. As Mannik explains, the latent trauma linked to photographs of the *Walnut*'s voyage sometimes caused her informants to leave the room or say that they had to stop looking. Here are some central questions to keep in mind through the research process: Are the informants fidgety? Did they stop looking frequently? Does the content of the photo match up with the story elicited? Are sensory memories being performed or expressed? As in all anthropological research, a reflexive approach that includes a deep awareness of the researcher's presence, intentions, and responses, as well as the interlocutor's feelings, reactions, and perceptions, is vital to understanding the data that is being gathered.

VIGNETTE

Lynda Mannik is a lecturer in the Anthropology Department at York University. Her research focuses on the links between photography, memory, and identity in relation to issues of migration and, in particular, migration by boat. She also focuses on linkages between media (primarily photojournalism) and memory.

THE VOYAGE OF THE SS *WALNUT* AND PHOTOGRAPHS
TAKEN BY REFUGEES

In 2006, I interviewed 32 of the SS *Walnut*'s surviving Estonian passengers who were living in and around Toronto, Canada. Their voyage began in 1948 aboard an old minesweeper, which was originally built for the British navy. Everyone had been living in Sweden as refugees for four years after escaping Stalin's takeover of Estonia in 1944. Sweden had positioned itself as neutral territory after the war; however, in 1945, under extreme pressure, 2,700 soldiers, including 175 Estonians, were extradited to the Soviet Union (Aun 1985). Even though the Swedish government continued to announce that it would not bend to Stalin's defiant push for repatriation, fears abounded among all Baltic refugees. In 1948, this group decided to move to Canada, and the *Walnut* was one of 50 boats that left Sweden between 1945 and 1951. They were all privately owned, most commonly small sailing vessels bought by two to four families and overhauled to cross the Atlantic. They also all had different destinations around the world, some went to South Africa, Argentina, Australian, England, Brazil, the United States, and 11 landed in Canada. The *Walnut* was the largest of these ships, with 347 passengers, and it was the largest vessel filled with refugees to land on Canadian shores in the twentieth century. Several of the younger men who were aboard took photographs of the entire voyage and the weeks spent in detention centers in Halifax, Nova Scotia. As a collection, these images provide a rare glimpse into migration by boat from the perspective of the refugees themselves (Mannik 2013).

Initially I decided to interview as many of the surviving passengers as I could, who were then between the ages of 65–95. I began this process with a set of 90 photographs that had been taken by Manivald Sein. He was 19 years old when he boarded the SS *Walnut* and turned 20 while crossing the Atlantic. Sein made no claims to serious journalistic or political intentions for his effort to document this trip, and he described himself as an amateur photographer only. The small two-by-three-inch black and white photos he created are fascinating because the visual content does not match up to the devastating details of the voyage, such as the severe winter storms on the Atlantic; the lack of food, water, or toilet facilities for 32 days; and the cramped quarters in a ship that was originally designed to house 17 crewmen. Most of Sein's images showed small groups of people standing or sitting together, seemingly in social poses, smiling and looking directly into the camera; in short, these photographs resembled tourist-styled shots (see Figure 10.1).

Each interview began with verbal questions about memories of the voyage. Although I had a predetermined format and a list of standardized yet open-ended questions, I also explored perspectives, ideas, and elements of life experiences differently with each participant. I began this way because the photographs depict a traumatic period in these individuals' lives. Gabriele Rosenthal (2003) makes note of the fact that there needs to be a certain structure to questions concerning traumatic events to encourage disclosure and to avoid feelings of exclusion when addressing certain topics. Throughout, my intention was to create a relaxed atmosphere in which sharing set the stage for

FIGURE 10.1: Group of men on the *Walnut*, November 1948. Photographed by Manivald Sein. Courtesy of Lynda Mannik.

remembering. Following the question period, we would then look at a collection of Manivald Sein's photographs.

From the onset, at every interview, people would also give me photographs they had in their personal collection to copy or keep. It was common for interviewees to leave the room spontaneously for a few minutes and then come back in with albums or with photos stored in envelopes or binders. Private collections consisted of between 5 and 20 images. In the end, I gathered over 200 photos, taken primarily by four different photographers. One outcome of the process of photo-elicitation as a method was my interest in the private and public circulation of photographs, which became a secondary topic in our conversations. And, interestingly, one of the things that happened during this practice was that while I was physically circulating photographs among this group, they were actually circulating photographs among themselves through me!

General Reactions to the Photographs

Approximately 30 percent of the *Walnut's* passengers had seen many of the photographs in question before, and, as I stated, many had their own small personal collections. Most of the passengers who had not seen any photos of the voyage prior, and who were interested in viewing them, said they definitely wanted copies for their private collections, which I made available. This group felt positively about the ability of photographs to rekindle old memories and feelings. However, a small percentage of the interviewees claimed that the photographs held little interest. Some found them confusing because the people and places in them did not match up at all with their memories of what had happened. Several said that the photographs made them feel too emotional and that they did not want to look at them at length. Some tried to avoid looking at them altogether, and most of these individuals did not want to have copies for use later.

Overall, there was quite a bit of confusion in the interview process concerning where these photographs had been taken and what they were depicting. Even the photographers themselves could not always remember exact locations after 60 years. Without prominent landscape markers (which most of these images did not have), these photos were difficult to identify, and people seeing the images for the first time found it hard to tell where they had been taken, which prompted many questions and a good deal of guessing. Complex and lengthy conversations took place over attempts to decide the location of certain photographs, and I was frequently called upon to fill in the blanks.

Naming was the most common reaction to the photographs.[3] Allocating names to faces and explaining relationships was one of the primary preoccupations. It seems that people are what make photographs interesting. Interviewees expressed happiness and excitement when they came across photographs of a relative, a friend, or others they recognized—and information was shared about relationships and life experiences as well as experiences aboard the *Walnut.* Comments about family relations, health issues, vocations, where those pictured lived now or how they had died were all included. The pride of those interviewed shone through when they were able to remember names, and, conversely, people became frustrated and apologetic if they could not remember someone's name. Their oral narratives were similar to the sort of dialogue that occurs in conjunction with family photo albums: personal, detailed memories told in an intimate atmosphere. Stories lay in and between the photographs, and these readings of them inspired statements about past lives.

The trauma associated with forced migration and the ill-equipped facilities aboard the ship remained in the forefront of our conversations. For many of the survivors interviewed, the only memories they had of the actual voyage on the *Walnut* revolved around being seasick. For these passengers, the photographs held little meaning, except for the images of the bunks or "cubbyholes" because this is where they had spent most of their time.[4] Others distinctly remember violent storms, very cramped quarters, rotting food, dangerous toilet facilities, and generally feeling panicked throughout this experience. Looking at the photographs would sometimes encourage details and more description.

For an example, this image (Figure 10.2) inspired expressive comments about feeling seasick. While looking at it one individual said,

> EM: I don't want to think about it anymore, how it was. We were sleeping head to feet. That is just the way we were on the boat. There were sick children, bringing up. They were seasick, so seasick. No food! Ohhhh! It was murder staying on a boat like that for one month. I was lucky though. I was healthy, I wasn't sick. I only brought up once, but then I was OK all the rest of the way (Martsen [indication in notes of person speaking]).

Interestingly, the same image frequently elicited positive or pleasant memories.

> VM: Yes, well I spent a lot of time right here [pointing to the crowded deck of the SS *Walnut*] .... all of the young people, we stayed in between the boats here because it was warm and there was a smoke stack up there. We put our back against the smoke stack to keep warm. All the children, you know, our age, 11–15, were here coming across the Atlantic. On a nice day, we could all sit up there (Muursepp).

FIGURE 10.2: On the deck while in transit, November 1948. Photographed by Manivald Sein. Courtesy of Lynda Mannik.

The point that I want to make clear here is that the content of a single photograph can elicit very different memories depending on the viewer. This finding suggests that, although photographs elicit spontaneous memories, as well as more rehearsed stories and memories, the type of memory they elicit can be random, unpredictable, and highly subjective.

Five of the passengers I interviewed did not want to look at the photographs at all. They glanced at them quickly as I passed around the collage boards, but did not comment during or afterwards. When asked if they wanted copies they said, "No." When asked how they felt about looking at the photographs, they told me that these images made them feel too emotional. They made them think about the trip again, which was something they did not want to do. Looking at photos became risky for these passengers due to the threat of "being caught up again in strong feelings," and it is also possible that the photographs caused the intensification of past experiences (Charmaz 2002, 311). As I mentioned previously, an outsider looking at the content of these images would find it difficult to detect the trauma or distress that was being experienced. The majority of photos show passengers smiling, physically active, and happy. Trauma is not evident, yet is obviously close to the surface of many of the passengers' memories about this voyage.

Looking at the *Walnut* photographs also triggered spontaneous, unrelated, and lengthy memories involving sensory experiences that had not been previously articulated. Memories of smells and of tasting food were common. One example, told to me by Max Kalm, involved looking at a partial view of the deck of the SS *Walnut* and then remembering the strong smell of oranges rotting on the deck. Mr. Kalm also said he remembered the taste of those same oranges and then not being able to eat oranges for five years afterwards. Spontaneous comments about feeling seasick, cold, hungry, or suffocated would be accompanied by a grimace, gasp, or shrug. More positive sensory memories of warmth or sunshine on the face were expressed with a smile, and the memory of fresh air was expressed through an exaggerated deep breath. Similarly, when people remembered the physical sensations of being on the ocean, they often tried to simulate those sensations and repeated their performances of these simulations for effect. While looking at one photograph, Enn Saumets remembered being near the stern of the *Walnut* during a storm. At the same time as he explained his experience—"That is the worst place to be: up and down, up and down, I couldn't take it"— he lifted his body and motioned with his hands to enact physically how he was moving and feeling at that time. These memories contradict Roland Barthes's (1984) argument that the power of visuality replaces full or total memory, which includes smells, sounds, and touch, and that, therefore, photographs actually block the things we feel by allowing us to remember the things we see so distinctly.

Overall, I would argue that looking at photographs of the *Walnut*'s voyage 60 years later had a powerful affect on those who survived this traumatic experience. The photo-elicitation method was effective in quickly creating a sense of intimacy and a safe atmosphere where personal memories could be shared. However, for some in this group, looking at old photographs reminded them of a time in their lives that was difficult, traumatic, and filled with uncertainty. Therefore, I would caution researchers using this method to make sure they are fully aware of the possible emotional responses they may encounter in reference to the subject matter of the photographs they are working with, whether these are historic images or contemporary images, because the relationship between feelings and photos is synergistic, yet not always visually obvious.

Making Connections

If you choose to conduct a research project that includes the method photo-voice, what sets of parameters would you include in describing the types of photographs you would like your interlocutors to take?

How will you prepare yourself in advance for some of the emotional issues that might crop up while you are conducting your photo-elicitation sessions? Also, how will you conduct yourself as a professional researcher during those emotional moments?

What steps will you take when conducting a basic content analysis of the photographs that you will be focusing on in your research project? As Mannik states, most cultural anthropologists are not also trained visual artists. If this is the case, then what steps will you undertake to train yourself in the art of visual content analysis?

Try This

You could do this exercise in class. Each student needs to bring three printed photographs that best describe her or his identity. During class, you will meet in groups of three. To start, all three students will put their photos on a tabletop, so everyone can see them. Then, each student will get a chance to explain what she or he thinks each photo represents. Next, all students, in turn, will explain why they brought these three particular photos, and what meaning the photos have for them personally. There will be many discrepancies between intended meanings and imagined meanings, so this exercise is valuable in prompting initial discussions about the ambiguous nature of photographs and the importance of contextualizing photographers' intentions and observers' readings.

Possible Projects

1. Try adding photovoice to your methods toolkit! Photovoice is a relatively new method in anthropology that is becoming increasingly popular due to digital technologies. It also incorporates photo-elicitation, which has been used since the late 1960s. In addition to the interview process and participant observation, this method involves asking your informants to take photographs. Afterward, sit down with them, either individually or in a group, and discuss these photos and why they took them. To assist in simplifying your research and to help you later in your analysis, you should create parameters limiting the number of photos and the reasons for choosing or taking each. For example, let's say you were working with ten women who had come from the Philippines to work in North America as live-in nannies. You might ask them to take five photographs each of places in their city that they feel safe and then five photos of locations where they do not. Conversations about the photographs will usually elicit comments about the locations themselves but also about other feelings they may have as temporary foreign workers living abroad.

2. Conduct life history research that includes photographs and old photo albums. This method provides an interesting comparative approach that allows you, as an anthropologist, to think about the different ways people remember. First, you will conduct two one-hour interviews with interlocutors, asking them to verbally tell you their life story. It would probably be best to go over the recordings and transcribe these before moving on. Second, ask them to bring old photo albums to the next two meetings. In these sessions, you will use traditional photo-elicitation methods—you and your interlocutor will sit and talk about the photos. Life stories will emerge from the pages of the albums. After those sessions are transcribed, you can compare each person's memories and try to find patterns within the elicited memories. In the end, you will have two

transcriptions, one based solely on verbal memories and the other based on memories gleaned while people looked through old photographs, which will provide valuable information for a good comparison.

Recommended Readings

Cappello, Marva. 2005. "Photo Interviews: Eliciting Data Through Conversations with Children." *Field Methods* 17 (2): 170–82.

Edgar, Iain. 2004. *A Guide to Imagework: Imagination-Based Research Methods.* London, UK: Routledge.

Harper, Douglas. 1986. "Meaning and Work: A Study in Photo Elicitation." *Current Sociology* 34 (3): 24–46.

Loeffler, T. A. 2004. "A Photo Elicitation Study of the Meanings of Outdoor Adventure Experiences." *Journal of Leisure Research* 36 (4): 536.

Pink, Sarah. 2015. *Doing Sensory Ethnography.* 2nd ed. London, UK: Sage Publications Inc.

Prosser, Jon. 1998. *Imaged-Based Research: A Sourcebook for Qualitative Researchers.* Edited by Jon Prosser. London, UK: Routledge.

Notes

1 An overview of the history of photography within the discipline of anthropology is discussed in the introduction of *Rethinking Visual Anthropology*, edited by M. Banks and Howard Morphy, 7–21 (Yale: Yale University Press, 1997).

2 A very similar process called photovoice is outlined by Hurworth (2004).

3 This is also discussed by Gaynor Macdonald (2003); see the article "Photos in Wiradjuri Biscuit Tins: Negotiating Relatedness and Validating Colonial Histories," *Oceania* 73 (4) (2003): 225–42.

4 This was the name most gave for the two-by-two-by-six-foot wooden boxes that they slept in that lined the inner walls of the SS *Walnut*.

CHAPTER 11

ETHNOGRAPHIC FILM AS ETHNOGRAPHIC METHOD

Introduction

Due to new cell phone technologies, people are quickly and easily making films and videos more often throughout their everyday lives. Think about how often you take a quick video of a cultural event, such as a concert or a parade, and then post it to Twitter, Instagram, or another form of social media within a matter of minutes. So what is the difference between those types of filmic representations of culture and an **ethnographic film**? Considering, as Jay Ruby (1975, 105) states, that "all products of human consciousness, *can be* considered anthropologically" and "all film displays information on the culture of the maker and the culture of the subject if, of course, the subject is human," then what is the distinction? One difference is discussed in Jennifer Cools' vignette below; she says that new digital technologies allow for more free-form videos and films but that this is primarily a solitary practice with less collaboration between filmmakers and their subjects than is usual in ethnographic films. As well, even though new technologies make it easier and cheaper to create videos and films, the editorial and directorial skills needed to create a quality film have stayed the same (Henley 1998). This chapter will begin with a brief overview of the history of ethnographic filmmaking and its relationship to mainstream **documentary filmmaking** practice. It will then explain some of the issues students face in terms of creating and publishing their own films as research projects. As well, ethical concerns will be considered along with the benefits of collaborative practices.

Since 1896, anthropologists have been involved in the production of motion pictures, creating hundreds of films and an immense amount of footage of rituals, dance performances, ceremonies, and other events. Mostly, anthropologists have filmed cultures that are *not* Euro-American (Ruby 1975). Initially, ethnographic films were thought to be in a **genre** of their own because they were created by anthropologists, almost exclusively, who were attempting to show a culture (or its performances, rituals, or dances) in its original form. By simply following the course of an event, the film, it was imagined, could "fulfil the **positivist** fantasy of 'being there'" (Marks 1995, 342), and the final product required little editing or alterations—that film could provide a true, detailed rendition of an event, a visual copy of what happened. Simply filming hours of community life and then editing it down to a manageable size was considered the way to create an ethnographic film, and it was believed that this "naturalistic" method of filming was innately objective, as long as the anthropologist documented everything that was happening. Obviously, this view is problematic.

In the 1970s and 1980s, theorists began talking about the ways that film and photography were not objective but must always be considered subjective due to the complicated production and editing process each film went through and, more simply, because every filmmaker (or photographer) takes different footage of the same event. Critics such as Jay Ruby (1975) argued that most films labeled ethnographic were about anthropology and the anthropologists who created them, as opposed to providing valuable objective information about the subjects of the films, and that the renditions of cultures these films provided were highly subjective.

There were two primary issues that contributed to the deconstruction of ethnographic filmmaking as a scientific practice. One of the biggest issues was that early ethnographic films were based on the same set of visual and auditory conventions and **humanistic ideals** used in mainstream documentary filmmaking. The consistent use of voice-overs as authoritative commentary aimed at encouraging the audience to think a certain way is one common convention. "These documentary conventions were employed because ethnographic filmmakers seem to assume that documentary film conventions are the most suitable conventions for their purposes" (Ruby 1975, 108). A second issue was that comprehensive training in visual media communication was not a commonplace experience in an anthropologist's education. It is rare to find an anthropologist who is also highly trained in filmmaking processes.

Nanook of the North

An interesting example of a film that speaks to this dilemma in the North American context is *Nanook of the North,* which was completed in 1922, before any established conventions in the art of documentary filmmaking. For years, up until the 1970s,[1] it was heralded as one of the most important "ethnographic" films ever made and widely shown to students of anthropology as an excellent example of how ethnographic films should look and how they could depict a culture. It was produced by Robert Flaherty, who was a filmmaker and explorer, but not an anthropologist. He had set out to the Canadian Arctic in 1916 to create an "ethnographic travelogue," but he decided that what he had filmed was too boring and lacked dramatic visual appeal (Flaherty 1950, 11). In his next attempt, he was determined to create a film that showed authentic primitive life. *Nanook of the North* was a silent film, crafted with **subtitles** in English and aimed at providing in-depth information about the daily lives of the so-called "Eskimos" (now referred to as Inuit). It was significant in methodological terms because he trained a cast of Indigenous actors and allowed them to assist him in the planning and production of the film (Marcus 2006). Flaherty claimed to have captured the daily life and real struggles of Inuk Nanook and his family in the Canadian Arctic, but, in fact, the whole film was staged and choreographed with a pretend family that Flaherty had created.

Scholarly critiques vacillate between viewing Flaherty's filmic rendition of Inuit culture as an extremely **ethnocentric** work seeped in the racist and sexist ideas of this period and considering it a good example of early collaborative work. Alan Marcus calls it an excellent example of a **"primal drama"** (2006, 201). In some ways, it represents an early documentary in which Flaherty claimed to want to show "the former majesty and character of these people" (quoted in Marcus 2006, 208), but it does so by creating scenes that often mimic white, Western lifestyles and ideals. This film's success and use in classrooms for so long was based on the fact that it did a good job of replicating **visual stereotypes** that proliferated in the early twentieth century. Conversely, Ginsburg reminds us that Flaherty was one of the first filmmakers to employ and collaborate with Indigenous people in filmic renditions about their lives. He hired community members as "technicians, camera operators, film developers, and production consultants" (Ginsburg 2002, 39). Even though his method was collaborative, Flaherty was still the director, and it was his vision that we still see on the screen today. The legacy of this film speaks to the subjective power of visual representation and film, as well as to the continuing confusion about what an ethnographic film is and what it should do. *Nanook of the North* is now viewed by the anthropological community as lacking in any analytical value because it was so highly scripted and staged (Marks 1995).

Documentary Film versus Ethnographic Film

According to Jay Ruby (1975), the difference between a documentary film and an ethnographic film is that an ethnographic film should attempt to mimic a text-based ethnography in visual terms. First, an ethnographic film should attempt to depict the essence and entirety of a specific culture. Specific, detailed visual descriptions are important but they are only part of the project. Second, it should be informed by and if possible represent the theoretical focus of the anthropologist. Third, it must express and justify the choices concerning methods and methodologies used throughout the research project. This consideration should happen at all stages of production including shooting, editing, and the selection of scenes. And finally, it should be visually recognizable as an anthropological film, meaning it should include visual signs that position it as a scholarly endeavor. One example of such a visual sign might be the use of multiple languages through layers of subtitles; another might be the use of specific anthropological terms in the narration. The idea is that an ethnographic film must be obviously anthropological in its form. Ruby (1975) says that most films designated as ethnographic have very similar styles to other types of documentaries and that anthropologists' reliance on mainstream documentary conventions has done little to establish a distinct genre.

Karl Heider (2006) outlines some specific visual aspects that he believes all ethnographic films should have. The first is "whole bodies." He says that close-up shots of faces should be limited and that it is more important to see the actions of people's whole bodies in the places you are researching (114). While filming, you need to think about pulling back to show longer, more sustained scenes of certain events that you deem culturally important. For example, if you were watching a Hollywood film about a group of men gambling, the camera would be cutting from one facial expression to the next and occasionally pulling back to establish the whole scene. In an ethnographic-styled film you would simply see a long, sustained shot of the whole group playing cards and talking. The shot would take in the room and people coming and going, as well. This aspect in filmmaking would be called a **"long take."** Most mainstream filmmakers hate to use them because they are afraid they might lose their audience's attention. This point leads to the second factor— that ethnographic films cannot stand by themselves in visual terms. They must be supplemented by written or oral narratives within the film, to create the context needed for the audience to understand the filmmaker's intentions, theories, and methods. This is important as well because much of the footage, such as the scene of the men gambling, could be nonverbal. Imagine you are shooting footage of a farmer's market with crowds of people milling around. As the narrator and anthropologist, it would be your job to explain to the audience, using voice-overs or some form of subtitles, what they are seeing and why the scenes are important to understanding the culture of the market.

The Ax Fight, which is an ethnographic film made by Timothy Asch and Napoleon Chagnon in 1971, is viewed as an excellent example of how film can expose the processes inherent to ethnographic fieldwork. The film is shot from a distance (wide angle), as a fight breaks out in a Yanomamo village in southern Venezuela. The film presents three perspectives of a single event unfolding, and it thereby problematizes issues related to objectivity in film. Asch and Chagnon were narrating the event from their anthropological perspective while they were filming. As Marks (1995) explains, the way they were "trying to make sense of it in anthropological terms is striking" (344). Asch and Chagnon's conversation of what they are observing is layered in voice-overs and positioned as distinct, scholarly narration. In this way, they attempted to teach their audiences as much about the actual fight and Yanomamo culture as they did about anthropology and how anthropologists practice ethnography. There has been a lot of controversy about this film. For some American scholars, it has been considered a good example of an ethnographic film because it shows layers of interpretation and how the method of observation works alongside scholarly theory. Others believe that it was staged in some of the same ways *Nanook of the North* was staged or that Chagnon provoked the conflicts and then filmed them. Peter Biella responds to these critiques by saying that they don't make sense: "I cannot conceive of making a film in which a main feature is the anthropologists' confession of confusion, when, by hypothesis, there was never any confusion at all" (Biella 2000). This is a good film for burgeoning ethnographic filmmakers to watch so as to learn about such controversies, long takes, voice-over narrative, and cultural critique.

How to Start

As in all decisions about ethnographic methods, it is important to decide from the onset why film is particularly important for your study. It is not enough of a justification simply to say, "Because I like to make films." Sometimes, choosing to film certain subjects is inappropriate. One example might be that a film representing certain people or a certain community could cause them harm for political or legal reasons, particularly if the film were published on the Internet. It is important to make sure that the visual methods you choose fit with your research objectives and the communities you are working with and that you have considered all ethical repercussions before starting. Therefore, the first step in any filmmaking project would be to proceed with a thorough background search concerning your topic, the history of the community you will be working with, and the viability of working with them in a collaborative way that includes obtaining full consent concerning how, where, and why you will be filming them, their culture, and community.

Heider argues that there are two basic ways to make an ethnographic film. The first and best way, he suggests, is to do your fieldwork, complete your data analysis, and write up your thesis (or book or paper) and then return to your fieldwork site and take footage that is closely related to your written work. A second way, which he says some use, is for anthropologists to shoot **film footage** while they are in the process of standard fieldwork. This way is obviously cheaper and faster, but because the full implications of a study are often not realized until the end of the writing process, using this method means that there may be some people, ideas, or places not covered by footage. Heider claims that the worst films are those produced when an anthropologist goes into the field and shoots a lot of footage but does not think in filmic terms and therefore ends up with useless images. To solve this problem, he argues, ethnographers should have two people produce the film: an anthropologist and a filmmaker (Heider 2006). For student projects, it would be a good idea to enlist a friend who is more familiar with filmmaking than you are to give you advice throughout the process.

Most films are created from numerous hours of footage, which is then edited down to a mere hour or so. Much information and visual content (and therefore also context) is lost during this process of reducing hundreds of hours of film to one or two. The job of a good filmmaker is to make critical decisions concerning what stays and what gets cut. It can be a very confusing process, though, because much of the visual "reality" that has been documented will be lost. The footage itself basically provides a chronology of what happened (MacDougall 1999). The idea is that, as an ethnographic filmmaker, you are skilled at keeping the most important scenes, condensing them without losing the essence of what happened, and creating continuity and a new storyline that explains your theoretical and methodological focus without disregard for "the moments" that were filmed. Sounds complicated, and it is! David MacDougall reminds us that much can be lost in this process; in particular, there may be a loss of meaning and a loss of the "sense of encounter" (1999, 299). When a film becomes too polished and standardized as a product, it can cease to express what it was like making it—the feelings and meanings inherent in the act of filming.

Some Ethical Concerns

Visual records, such as videos and photographs, hold a lot of weight in terms of evidence. Making a film about someone can have serious ethical implications. The first thing is to consider whether the actual making of the film and the publishing of the film will harm the subjects of the film in any way.

For example, if your film or video were to circulate on the Internet, would it damage the reputation of anyone depicted in it? There are also cultural differences pertaining to how people view visual imagery and its production. Protecting the people you are working with involves making sure they do not experience any undue stress or angst (Pink 2001). Consent forms should be obtained from all individuals who are being filmed, although sometimes getting consent can be difficult if you are filming a large celebration, for example. In this case, it would be appropriate to ask the permission of the organizer at the venue. Obviously, if people come up to you and ask why you are filming them, then you have to provide full disclosure. Consent would necessitate people knowing where the film will be displayed after it is completed—to make sure everyone is comfortable with, for example, your film being published online.

Cool argues that the collaborative aspects of ethnographic film help us distinguish between this type of film and the documentary. As we have discussed in terms of written ethnographies, there is a similar, contemporary focus on diffusing authority—the authoritative voice—in all ethnographic films. Films that have been described as ethnographic, going back to Flaherty's *Nanook of the North* (1922), have often, if not always, involved the protagonists. However, more recent collaborative projects are designed with a political agenda that favors exposing the injustices experienced by the protagonists. Take, for example, films in Canada and the United States that focus on Indigenous land claims; in these films, the input of the protagonists is critical to creating ethnographic records that will further their political goals (Henley 1998). Contemporary films also rely more on film-elicitation as an added method. After a film is completed, it is shown to the people in the film, and they are asked to critique it. The anthropologist takes their comments and concerns back to the editing room and starts over. This practice can be repeated until both parties feel that the film's images and sounds provide a good representation. Scholars such as Heider have argued that filmmaking in anthropology merely reproduces insights and ideas that have been found through other fieldwork methods. But in collaborative work, it is what happens between the protagonist and the anthropologist during the process of making a film that can reveal new ideas, new insights.

Ethnographic film will never fully replace written ethnographies. Perhaps these films are best suited to remaining as visual and auditory accompaniments of text-based projects, or, in the least, perhaps every ethnographic film should be accompanied by some sort of explanatory written text (Henley 1998). Multimedia projects may be the way of the future, and using multimedia technologies is certainly a good way for students of anthropology to disseminate their research and ideas to the public. If you do choose to include filmmaking in your methods toolkit, make sure you familiarize yourself with the genre by watching classic ethnographic films and thinking critically about how they handle issues of representation and about what methods of depicting informants they use. Also, be conscious of *all* ethical issues before turning on your camera.

Examples of Early Classic Ethnographic Films (according to date)

1922	*Nanook of the North*, Robert Flaherty (65 min.)
1947	*Au pays des mages noirs* [*In the Land of the Black Magi*], Jean Rouch (12 min.)
1949	*Initiation à la danse des possédés* [*Initiation into Possession Dance*], Jean Rouch (36 min.)
1949	*La circoncision* [*The Circumcision*], Jean Rouch (22 min.)
1952	*Trance and Dance in Bali*, Gregory Bateson and Margaret Mead (20 min.)
1958	*The Hunters*, John Marshall (73 min.)
1963	*Dead Birds*, Robert Gardner (83 min.)
1965	*La Chasse au lion à l'arc* [*The Lion Hunters*], Jean Rouch (68 min.)
1967–68	*Netsilik Eskimo Series*, Asen Balikci and Guy Mary-Rousseliere (a dozen films are in this series)
1969	*Desert People*, Ian Dunlop, Robert Tonkinson, Richard Howe (51 min.)
1970	*The Nuer*, Hilary Harris and George Breidenbach (73 min.)
1970	*The Feast*, Timothy Asch and Napoleon Chagnon (29 min.)
1972	*Towards Baruya Manhood*, Ian Dunlop (535 min., 9 episodes)
1975	*The Ax Fight*, Timothy Asch and Napoleon Chagnon (30 min.)
1976	*Trobriand Cricket*, Gary Kildea and Jerry Leach (54 min.)
1980	*A Balinese Trance Séance*, Timothy Asch, Patsy Asch, Linda Connor (30 min.)
1980	*N!ai, the Story of a !Kung Woman*, John Marshall and Adrienne Miesmer (59 min.)
1986	*Forest of Bliss*, Robert Gardner (90 min.)
1988	*The Goddess and the Computer*, André Singer and J. Steven Lansing (58 min.)
1989	*Djungguwan at Gurka'wuy*, Ian Dunlop, Bruce Moir, Dean Semler, Dundiwuy Wanambi (233 min., 5 videocassettes published in Lindfield, NSW by Film Australia)

VIGNETTE

Jennifer Cool is a media anthropologist and ethnographic filmmaker at the University of Southern California (USC), where she leads the Masters in Visual Anthropology (MVA) program and teaches the yearlong course sequence in which students research and produce thesis videos. Before the launch of the MVA program in 2009, she taught in the Department of Art and in the Donald Bren School of Information and Computer Science at the University of California, Irvine, and in the School of Cinema at San Francisco State University. Her film Home Economics: A Documentary of Suburbia premiered nationally on the PBS television series POV. Her recent publications include an essay on working with anonymous subjects in ethnographic film (Cool and Mulcihy 2015) and a manifesto for creating an open, crowd-sourced catalog for ethnographic film (Cool 2014).

LESSONS FROM THE ANALOG: ETHNOGRAPHIC FILMMAKING AS SOCIAL PROCESS

"Stay Where You're At": Discovering the Suburban Other

In the summer of 1990, I took a video camera to the suburbs of Los Angeles to begin research on homeownership. After a year of coursework in anthropology and visual representation, I was eager to put study into practice in a five-week course on ethnographic filmmaking. It was my first experience using video as a means of ethnographic inquiry. Working in pairs, students chose local subjects and headed out each weekend—with class-issued camcorders—to research, shoot, and edit a short video to show in class each week.

My project partner and I decided to focus on the tract home developments of Antelope Valley[2] (55 miles from Los Angeles) and to look into the cultural meanings of homeownership, a cornerstone of the American Dream that we assumed factored in the enormous growth of "bedroom communities" outside urban areas in the United States and other postindustrial nations since the 1980s. We started with home sales showcases because these were public and busy on weekends when Los Angeles area residents drove out to developments with names such as Marbrissa, Rancho Vista, and Anthem to walk through model houses, each furnished down to the last detail with items such as framed prints, children's toys, place settings, and kitchenware. The model homes were a research bonanza: multiple, accessible field sites at which to observe homebuyers, sites that were also veritable theme parks of symbols of *home* and *homeownership*

FIGURE 11.1: Theme parks of the American Dream, a model home sales showcase, Palmdale, CA, 1992. Photographed by Jennifer Cool.

in America. We videotaped model homes and a few vox populi[3] interviews and did ethnographic interviews with first-time homeowners, who, at our request, walked us through their homes, talking about furnishing each room. We also shot lots of footage from the car, driving through neighborhoods and past billboards advertising new homes along the freeways.[4]

Each week in class, we screened and discussed videos edited from our weekend ventures. Each week, we were struck that classmates and faculty did not view our suburban informants through a lens of cultural relativism. Instead, they responded emotionally and bodily to their ideas and practices of homeownership as "tacky," "in bad taste," and emblematic of all the social and environmental ills of mass consumer society. After viewing several minutes of footage, one faculty member who would have defended the cultural logic of any number of alien social practices, exclaimed, "What empty lives these people lead!"

As a fledgling cine-ethnographer, I was uncomfortable with these reactions. The homebuyers whose images and speech we captured, cut, and circulated in our weekly screenings were no longer strangers or simply human subjects. They were already collaborators. Feeling complicit in the harsh judgment our suburban informants received

FIGURE 11.2: Kitchen conversations: Jennifer Cool (right) with an informant. Still from *Home Economics: A Documentary of Suburbia* (1995) by Jennifer Cool. Courtesy of Jennifer Cool.

during the class screenings nagged at me. Later, when I returned to the project for my thesis, this feeling shaped my dialogic approach of speaking to rather than describing subjects, as well as my attitude toward relations of power and knowledge between ethnographers and those they represent on page or screen. The experience led me to see that "anthropology as cultural critique" (Marcus and Fischer 1986) cannot begin from criticism but must start by looking to the self-understandings of the subjects themselves. My thesis work set out to make a quintessentially anthropological argument—it aimed to show the logic and validity of a particular way of life, that of suburban homeowners, and then turn this showing into a critique of contemporary American society.

The Saturday before the final week of our summer class was a hot day. We set out early on the two-hour drive to Antelope Valley, and it was already sticky as we rose onto the high-desert plateau north of Los Angeles. We had a long list of shots and sounds to capture: home residents, prospective buyers, salespeople. By mid-afternoon we had recorded everything that didn't require talking to people. We had been working from a car with no air conditioner for several hours and had not yet tackled the chore of walking up to strangers and asking them to participate in our study. Doing impromptu street interviews did not feel like the ethnography we had been trained to do. Yet we knew it was important, and clearly ethnographic, to talk with people we encountered in the field. We went looking for interview subjects.

We drove back to the model homes in search of someone to interview and succeeded in videotaping conversations with a middle-aged Filipino-American woman and two young couples (one white, one black), all looking at homes. By late afternoon, visitors dwindled, and it was time to move to another field location, or head home. We were leaning toward the latter but decided to drive around looking for residential street life on our way out of town.

We turned into the first tract neighborhood and followed our ears to a cul-de-sac. Kids were playing in the road. Three garage doors were up. We parked. A man and woman were moving things around their garage. A woman came out and called to the kids. We sat there, trying to figure out what to do. Soon, everyone had seen us. It would now be awkward *not* to get out and talk to someone. Just as we realized this, the man organizing his garage came over, leaned against the top of

FIGURE 11.3: Young woman in her backyard, a still from *Home Economics: A Documentary of Suburbia* (1995) by Jennifer Cool. Courtesy of Jennifer Cool.

our car, and asked if he could help. It was just the assist we needed. I hopped out and started explaining that we were graduate students doing research on new home communities in Antelope Valley.

We walked across to the man's garage where Rob introduced himself and his wife, Abby. Before the momentum shifted, I asked if we could shoot an interview, assuring them it would be quick. Abby said she was camera shy and went in the house. Rob said, "Yeah, I'll give you a couple minutes." My classmate switched on the camera and handed me the microphone. I asked Rob a set of standard questions: When and why had they moved to this home? Where had they lived before? Did they have children? What type of work did he do? Just as I began to sense that he wanted to wrap things up, I asked one last question. "What would you say to the city dwellers and, you know, college folks and young people who say, 'Gosh, I'd never live in a tract house! They're all so alike and cookie cutter, not umm individual...'" I trailed off, worried I was insulting him. Unfazed, Rob cocked his head at the camera and smiled. "Stay where you're at," he shrugged.

A Sweet Spot

Today, practically anyone with a smartphone can shoot and edit video, but things were different in 1990. Analog film (Super 8mm and 16mm) was the primary format of instruction in our visual anthropology program, and students took a year of film production coursework before even embarking on thesis research. Analog film was also expensive.[5] Shooting in black and white without synchronous sound was a common cost-saving measure. In contrast, by using consumer video, our summer seminar enabled students with no prior technical training to explore filmmaking as ethnographic research.

Looking back, two things strike me. First, we were working in a transitional period: after the development of consumer video but before media production moved to the computer. And, second, this was a sweet spot. We had the best of both coming and passing worlds. We had tools we could use without much training, and videotape was cheap, so we could record as much color, sync sound as we liked. Yet, we were also constrained by conditions—shared cameras, shared editing suites, regular group screenings—that articulated filmmaking as a social, rather than simply technical, process. In part, these conditions were material in that the monetary cost of consumer equipment made sharing a practical necessity. Yet these constraints were also cultural because they extended norms of teaching analog filmmaking to the video format. Far from being setbacks, I think these constraints were actually advantages for neophyte ethnographers exploring camera and sound in their work.

One constraint that turned out to be advantageous was working in a consumer, rather than professional, format. Our sense that "real" filmmaking was done in professional formats led us to approach our work as practice—as research process, rather than film product. Although we aimed to record footage that was technically and aesthetically strong, we were freer to experiment with cine-ethnography as a mode of discovery.

Having to share cameras was another beneficial limitation because working in pairs eased the learning curve for both technical and ethnographic skills. Rather than a single person having to divide attention between informants and equipment, one could focus on each and the two could trade off at regular intervals to learn both roles. Using the campus editing facilities (rather than working individually on one's own computer as people tend to today) had similar benefits. Everyone in the class was using the exact same equipment and, thus, could help troubleshoot technical problems when they arose. With many students sharing, the editing rooms were in high demand, and we had to sign up in four-hour blocks, which required us to schedule editing sessions into our process. This arrangement also provided a common space that fostered social learning among students in adjacent rooms or those coming in and waiting for the next time slot; troubleshooting and giving feedback happened spontaneously because of proximity.

Screening something every week was another constraint that enhanced the social dimensions of our work. Although video can be played back instantly in the camera, with film one has to wait for footage to be developed to see how it turned out. Thus, the practice of screening "dailies"—processed, unedited footage, synced to sound—

FIGURE 11.4: Approaching suburbia, frames from *Home Economics: A Documentary of Suburbia* (1995) by Jennifer Cool. Courtesy of Jennifer Cool.

as soon as possible after they came back from the lab was integral to analog filmmaking and, because it required projection facilities, was conventionally a group activity. Although we were working in video, the practice was carried over to our summer course with the modification that we screened *edited* rather than raw footage.

The theme of how we, as ethnographers, study people we recognize as distinct from ourselves yet bound with us politically, ethically, and epistemologically in a common global economy has been central to my work ever since this summer course. It framed my master's thesis on homeownership (Cool 1993), my doctoral research on social media, and my writing on anthropology as cultural critique (Cool 2001). Although the relations between "field" and "home" differ for every project, weekly screenings bring them into the foreground, reminding us that our ethnographic work is always situated in complex webs of significance and power.

Attention to features and freedoms dominates popular understandings of the digital technologies that have proliferated in everyday life over the past 25 years, and this focus constructs filmmaking as an individual and technical pursuit. In contrast, each of the productive limitations I discussed frames ethnographic filmmaking as a collaborative, social process—working in teams eased the learning curve; weekly screenings structured the work; and the focus on process over product spurred discovery. Despite the many benefits, these ways of working have become less common because they fly squarely against the individualizing currents of contemporary, digital media. As an instructor, I have prescribed the group work that was integral to my own training in cine-ethnography. Although students of my generation rushed to screen dailies together, in the twenty-first century my students often need to be reminded to watch the footage they record! Though filmmaking was for us a structured and intensely social activity, for my students it tends toward the opposite— free-form and solitary. In a context where making and sharing media has become commonplace, it is crucial to think critically about what distinguishes ethnographic film from the many other forms of documentary and "reality" media that are now common. Filmmaking practices of an earlier era offer insight into such contemporary challenges.

Making Connections

What are the myriad ways you can make your ethnographic filmmaking into a more social activity, from the very beginning of your fieldwork?

What does Jay Ruby (1975) mean when he says that ethnographic film is very different than documentary film? Watch five ethnographic films from the list above, either alone or with friends, and think about the various elements of this question. Flaherty's *Nanook of the North* (1922) should be included in this list.

How do you think that extensive field notes, taken while filming, would change the outcome of your editing process and therefore the finished film?

What is the problem with "long takes"? Why are they essential to ethnographic filmmaking, and how will you incorporate them into your project?

Try This

This exercise will help you think about "long takes" and how you can use them to understand culture. Go to an event that you are very familiar with (one you have been to many times) such as a baseball game or a dance class or even the cafeteria at your university. Sit and hold your camera steady for five full minutes while you take a "long shot" of the event. Make sure you are positioned to get a good overall view before you start. Five minutes will seem like a very long time. Afterward, watch this video three times, and each time write a response to these three questions. Did you learn about anything new about this event via the video? From an etic (outsider's) perspective, how would you describe aspects of culture that are taking place? If you had to edit this footage down to one minute, which seconds and minutes would you edit out? Afterwards, think about the complexities of film and the importance of repeatedly reviewing your work.

Possible Projects

1. After you have completed your ethnographic film project, create a group film-elicitation session for a collection of people that are outsiders to the project, meaning they know nothing about it and are not affiliated with anyone in the film. Take field notes during this viewing, and afterwards conduct a brief question period with the group. In particular, take notes about how they receive the information in the film, what they come away with in terms of knowledge about the culture represented, and how they say they would have filmed and edited it differently. Next, show the film to approximately the same number of people in Group "B," whose members are people who were either in the film or somehow related to the people in the film (e.g., from the same community) Take field notes throughout as well, and follow up with a similar question and answer period. Analyze and compare the results of both meetings to revise and reedit your film. A good

complimentary additional exercise would be to write a paper that first explains your reasoning and experience during the time you created the film, then your analysis of the audience responses, and then your decision-making process in terms of revisions.

2. This project is focused on Jennifer Cool's recall of social practices that used to be more prevalent during filmmaking classes. After you have taken at least one hour of raw film footage, divide it up into 20-minute segments and show each segment to three different students in your class. After explaining your project to them, ask each of them to edit the 20 minutes of raw footage down to 10 minutes and then to send you the newly edited clip. Recirculate the 20-minute segments one more time, sending each to a different classmate within this group of three, and ask them to do the same thing. At the end of this exercise you will have two different 10-minute, edited versions of each 20-minute segment of your raw footage. Going over the different editing strategies alone or with a small focus group should help you decide what the final project will look like. Although your classmates' opinions are somewhat outside of the project, considering them will make your project more collaborative; force you to review your work through others' eyes; and, as Cool explains, turn filmmaking into a more social activity.

Recommended Readings

Asch, Timothy, John Marshall, and Peter Spier. 1973. "Ethnographic Film: Structure and Function." *Annual Review of Anthropology* 2: 179–87.

Ginsberg, Faye. 2002. "Screen Memories: Resignifying the Traditional in Indigenous Media." In *Media Worlds: Anthropology on New Terrain*, edited by Faye Ginsburg, Lila Abu-Lughod, and Brian Larkin. 41–44. Berkeley, CA: UCP Press.

MacDougall, David. 1978. "Ethnographic Film: Failure and Promise." *Annual Review of Anthropology* 7: 405–25.

Pauwels, Luc. 2000. "Taking the Visual Turn in Research and Scholarly Communication." *Visual Sociology* 15 (1): 7–14.

Pink, Sarah. 2013. *Doing Visual Ethnography*. 3rd ed. London, UK: Sage Publications Inc.

Prosser, Jon. 1998. *Image-Based Research: A Source Book for Qualitative Researchers*. London, UK: Routledge.

Ruby, Jay. 2000. *Picturing Culture*. Chicago, IL: University of Chicago Press.

Schneider, Arnd, and Caterina Pasqualino. 2014. *Experimental Film and Anthropology*. London, UK: Bloomsbury.

Notes

1   This coincides with the beginning of Inuit television and film, and Ginsburg suggests that *Nanook of the North*, due to the collaborative nature of its production, had an influence on this trend. For an overview of this history, see Ginsburg (2002).

2   According to the 1990 Gobar Report, prepared for the Lancaster Economic Development Corporation, 57 people a day moved to the Antelope Valley between 1986 and 1990. In this period, 33,989 new houses were built, an average of 23.3 houses per day (Gobar 1990). Antelope Valley's estimated 1990 population of 250,000 represents a 168.4 percent increase for the City of Palmdale and an 80.2 percent increase for the City of Lancaster, since 1980 (Cool 1993).

3   This term is from the Latin and can be translated as "voice of the people," meaning "popular sentiment"; vox populi interviews are also known as "man in the street" interviews.

4   At this time, 100 feet of 16 mm film stock (fewer than three minutes of footage at 24 fps) cost about US$18 for black and white and US$25 for color; and film processing cost about .25 cents per foot.

CHAPTER 12

DOING RESEARCH WITH AND IN VIRTUAL COMMUNITIES: CULTURE, COMMUNITY, AND THE INTERNET

Introduction

In this age of digital technologies, you never know where and when you might bump into an anthropologist or an anthropology student doing research. In the early twenty-first century, anthropologists have been masquerading as **avatars** in a variety of virtual communities, where standard ethnographic methods such as participation observation and interviewing have been tailored to document the social activities of groups online. Online communities are now considered just another aspect of what it means to be human, just another platform for creating meaning, relationships, careers, and even culture. Tom Boellstorff (2008) coined the phrase "Age of Techne" to explain how digital technologies have changed the way we think about information and also the world. He says that we are now crafting ourselves within technology in virtual worlds, not just exchanging information, and that there is a marked shift toward more individual agency with respect to creating these worlds, which in turn leads to the creation of new kinds of cultural practices. Boellstorff also claims that virtual worlds, such as *Second Life,* are not just networks but actual places because culture is created within them. Although this virtual culture is unique, it also mimics and often replicates so-called "real" lives. Virtual worlds are also not completely outside of everyday life but are an integral part of the ordinary lives of the people who participate in these worlds (Carter 2005). Qualitative methods and the ethnographic documentation of social activities can help us understand the similarities and differences between these virtual and the face-to-face worlds.

Digital technologies have expanded and altered the ways qualitative research is conducted. Over the past decade or so, theorists have developed a range of terms and methodologies to describe ethnography that takes place in virtual worlds, including **virtual ethnography** (Hine 2000), **cyberethnography** (Carter 2005), and **netnography** (Kozinets 2010). However, as Driscoll and Gregg (2010) explain, it is important to make a clear distinction between real-life ethnography and virtual ethnography; imagining that you are traveling to an intact virtual community, which you will then study, will not work because, compared to a "real" world community, a virtual world and its various subcultures often exhibits an increased lack of stability in terms of identity, culture, and personal investment. This instability that Driscoll and Gregg (2010) are referring to is the consequence of the loose social fabric of virtual communities: people regularly move in and out of them easily and commit more or less time in terms of sharing these social spaces. Also, some participants (i.e., lurkers) remain relatively invisible to researchers. Christine Hine asks us to think about shifting the anthropological focus from holism and locales to connectivity because virtual worlds are field sites of flows, in which understanding culture is based on understanding "connections, differences, heterogeneity and incoherence" (2000, 61). Despite these complexities, researchers to date have successfully studied the cultural values, meanings, and objects created within online communities to help us understand how traditional ethnography applies.

Why Virtual Worlds Are Good Places to Do Research

Understanding culture is the cornerstone of cultural anthropology and the primary aim of traditional ethnographic study. Through observation and participation techniques, ethnographers have as a main purpose to gather as much information as they possibly can about the different cultures they are working within. **Virtual worlds** are defined as "electronic places that mimic complex physical spaces, where people can interact with each other and with virtual objects, and where people are represented by animated characters" (Bainbridge 2007, 472). They are visual spaces where buildings, landscapes, and creatures exist and where objects become part of economies and identities. There are many different types of virtual worlds; some of those developed for adults include *Chathouse 3D, Smeet, Second Life, There, InWorldz, The Sims, IMVU, Kaneva, Utherverse,* and ***World of Warcraft***. *Second Life* (SL) and *World of Warcraft* (WoW) are two good examples (and the most thoroughly researched). In these worlds, users create avatars that can walk, fly, and swim through three-dimensional landscapes; talk to each other; and participate in internal economies. Not only can researchers observe and follow participants' actions and relationships, but the software also facilitates interpersonal interviews and the collection of other forms of data. In SL, for example, researchers can, and have, set up virtual laboratories where they invite residents to come and participate in various social experiments and interview sessions.

There are lots of good reasons for conducting research in virtual worlds: one is that some of what is attainable in virtual reality is not possible in offline situations. Online, thousands of people are available from all walks of life and all cultures. In 2016, it was estimated that SL had approximately 6.5 million subscribers and WoW had approximately 10 million. Participants are often readily available and interested in being a part of long-term anthropological research projects. Research online is inexpensive, which is particularly important for student projects. And it can allow for innovative studies that combine real-world ideas with new technologies. For example, Bainbridge (2007) says that research experiments can be designed to compare the socioeconomic effects of unconventional government policies focused on eliminating environmental pollution, an issue already being fervently discussed in WoW. Virtual worlds are also good places for studying emerging issues related to other aspects of digital technologies including intellectual property rights, the implications of online misbehavior, and the adaptations of cultural and gender stereotypes.

The Online Self-Other Dilemma

There are many new issues cropping up that are related to the age-old dilemma in cultural anthropology of understanding the relationship between the anthropologist and the people he or she is studying. In virtual worlds, people are avatars and although avatars can be seen as extensions of the self, like puppets in some ways, they also are usually designed to express latent desires and alter egos. Thus, avatars express and perform identity in a very different way than their owners do in the "real" world. You may have secretly fantasized about studying to become a priest or fancied yourself as naturally inclined to be a physician; in WoW you can instantly take on these roles and develop them, as time goes on. Having the ability to create and pursue alternative identities with an avatar complicates any sort of boundary between the self and Other, and it further leads to a myriad of questions about the relationship between professional anthropologists and the participants of their studies. How do people in their roles as avatars react differently to interview questions than they would offline? Do they interact differently with other avatars—differently than they would with people in "real" life? Did a person create a specific avatar just for the researcher's interviews? Do the nicknames of avatars count in consent forms? We are also frequently online as ourselves during our daily lives. Some theorists have argued that we live virtual lives. If this is true, then it is important to think about how your identity as a researcher is affected by the ways you interact with digital media, and how your daily practices online affect the ways you analyze and critique others' virtual lives.

The first thing to consider carefully is what kind of avatar you will be as a researcher. Your choice can speak volumes about your identity and how others perceive you. If, for example, you choose to be a priest in WoW, others will think that you have certain values, perspectives, and mandates, and will act accordingly when in your presence. Choosing to represent yourself as a priest might not be the best way to enter a virtual world if you are planning on doing a lot of observations because you will be more conspicuous, and you will seem less approachable to some. Matthew Williams (2007) explains that, in cyberworlds, choosing a tourist avatar as opposed to a citizen avatar allows a researcher to pose as an "incompetent newbie," which in turn creates an impression of naiveté and the expectation that this avatar will need help with learning about the game and the culture (14). Some worlds allow you to change identities easily while others do not. As François Dengah explains in his vignette, researchers also might create several avatars before they settle on the one they will use for their projects. Initially switching between avatars allows them to experiment with the ways others will react to them because of gender, race, and first impressions.

Another issue in regards to avatars is that residents of virtual worlds can have multiple identities, and these identities can be intertwined in complex ways, which further complicates the research process. One consideration is the fact that the research population cannot be distinguished in traditional ways, which conceived of place as the primary indicator of identity. Virtual worlds, as special spaces, contain diverse populations that are multifaceted and always changing in terms of race, culture, community, class, and other identifiers. Also, some virtual worlds allow participants to have several avatars, and they frequently switch between these characters depending on the activities and other avatars they are involved with. Conversely, two or more people may share one avatar, which allows for a different type of anonymity and a different sort of "self." One example would be an avatar that is shared by members of a family. Boellstorff et al. use the example of a married couple that switched genders when they created their avatars. In terms of an anthropologist accounting for these multiple identities, Boellstorff and colleagues advocate for following the policies set out by the participants in the virtual world:

> If two avatars of the same person are treated as a single person, we should follow suit; likewise if they are treated as different people. If a female avatar we know to be inhabited by a male person is treated as a woman and addressed as a female, then we should do the same. (2012, 100)

How Basic Methods in Virtual Worlds Differ

Scholars have been discussing the new methods and methodologies emerging due to research conducted online since the 1990s, but the beginning of the twenty-first century has been heralded as the perfect time to conduct online studies because we are still in a transformative phase, so it is easier to see the differences between virtual and traditional ethnography as a practice, as well as the potential of new digital and online methods. On the positive side, conducting an ethnographic study primarily in a virtual world is cheaper and more convenient because it requires less travel time (and fewer travel costs) and allows for flexibility in terms of where the researcher works and when. It also allows researchers to retain a video diary of interviews and of their experiences, which they can repeatedly view for in-depth analyses. However, there are several common practical problems: time lags between audio and visual representation; disconnections due to technological failures; and, most important, difficulty in reading facial expressions and body language as well as other physical cues that are more obvious in face-to-face interviews. These cues are essential in the creation of intimacy and rapport with research participants. Jeffrey Snodgrass (2014) provides an excellent overview of some of the challenges researchers in online communities initially face. He alludes to "environments that are shorn of paralinguistic flavor" and "large amounts of text and images, which are at once overwhelming and denuded of meaning" (474).

Participant Observation Online

All fieldwork commences with a period of preparation. For research that takes place in virtual worlds, this entails learning about how the various technologies work, the history of the game, the demographics, and the cultural rules as understood by all participants. Generally speaking, as in all fieldwork, it is a good idea to find one or two seasoned players who can explain the subtleties of the culture and social practices. Another issue is that, in some virtual worlds, such as WoW, you must pass certain levels to be able to study participants meaningfully at that level, and being able to do so requires dedicated participation and practice (Boellstorff et al. 2012). In contrast to when you conduct traditional fieldwork, you will be working at home most of the time. Conducting thorough ethnographic research means committing to immersing yourself (being there) and devoting much of your time, day or night, to your project. The amount of time needed can cause problems with family members, for example, who might expect you to participate in everyday family culture, to quickly quit "the game" and make dinner! Getting in and gaining rapport is the next step. Tom Boellstorff (2008) began his ethnography in *Second Life* by buying land and learning how to build a house. This gave him some status, and provided him with a place to do research, where he could invite other community members to gather and get to know him.

A central component of traditional observation revolves around bodily activities. In virtual worlds, watching and taking note of avatars' movements and gestures will be just as important. For example, the ways a user controls her or his avatars to jump, fly, or dance can influence how others perceive them. If an avatar flaps its arms around while standing and talking to someone, then this could be interpreted as awkward or inappropriate, causing that person to leave the area. For an avatar, mimicking offline movements and attempting to "fit in" with appropriate body language can sometimes take a lot of practice.

One unique aspect in virtual worlds is "lurkers." Lurkers are usually defined as people who do not identify themselves but just watch and read text chats in the background. They never participate, so it is impossible to know what their identities or intentions are. For the anthropologist, lurkers are almost like ghosts, and even though they have a significant presence, studying them is nearly impossible (Jordan 2009). In public virtual spaces, lurkers may look like regular avatars, but they do not move or speak, and they stand off to the sidelines seemingly frozen. Ethnographers can also do research *as* lurkers because, in some ways, they are perceived as just hanging out. As Dengah explains, "lurking" can be an advantageous research method for anonymously collecting data because researchers can just observe without participating. Some have argued that lurking is an excellent method of "pure" observation, but lurking does present some ethical concerns in terms of consent and disclosure.

In offline research, there is always a balance between participating, observing, and documenting what you see and hear. Being online complicates this equilibrium. For one thing, multiple interactions are going on at the same time, yet the researcher cannot be in two places at once. For an example, Bonnie Nardi (2010), in her ethnography *My Life as a Night Elf Priest: An Anthropological Account of World of Warcraft*, talks about how she missed raids because she was in the middle of interviews. Some researchers are good at managing multiple tasks through multiple modalities, but if you miss participating and observing in too many events then you can fall behind in terms of what the group focus is. The online environment provides ways to take field notes that are not available in traditional observation: for example taking screen shots, which are faster and easier than taking regular photos, or using two computers, one that your avatar is participating in and one for creating field notes.

Interviewing as an Avatar

As we discussed in Chapter 4, the interview process is integral to any ethnography. In basic terms, interviews provide a more intimate sense of cultural meanings and personal identities than does using participant observation only, which is more focused on what people do than on what people say. Interviews provide in-depth narratives about the past and the present, along with detailed information about people's beliefs, motivations, and desires, as well as internal perspectives and unconventional practices. Interviews in virtual worlds are conducted in a similar way, except that the researcher and the interlocutor are usually in avatar form. One main difference occurs in sites that do not have voice options. In this case, all communication takes place through **text chats**, so, obviously, there are far fewer bodily cues such as facial expressions, voice tone, voice volume, and eye contact. The lack of these cues can increase miscommunication. The pace of text chats is also very different, and it can be difficult to tell if the person you are communicating with is alone or in a group, for example. Even in virtual worlds where voice is an option, avatars do not have the same ability to be expressive through their bodies and faces; therefore, there is a greater reliance upon verbal cues (Boellstorff et al. 2012). And finally, there are always the issues of **time lags** or disconnections. These technical difficulties are common problems due to Internet connectivity, and they can leave people on either side of the communication waiting to receive answers and comments. If the lag or disconnection is severe, it can disrupt the flow of the conversation and sometimes stop the interview process completely.

Collaboration and Ethical Concerns

As we have been discussing, when doing research in virtual worlds, you will experience an overall shifting and blurring of boundaries, both in terms of relationships and in terms of thinking about a specific virtual space as an intact culture. People move in and out of virtual worlds, which complicates any perceived boundaries between researcher and research participant. Many researchers begin as players and therefore identify as both members of the group and "outsiders" looking in. The ethnographer's traditional fear of "going native" does not apply in this case. If you are both a participant and a researcher for your project, open and full consent and collaboration from the beginning are probably the best ways to maintain rapport. If you are part of the group, it is often easier to make public announcements, to recruit willing participants, and to make group decisions about how the research will be disseminated.

Collaboration is a central aspect of most online research because the Internet is a space where networks of knowledge, often via open sources, proliferate (Gubrium and Harper 2013). As cultural anthropologists, we welcome exclusively participatory online projects that benefit the communities that researchers are working with. Due to the very public nature of the Internet, it follows that the dissemination of research findings should have the consent of all involved. There are many good sources that can assist you in designing such a project; one is Gubrium and Harper's new book, *Participatory Visual and Digital Methods* (2013). Also, many of the methods discussed in Chapter 8 apply, including returning transcripts to participants for them to check, and collaborating with them when designing the research questions. Specific plans might include using methods or technologies such as photovoice, digital storytelling, participatory film or video making, the creation of community websites, and the creation of interactive websites focused on archival materials. Projects of this sort will become more prevalent and important in the future, as will jobs for ethnographers and anthropologists. Anthropologists are already being hired to assist in the development of virtual worlds and in the important job of finding out how virtual worlds are affecting real worlds. Dengah's vignette demonstrates how collaboration works between students and their professor and between researchers and participants. The students he teaches are learning firsthand some of the ways that virtual worlds influence their everyday lives.

VIGNETTE

H.J. François Dengah II is an assistant professor of cultural anthropology at Utah State University, where he teaches Ethnographic Methods, among other courses. His research focuses on the intersection between culture and well-being in various contexts, including among Brazilian Pentecostals, Utah Mormons, and online gamers. Dengah wrote this vignette in association with Jenni Budge, Logan Broadbent, Jill Davis, Canyon Neal, Kylie Searle, David Tauber, and Joshua Wanner.

VIRTUALLY TOGETHER: COLLABORATIVE EXPERIENCES IN AN ONLINE WORLD

Why Virtual Worlds?

In 2008, I started my first ethnographic study of a virtual world. I was a night elf hunter named Tarwen—a master with the bow and arrow. With my faithful jaguar, Malinowski, we ran through the savanna grasslands of the Barrens, trekked through the Swamp of Sorrows, and partied with pirates in the hidden alcove of Booty Bay. A motley crew of gnomes, elves, humans, and dwarfs joined Tarwen on these adventures; some were men-at-arms, soldiers and warriors wielding swords and battle-axes; others were hunters like me who traveled with their pets—wolves, falcons, and even giant spiders; still others were magic users—shamans, mages, and warlocks—who bent elemental forces to their will. Together we formed a guild, Virtual Worldz, an organization that allowed us to combine our powers to achieve common goals. Like the fabled Fellowship of the Ring, the brave souls of Virtual Worldz engaged in perilous quests to rid the world from demonic dragons, undead kings, and other forces of evil.

The offline identities of Virtual Worldz members are slightly more grounded. We are students and professors of anthropology who play, research, teach, and learn, within the fantastic and imaginative virtual spaces that are characteristic of massively multiplayer online games (MMOs). Besides the research importance of these virtual places, they also serve as spaces for teaching and "doing" anthropology. Virtual worlds provide opportunities for anthropologists to travel to "exotic" places with relative ease. These online communities, often as vibrant and rich as their offline counterparts, can be subjects of ethnographic inquiry that are studied in much the same way as one would study a culture in "the real world" (see Boellstorff 2008). For nearly a decade, my research in these virtual spaces has been intertwined with the process of teaching the next generation of anthropologists the tools of the trade. I conduct nearly all of my virtual ethnographic research alongside undergraduate and graduate students in joint studies. In this vignette, I highlight their voices and experiences to show how students can be valuable collaborators in real anthropological research projects. I conclude with a brief reflection on the nature of collaborative research and its role in the ethnography of virtual cultures.

Getting into the Field
In the fall of 2015, I recruited a new crew of adventurers to explore, play, and do research in *Guild Wars 2*'s high fantasy world of Tyria. Like any ethnographer entering a new field site for the first time, some recruits found visiting this world a jarring experience. Indeed, I remember feeling trepidation during my first foray into an MMO for research purposes, unsure of my ability to conduct research in such a "foreign" environment. This feeling can be somewhat compounded by the initial task of creating a personal avatar. Many MMOs offer an overwhelming set of options to customize one's avatar, and these choices are often permanent. My student, Jenni, describes this in detail in her field journal:

Appearance was the most detailed portion of the creation: height, body type, hair color, eye color ... skin shade, hairstyle, eyebrow angle, [etc.].... It was a daunting task, but in the end I discovered that the effort I put into my avatar reflected a lot of different things. She reflected who I am, a bit of who I want to be, and what I want to be seen as in the virtual space. (This made me think.) Do gamers create who they are, in their minds, themselves as they are, or themselves as they wish to be?

Many researchers create several characters, only to settle on one "main" avatar that they use for research purposes. Others create several characters, switching races and even genders to get a sense of how avatar characteristics influence how players interact with one another. In fact, the researcher's own avatar appearance can influence informants' reactions and impressions of the study (see Snodgrass 2014). For example, my avatar "Subutai," an imposing eight-foot-tall feline warrior, has better success recruiting informants than my diminutive three-foot-tall gnomish thief. The likely reason is what Nick Yee (2014) calls the "Proteus Paradox": although reinventing oneself in the virtual world offers the promise of escaping physical and social constraints, subconscious (and erroneous) appraisals manifest in online realities—in this case, height discrimination.

Observing and Listening to Gossip

Soon after creating our (tall or short) avatars, we began doing the serious business of conducting research in this virtual world. The core of any ethnographic study is participant observation: hanging out and watching what people say and do and participating in the activities of the community. This may also include "lurking" and listening to gossip (Garcia et al. 2009):

> P1: *Pretty sure there's less elitists jerks in this game than you think >_>*
> [sideways glance emoticon]
> P2: *Newsflash, there's elitist jerks no matter what game you play*
> P1: *True*
> P3: *newsflash! I forgot having an opinion on the internet is worse than elitism...*
> P4: *newsflash, don't write anything on the net if you can't handle criticism*
> P3: *and for having an opinion about the elitism in this game I am worse than the elitists...lol this community is funny*

Guild Wars, like many virtual spaces, utilizes a "chat room"–like dialogue function; people can converse within public spaces and these conversations are visible to any passersby. In this case, Jill was able to "listen in" on a conversation between friends, much like an anthropologist would do in an offline research setting. But rather than having to quickly take notes on everything said, Jill took "screen shots" of the conversation for later analysis.

Similarly, I find that "lurking" is a viable and advantageous methodology, particularly in online settings, where such nonparticipant observation is easily and anonymously conducted. By simply "listening" to the ambient chat, the researcher can be privy to much that is of central interest to the community, including gossip, opinions, and debates.

Hanging Out and Gaining Rapport

Eventually, the ethnographer needs to make connections within the community, gaining rapport and trust with the group. As Kylie shows, it often requires putting yourself "out there" and taking advantage of opportunities.

> This week I made the goal to join a guild. While playing, I saw a guild advertisement on my chat. I quickly responded requesting how to join, and they added me. I had a quick chat with them. They were very friendly and helpful. I told them that I am an anthropology student conducting research.

Guilds are smaller groups of like-minded players, often composed of friends and family, which exist within the larger virtual world. Soon after Kylie's induction into her guild, the Emerald Pirates, she was making friends, gaining rapport, and even finding potential informants to interview. From an ethics standpoint, she identified herself as a researcher, which is important because discussions taking place within the guild are considered private (compared to the general chat, which can be considered open to "public observation").

In my own experience, guilds are great communities for ethnographic research. I have spent countless hours conducting participant observation in various guilds and, as a result, met a diverse range of key informants. One particular guild stands out from the rest, however. This guild, the Choir of the Quiet Knights, comprised graduate students, business owners, lawyers, medical doctors, and stay-at-home parents (accompanied by some of their children). The leader of this group was an elderly woman many referred to as "Grandma." Although no one in the guild ever met in real life, every year, Grandma sent out birthday and Christmas cards to each of the members.

The Offline Places of Virtual Spaces

Membership in some guilds, such as the Quiet Knights, is diverse, with participants located in different parts of North America. When primary forms of interaction take place in virtual spaces, it can be easy to forget that behind the avatar is an actual person in some physical location. The physical contexts of these virtual spaces are also worthy of ethnographic inquiry. As my student Joshua noticed, combining both virtual and physical space can have important implications for relationships and community development:

> Gaming with friends and family is much better than gaming alone.
> Last night I went to the Cyber Café, a gaming center, which has walls
> lined with computers and TVs with game consoles. It has the feeling
> of the old nickel arcade I went to a few times as a child. I thought that
> they had all died out because most entertainment is now accessed

FIGURE 12.1: Jenni and Kylie conduct participant observation together in virtual and actual space. Photograph courtesy of François Dengah.

from the comfort of your own home. It had the feel of "third places"—places where individuals can gather to socialize informally beyond the workplace and home.

Indeed, our research has recently led me to consider how these blurred "virtual" and "real" world groups shape patterns of social interaction and mental health. One of the groups I am working with is my university's eSports (electronic sports) club. These eSports clubs are quickly growing on North American college campuses; these are places where students meet in physical and virtual space to compete in online sports. In fact, a half dozen North American colleges offer scholarships in eSports, and even ESPN has started covering these competitions.

Conducting Interviews

Every single tool in the anthropologist's tool kit used to study offline cultures can be used to study virtual online cultures. Interviews can be done in both offline and online contexts, with each approach having its own strengths and weaknesses. In my experience, however, offline

FIGURE 12.2: USU students play together during the eSports Club meeting. Photograph courtesy of François Dengah.

interviews provide a wealth of knowledge from the paralanguage—nonverbal communication and signals—that the participant conveys.

During the course of an interview, such paralanguage can be incredibly useful—revealing places to probe or to avoid—and it can be helpful in the later analysis of the interview. That is not to say, however, that online interviews are not valuable. They provide their own unique atmosphere and, in some respects, are more honest and representative of the ways in which members of these virtual communities interact with one another in these virtual spaces. Tom Boellstorff (2008), for example, conducted an entire study on the virtual world of *Second Life* solely through in-game ethnography and interviews.

An in-game, online interview is the approach Logan used in her social network interview with an informant 800 miles away. Logan writes the following in her journal after the interview:

> I had to conduct the [social network] interview in-game because my interviewee lives in Washington state. One thing I found interesting with the interview with Karen was that she met several of her friends online playing various MMO's. [For example,] she met her husband on *World of Warcraft*. She is a great example of someone who takes her online friendships very seriously, equally to those she has in real life.

This online interview was apropos to the research topic of online social networks and the nature of online communities. In my own research, I found that I could not limit my interviews to those informants in close geographic proximity. To understand the composition and culture of online communities, I had to engage in a substantial number of online interviews.

Collaboration in Virtual Worlds

Our virtual ethnographic work has made me realize that a single researcher cannot describe, study, or even access every part of a community that researcher is studying. Collaboration helps researchers achieve a more holistic approach to understanding virtual cultures by allowing the integration of more views, experiences, and methods. This tactic can be incredibly useful in online contexts, where the community may lack clearly defined boundaries and is composed of an amalgam of diverse individuals and subcultures. Some of my most insightful respondents were introduced to me by my student collaborators, including a gamer who was using virtual worlds to explore her

FIGURE 12.3: Conducting an "in-game" interview with the Quiet Knights. Photograph courtesy of François Dengah.

new gender identity and a young man with muscular dystrophy who uses his abled-bodied avatar to do things and meet people inaccessible in offline contexts.

Virtual Worldz

Almost ten years ago, while researching *World of Warcraft* with my adviser, Jeffrey Snodgrass, I learned how to conduct participant observation and use various interviewing techniques, as well as how to analyze the data and present findings at conferences and in publications. The collaborative nature of this research, bringing together professors and students in joint research, has been the hallmark of our research ever since and has trained dozens of students who have since gone on, like myself, to be academic and professional anthropologists. Yet these communities are more than great locations for learning research methods; they are important spaces for ethnographic inquiry, as more of our time is spent forging relationships within these online spaces and places. Some of the most exotic locales for anthropological research are now just a mouse-click away.

Making Connections

Why does François Dengah say collaboration is so important in terms of both the relationship between researchers and the relationships between researchers and interlocutors?

Can you see there being any issues within your specific project if you decided to create two or three avatars instead of only one for your research purposes? How might some of these issues change your project?

Why is it important to consider the links between online and offline identities, as well as the daily lives of research participants?

Every virtual world can be considered a culture in and of itself. Why is it necessary, then, to contextualize and compile a history of the development of any virtual world you plan to do research in before beginning the actual fieldwork?

Try This

Download *Second Life* software, create an avatar, and then spend at least three hours wandering around and observing other avatars. Before you begin, make sure you read about the ways to protect yourself from avatar predators. There are several good sites online. One popular site is https://sl4nowt.wordpress. com/2009/01/30/30-things-every-newbie-should-know-before-starting-second-life/. After doing your observational research, write up a report that describes various aspects of your avatar identity as compared to the identities of other people's avatars. Consider aspects such as clothing, hair, body size and shape, inclusion of animal body parts, gender, and body movements. Are there any similarities that you can describe? Did anything surprise you? Did other avatars approach you? If so, what was that experience like?

Possible Projects

1. Choose a virtual world website that interests you. Then spend a lengthy period (about one or two weeks) lurking on the site. In this capacity, you will just be observing activities and relationships from the outside, and you would remain invisible to all other players and avatars. Next, spend the same number of weeks as a full participant who is identified by the community as a researcher. Through a comparison of these experiences, you could start to think about how people react and act differently in respect to identity. Do they present themselves differently to researchers?

How do they do this? Were some people more receptive than others? Does this comparison affect the type of research data you imagined you would be gathering? What does this comparison suggest about the difficulties and benefits of online ethnographic research, especially considering the type of data you plan to collect?

2. Understanding how virtual worlds are affecting individuals and offline cultures is as important as understanding the online cultures they create. Many contemporary anthropological studies include online methods as well as offline interviews and participant observations. There are several ways you could combine online and offline research when completing your project. First, if the people you are working with online live fairly close to you, you could interview them in person. If this is not the case, then you could interview them through **Skype** or ask them sets of questions via email. The questions could also be varied. Some might have a life history focus: you could ask them simply to explain in their own words their personal histories of participating in the virtual world and how this participation has affected their family lives and careers, or you could ask each of them to keep a diary for a time. Other questions could be more specific but still open ended: Has this practice affected your personality (i.e., made you less shy, for example)? How does your online life affect your offline life? What is the difference between your online and offline relationships? Can you ever see yourself quitting virtual world participation altogether?

Recommended Readings

Bainbridge, William Sims. 2012. *The Warcraft Civilization: Social Science in a Virtual World*. Cambridge, MA: MIT Press.

Castronova, Edward. 2008. *Synthetic Worlds: The Business and Culture of Online Games*. Chicago, IL: University of Chicago Press.

Golub, Alex. 2010. "Being in the World (of Warcraft): Raiding, Realism, and Knowledge Production in a Massively Multiplayer Online Game." *Anthropological Quarterly* 83 (1): 17–45.

Hine, Christine. 2000. *Virtual Ethnography*. Los Angeles, CA: Sage Publications Inc.

Landzelius, Kyra. 2004. *Native on the Net: Indigenous and Diasporic Peoples in the Virtual Age*. London, UK: Routledge.

Sundén, Jenny, and Malin Sveningsson. 2012. *Gender and Sexuality in Online Game Cultures: Passionate Play*. London, UK: Routledge.

Taylor, Tina L. 2009. *Play between Worlds: Exploring Online Game Culture*. Cambridge, MA: MIT Press.

GLOSSARY OF KEY TERMS

academic anthropologists. Anthropological researchers who are employed by universities or academic research institutions.

analysis. The process of "making sense" of the data that you collect during your ethnographic research. This is a cyclical process of the refinement of data that is achieved through multiple readings of your transcripts to identify the key themes or issues that you will discuss in your final research project.

applied anthropology. A type of anthropology, also referred to as "practicing anthropology," that seeks to find solutions to practical problems. Increasingly, many anthropologists find employment in this type of anthropology.

archival photographs. Historical photographs that are stored in either official government archives, community archives, library archives, museum archives, or in personal archives (such as a cardboard box or family photo album).

armchair anthropology. A late nineteenth- or early twentieth-century anthropological approach to studying various societies. It involved drawing conclusions and making generalizations about various aspects of society based upon the use and interpretation of secondary sources written about different cultures (e.g., missionary reports, travel writings, explorers' accounts). Armchair anthropologists did not go into "the field."

autodriving. A term used to indicate that the interviewees took the photographs being talked about in the photo-elicitation process. Therefore, the interviews are "driven" by how the interviewees see themselves, their lives, and their life experiences, and by how they want to be seen.

autoethnography. A research method and form of writing that systematically analyzes the personal experiences of anthropologists to interrogate the methods and theories of the discipline.

avatars. Visual figures that have been designed to represent a certain person or certain people in a virtual world. All virtual worlds have specific rules around how a personal avatar should look, with some being more complex and flexible than others.

big data. Information derived from a variety of relational databases and "unstructured" data sources, such as blog posts or online photographs.

closed questions. Questions designed by the interviewer to glean specific information needed for a research study. "How old are you?" or "When were you last employed outside of the home?" are closed questions. See also *open-ended questions*.

code of ethics. A set of rules outlining in detailed and precise language all of the ethical imperatives that need to be followed by practitioners of an academic discipline or members of an organization or business. Each discipline has its own specific code; in anthropology and ethnography, the code of ethics regulates how people conduct research. Codes of ethics in North American anthropology follow ethical concerns that have been debated throughout the history of the discipline.

coding. A three-step process (open, focused, and selective coding) that involves looking for repeated or key themes or issues that emerge from data.

collaborative research. Research that emphasizes deliberate and explicit collaboration, especially between the investigator and the community being investigated. In ethical terms, collaborative research means making sure that the people you are working with are consulted at every level of the research process, including the proposal stage. It rests on voluntary participation that benefits research subjects.

comparative approach. A research method employed by armchair anthropologists in the late nineteenth century. It involved the cross-cultural comparison of the customs and beliefs of different cultures through the acquisition and interpretation of secondary data (e.g., the reports and writings of missionaries, sailors, or others who came in contact with various Indigenous people).

cyberethnography. One set of research methods designed to assist in understanding how to do ethnography online in virtual worlds. This particular term was coined by Denise Carter in 2005.

decolonizing. The process of critically exploring the effects of colonialism on different societies and examining how anthropology was an outgrowth of colonialism itself. As such, it involves a reassessment of relationships between anthropologists and their informants, with a movement away from subject-object dichotomies to collaborative efforts of knowledge production.

descriptive notes. The initial notes or jottings that an anthropologist takes while in the field based on what that person sees, hears, smells, and experiences. The intention of taking descriptive notes is to write down (in shorthand) in a highly descriptive manner everything that is perceived in a certain environment and situation.

dialogic anthropology. Anthropology that focuses on the dual role played by both anthropologist and interviewees during the research process. The collaborative nature of ethnographies extends to the resulting production of knowledge in which relational meanings are analyzed.

diary notes. Very personalized written expressions of feeling, insights, ideas, and observations. They are written in the first person and describe experiences from the writer's perspective only.

do no harm. The primary focus and maxim of all anthropological research in North America, including in all four fields of this discipline. As an ethical and moral imperative, anthropologists design and conduct research that will not harm the people they are working with, either during the research process or afterwards.

documentary filmmaking. Films and filming processes that are considered to be nonfiction and that accurately depict some aspect of reality based on "facts." They are used for teaching purposes and often contain historical information.

dyadic relation. The interpersonal relationship that develops between the anthropologist and his or her informant. Of importance is the fact that the nature of this relationship, whether positive or negative, can impact the level of rapport that you develop with people and, ultimately, the data that you acquire during your fieldwork.

elicitation. The standard definition focuses on provoking or drawing out a comment or emotion from someone, but in this context, the term refers to a nonaggressive form of encouragement or inspiration.

engaged listening. Combining listening with seeing and observing, and then connecting what you see with what you actually hear. In an interview setting, this form of listening means paying attention to the body language, facial expressions, and physical movements of both you and the interviewee as well as to the environment in which the interview takes place.

epistemology. The study of the production of knowledge. Within the context of anthropology, this refers to the act of being critical, reflective, and reflexive about the kinds of knowledge that we produce ethnographically, as well as being attuned to the social, historical, political, and economic conditions that affect how we do fieldwork and how we write.

essentialist representations. The construction, via writing or images, of generalizations (usually based upon stereotypes) about a group of people.

ethics. A set of rules and philosophies that explain the moral values of a culture or society. Cultural anthropologists follow the ethics that are outlined in the discipline's "code of ethics"; they also follow the ethics of their own culture, the ethics outlined by the United Nations, and the ethics of the other cultures they are working with.

ethnocentric. The belief that the people, culture, customs, and practices of one's own group (e.g., nation or race) are better, moral, and right compared to those of other groups.

ethnographic authority. The common conception in modernist anthropology that anthropologists, through their direct experiences of fieldwork, had specialized and inside knowledge of the cultures they studied. As such, they were "authorities" about various cultures, and their observations were perceived as objective and infallible.

ethnographic film. A film that is made with the purpose of representing an ethnographic study. It should include narratives or visual references that express the methods used and any theoretical perspectives.

ethnographic methods. Techniques of data collection used by anthropologists, which may be qualitative or quantitative. Some examples of methods include surveys, interviews, or participant observation.

ethnography. A written analysis and documentation of an anthropologist's fieldwork experiences.

etic. An adjective meaning "from the outside" or from the perspective of an anthropologist. Etic anthropological research describes a culture from an outsider's perspective, so these descriptions depend on the ethnographer's criteria of significance. The opposite is emic anthropology, which tries to capture the "insider's" point of view.

field notes. Written notes and other forms of visual information created by anthropologists during participant observation and interviewing to capture what they see, hear, smell, and feel. These notes later become the data used in scholarly analyses.

film footage. The raw, unedited visual material that someone takes with a camera, whether it is digital or videotape. The term footage used to refer specifically to the length of the film tape.

film-elicitation. A research method that is very similar to photo-elicitation except that various forms of films and videos are watched and talked about instead.

focus group. A small group of people (2–12) gathered together by a researcher to discuss open-ended questions about a certain research topic or focus. In anthropological research, members of a focus group usually know each other and the anthropologist.

focused coding. The second stage of the coding process, which involves more critical thinking than the open coding stage. During this stage, your goal is to refine and reduce the plethora of open codes that you have accumulated in an effort to relate your codes to one another and identify several key codes for addressing your topic of concern.

genre. A category of an artistic endeavor, which can be writing, film, or music. All genres have standardized forms, styles, and subject matter.

globalization. A process of increasing cultural, economic, and possibly political connectedness among different nations and communities. Although globalization has been ongoing since the beginning of European colonialism and industrialization, it has accelerated in the past 50 years due to changes in communications technologies, transport, and other factors.

historical particularism. A concept popularized by Franz Boas that posits that every society should be explored in relation to its own unique history and context of development. In many ways, it represented a reaction against universalizing and generalizing theoretical orientations of the late nineteenth and early twentieth centuries, such as unilineal evolution.

Human Terrain System. A project initiated by the US Department of Defense in 2007. It involved hiring civilian anthropologists and embedding them with armed military forces in Iraq and Afghanistan. Anthropologists were expected to conduct interviews and other forms of research with local communities in an effort to prevent counterinsurgency.

humanistic ideals. Principles based on the philosophy of humanism that emphasize the value and welfare of human beings. If you were a humanist, your research would focus on human activities, societies, and cultures and on social justice for all peoples.

identity. One's perception of self as an individual and as part of a social group. Some examples include age, gender, sexuality, nationality, and race.

inductive. A form of analysis that avoids imposing theories or generalizations upon one's data. In an inductive approach, theory and key themes emerge from the careful analysis of the data derived from fieldwork.

informed consent. The voluntary agreement of an individual with an action proposed by another, such as participating in research, after having full knowledge of what is proposed and of the potential benefits and risks. "Informed" is the operative word in discussions of "informed consent," and it refers to an ethical stance in anthropology that focuses on making sure that the participants in research studies are very clear about exactly what their role will be and how their participation might impact their lives afterwards.

integrity. Adherence to the moral and ethical principles of honesty, trust, fairness, respect, and responsibility. Having integrity as a researcher means you are honest with the people who are participating in your projects and that you consistently follow your discipline's code of ethics and your own cultural moral values throughout all aspects of the research process.

iterative. Characterized by repetition. An iterative process of assessment refers to a nonlinear means of analyzing your data, a process in which you are continually going back to think about and analyze data, looking for key issues that emerge from these data. In other words, it is an inductive method that avoids having the researcher impose etic categories upon data.

jottings. Brief shorthand notes taken during participant observation and interviews. They are often called "jottings" or "scratchings" because that is what they look like, and usually only the person who has written them can understand their full meaning.

life history. The overall picture of the life of an informant or interviewee. Life histories are conducted as unstructured interviews on an ideal basis; in these interviews, the interviewee is basically asked to tell the interviewer his or her life story. Several sessions are often required to give each individual enough time to narrate this life story, which does not have to follow a chronological order.

literature review. A critical summary and analysis of key anthropological and other academic literature that relates to your topic. Most ethnographies contain a literature review, which is either a separate section (or chapter) or interwoven throughout the entire narrative of the ethnography.

long take. A filmic term that refers to a wide-angle image that is sustained for a long period to show an event or activity in total.

magical realism. A genre of writing and representation that attempts to challenge modernist forms of representation.

medical anthropologists. Applied anthropologists who specialize in the study of health and health care systems in cross-cultural contexts. Medical anthropologists often work as faculty in universities or in nonacademic settings, such as development organizations, hospitals, or government.

memoing. The process of writing notes or phrases on transcripts (handwritten or digitized) during the analysis process. Memos often include comments about observations gleaned during fieldwork and subjective feelings and perspectives.

methodologies. The critical or theoretical analysis of various fieldwork methods and forms of representation. For example, a critical interpretation of participant observation might ask questions about the ethics of this method, how the anthropologist's presence in a society could influence people's behaviors, or how participant observation has changed in response to factors like globalization.

modernist anthropology. The anthropology produced in roughly the first half of the twentieth century. During this period, anthropology was considered scientific and was based on the idea that an external and objective knowledge existed independently of culture or individual perspective.

morals. Culturally based principles of conduct that distinguish between right and wrong. Every culture has a certain set of morals and values that define what its members consider socially acceptable and are concerned with the correct way to live. Morals and values help us understand what is right and wrong according to the cultures and societies in which we live.

multisited fieldwork. A term coined by George Marcus to describe the act of conducting fieldwork among disparate sites (geographical, ideological) in an effort to understand the linkages between localized ethnographic events and international or global concerns.

"native's point of view." A term used and popularized by Bronislaw Malinowski to describe an "insider's" perspective. Malinowski felt that participant observation was necessary to develop rapport with people and acquire an intimate, firsthand, or "emic" perspective on the lives of one's informants.

netnography. A branch of ethnography originally designed to assist in the development of marketing research techniques online. It is focused on finding patterns concerning symbolism, meaning, and consumption in online communities.

ocularcentric. The privileging of vision over the other senses. According to many anthropologists, Western cultures have tended to value vision as the most important sense. Vision thus frames how Westerners view the world and those around them.

open coding. The first of a three-stage process of analyzing qualitative data. It is arguably the most labor-intensive stage, as it involves word-by-word and line-by-line coding of data to generate multitudes of key words and themes. It is also the least analytical of the three stages; at this stage, researchers are not attempting to "analyze" data or impose theory upon these data but to generate codes that summarize the actions, key conversational topics, and other phenomena that we ethnographers experience in the field and record in our field notes and interviews.

open-ended questions. Questions that give interviewees free rein to talk about what they want for as long as they like. Open-ended questions are nonspecific and therefore facilitate an opposite style of interviewing compared to closed questions. Here is an example of an open-ended question: "What is life like in Independence, Virginia?" See also *closed questions.*

partial perspectives. Observations made by particular individuals from various standpoints. When anthropologists use the term, they are acknowledging that perspectives are not only "partial" in that they are *subjective* (or from particular positionalities) but also that they are *incomplete* (the two meanings of the word "partial").

participant observation. A method of research in which the researcher or "observer" participates in the ongoing activities or the daily life of a group and records observations. Normally, participant observation refers to long-term engagements (face to face or virtual) with a community of people, and the researcher participates in various activities while observing people's behaviors.

participatory research. A form of collaborative fieldwork and research that is grounded in a desire to give one's informants a voice and a say in policy development and implementation.

photo-elicitation. A research method used in the social sciences in which researchers sit with interlocutors and talk about photographs. A wide variety of photographs can be used, including archival photographs, photographs taken by the researcher, photographs taken by the interlocutors, or photographs found by consulting other, outside sources such as media advertisements or Internet websites.

photovoice. A form of participatory research in which informants are asked to create photographs based on a specific research question or topic and then talk about them with each other and the researchers involved. This method is intended to empower individuals, create collaborative research environments, and help community advocacy groups.

polymorphous engagement. A term coined by anthropologist Hugh Gusterson. It refers to a type of participant observation that makes use of mixed methods.

positionality. How you perceive yourself and how your interlocutors perceive you, in terms of your identity, within the context of fieldwork. Increasingly, anthropologists must acknowledge how their own positionalities affect fieldwork and writing.

positivism. A philosophical tradition that dominated modernist scientific traditions. It presupposes that researchers can only comment upon and draw conclusions about data that are directly observable and measurable. Information that is obtained through human senses (e.g., sight, smell, sound) is deemed true and capable of representing scientific truths through facts. Within this context, there is little, if any, room for an exploration of the subjective elements of field-work experiences. More contemporary theories that include cultural relativity argue that it is impossible to be positivistic because truths shift depending on your cultural beliefs and perceptions.

positivist. An adherent or student of positivism, the philosophical system that bases knowledge on natural phenomena and their properties and relations, which can be verified by the senses and by the empirical sciences.

postmodern crisis. A period in sociocultural anthropology's history in the mid-1980s when many anthropologists began to critique dominant ideals of modernist thinking, including notions of objectivity and the concept that there is a singular "truth." Anthropologists began to acknowledge their own subjec-tivities and to be more reflexive about their fieldwork experiences.

primal drama. A term coined by Alan Marcus (2006) to describe a filmic genre that "often features representations of the Other as its subject[;] it does so in an attempt to present its core theme—that of man's relationship with nature and his primal instinct for survival" (202).

problem-oriented research. A form of anthropological fieldwork and writing that is informed by the desire to solve a specific "problem" or answer a series of questions. Many applied anthropologists engage in problem-oriented research.

rapport. The feelings of connectedness and trust that are needed to conduct good interviews or other forms of ethnographic research. A researcher needs to get to know and create intimate bonds with interlocutors before they will agree to be interviewed and share information about their lives. Positive feelings of trust and respect should continue throughout the interview or research process.

realism. A form of writing and representation that dominated modernist anthropology. Ethnographies that are "realist" posit that the ethnographer is an objective observer of culture and that it is possible to obtain and represent "the truth" about a culture. There is generally little or no reflexivity in such ethnographies, as the dominant perception is that the identity or positional-ity of the anthropologist should have no effect on the outcome of fieldwork.

recursive. Characterized by recurrence or repetition. Within the context of writing, this means viewing writing as a cyclical process in which you continually rethink and review and rewrite sections of your work and reflect critically upon your research question. Indeed, most stages of research are recursive, including data analysis. You may even find that you revise your research question after you begin fieldwork.

reflective notes. Formalized sets of typed notes that include elaborate description, reflective thoughts, and personalized perceptions. These notes should be written shortly after field experiences so that you can document as much information as possible.

representation. The practice of constructing visual or written depictions of a group of people when you, as an anthropologist, produce a written document, film, or other form of visual media about your fieldwork experiences. Anthropologists need to think critically about the political and ethical implications of the images and texts that they produce, and especially about how their depictions affect the people they work with.

salvage ethnography. A form of ethnography popularized by Franz Boas that involved collecting Indigenous material culture, oral histories, songs, and other "data" to record the practices and folklore of threatened cultures in the early part of the twentieth century. Boas feared that processes of assimilation and acculturation would lead to the "extinction" of Indigenous cultures, so it was necessary to rapidly record their cultural traditions.

Second Life. A 3-D, online virtual world that was created in 2003 by a company called Linden Labs. Users can customize avatars, build homes, develop businesses, and design objects. To date, millions of users from around the world have participated, and many have made hefty incomes buying and selling online real estate and material goods.

selective coding. The final stage of coding and analysis. In this step, you reread your data to try to narrow down the key concepts that you will focus upon in your paper. During this stage, you will find specific ethnographic examples from your transcripts and field notes that discuss or relate to these key issues.

Skype. A system that is downloaded for free and that allows free calling for anyone on the Internet. Skype is most commonly used for video chatting, which allows you to see the person you are talking with in real time.

snowball method. A method for acquiring more research participants that calls on existing participants to help recruit others of their acquaintance. The researcher might ask everyone interviewed to name other people that might also like to be interviewed. Snowball sampling can be directed toward a certain demographic or be more open and start from multiple points to create a more diverse group.

structured interviews. Formal interviews during which preset questions are asked. In very structured interviews, the interviewer asks direct questions and strictly controls the timing and topics discussed. Interview styles range from the very structured to the very unstructured, with life history interviews being the least structured. See also *unstructured interviews*.

study up. The act of studying and conducting fieldwork with interlocutors who are generally more powerful (e.g., economically or socially) than the anthropologist. Studying up represents a reverse trend from the long-standing ethnographic tradition of studying marginalized peoples.

subtitles. A title or caption at the bottom of a television or movie screen that textually describes dialogue in another language than the one heard. Usually subtitles are a direct translation, but sometimes they are used to express other ideas that compliment or contradict what is being heard.

text chats. Talks or chats using texted words to communicate. In virtual worlds, a text chat happens in real time on blogs and chat forums, and the form of the written words closely resembles texting.

theorize. The process of considering how your data relate to existing literature and theories about your research topic or to the issues addressed within the context of your research. Theorizing means that you will need to read, reflect upon, and integrate existing anthropological and related research into your written ethnography or final paper. You may address how your research fits with existing literature, how it is similar, how it differs, or other factors.

thick description. A term popularized by anthropologist Clifford Geertz to describe his preferred method of doing and writing about his fieldwork experiences. Geertz stressed that written representations of fieldwork should be detailed, contextual, and should position the ethnographer within the context of the ethnography.

time lags. A period between events. In virtual worlds, this refers specifically to the lag between what is seen online and what is heard offline by observers.

transcriptions. Commentary that is transcribed, or turned into writing, from a spoken, sung, or dictated form. Often, a voice recorder will be used, and then a researcher will access an audio to text program to produce a transcription. The researcher can also type up a transcription in a standardized manner as part of the field note process.

transparency. Being open, frank, candid, and honest in discussions about your research focus, your methods, and how you plan on using the data you will gather. It is imperative that all anthropological researchers maintain a certain level of transparency in all aspects of their research.

tropes of entry. Narratives written by early twentieth century anthropologists that describe their experiences of entering their fieldwork sites. Such stories often functioned to bolster the authority or legitimacy of the claims that anthropologists made.

unilineal evolution. An outdated social evolutionary theory that posits that all societies go through a series of standardized stages from simple to complex. Lewis Henry Morgan, for instance, suggested that all societies "progress" through the stages of savagery, barbarism, and civilization, with each stage marked by various technological changes.

unstructured interviews. Informal interviews in which questions are frequently not prearranged. The unstructured interview is often like a friendly conversation; the interviewer can follow the interviewee's lead and base questions on the interviewee's comments and responses. See also *structured interviews*.

verandah anthropology. A type of anthropological fieldwork popularized in the late nineteenth and early twentieth centuries that involved limited and short interactions and engagements with informants. As the guests of colonial government administrators, many anthropologists would invite their informants, often Indigenous peoples, onto their verandahs where they conducted short interviews, frequently with the help of a translator.

virtual ethnography. A blanket term used to describe the various methods ethnographers are developing in regards to shifting a traditional ethnographic approach to research that takes place with online communities.

virtual worlds. The worlds created through online, computer-based games. In these worlds, many users create their own avatars, participate in activities, create context, communicate with others, and meet people from various (and actual) geographic regions. Complex two- and three-dimensional digital technologies are used to mimic real-life places and activities.

visual field notes. Field notes primarily created through drawing, painting, diagrams, and photographs. The use of words is limited, and there is a focus on combining types of imagery, either in a collage or bricolage form or in a diary form, to express personal and theoretical ideas and perceptions alongside observed actions and environments.

visual stereotypes. Visual misrepresentations of certain groups (e.g., nation, race, class, gender, or age) that are generalized and most often negative. Visual stereotypes have long histories in all forms of media representations, and over time, they create mental and cultural constructs that people come to believe are true.

World of Warcraft. A very large, popular, role-playing game first created in 2004. It is set in "Warcraft," a complex fantasy world filled with magic and adventure as well as unusual creatures, monsters, shamans, warriors, and elves. In the game, you have to choose a realm, a race, and a class. Millions of people (approximately 10 million in 2014) from around the world have socialized and participated in quests and battles in this virtual world.

REFERENCES

AAA (American Anthropological Association). 2002. *El Dorado Task Force Papers.* Submitted to the Executive Board as a final report May 18, 2002. 2 vols. Washington, DC: American Anthropological Association. http://www.nku. edu/~humed1/darkness_in_el_dorado/documents/0535.htm.

AAA (American Anthropological Association). 2012. "AAA Statement on Ethics." *AAA Ethics Blog.* http://ethics.americananthro.org/category/statement/.

Atkinson, P., and D. Silverman. 1997. "Kundera's Immortality: The Interview Society and the Invention of the Self." *Qualitative Inquiry* 3 (3): 304–325. https://doi.org/ 10.1177/107780049700300304.

Aun, K. 1985. *The Political Refugees: A History of Estonians in Canada.* Toronto, ON: McClelland and Stewart Ltd.

Bainbridge, W.S. 2007. "The Scientific Research Potential of Virtual Worlds." *Science* 317 (5837): 472–476. https://doi.org/10.1126/science.1146930.

Banks, M. 2001. *Visual Methods in Social Research.* London, UK: Sage Publications Ltd. https://doi.org/10.4135/9780857020284.

Banks, M., and H. Morphy. 1997. *Rethinking Visual Anthropology.* New Haven, CT: Yale University Press.

Barthes, R. 1984. *Camera Lucinda.* Translated by R. Howard. London, UK: Fontana.

Bear, L., K. Ho, A. Tsing, and S. Yanagisako, 2015. "Gens: A Feminist Manifesto for the Study of Capitalism." Generating Capitalism *Cultural Anthropology Blog*, March 30. https://culanth.org/fieldsights/652-gens-a-feminist-manifesto-for-the-study-of-capitalism.

Bennett, J.W. 1996. "Applied and Action Anthropology: Ideological and Conceptual Aspects." *Current Anthropology* 37 (1): 23–53.

Berman, T. 2003. *Circle of Goods: Women, Work, and Welfare in a Reservation Community.* Albany, NY: State University of New York Press.

Biella, P. 2000. "The Ax Fight a Film Maker's Response." Email correspondence to Raymond Hames (see http://online.sfsu.edu/biella/biella2000a.html).

Birx, H.J., ed. 2010. *Twenty-First Century Anthropology: A Reference Handbook.* Thousand Oaks, CA: Sage Publications Inc.

Boellstorff, T. 2008. *Coming of Age in Second Life: An Anthropologist Explores the Virtually Human*. Princeton, NJ: Princeton University Press.

Boellstorff, T. 2013. "Making Big Data, In Theory." *First Monday* 18 (10). https://doi.org/10.5210/fm.v18i10.4869.

Boellstorff, T., and B. Maurer, eds. 2014. *Data: Now Bigger and Better!* Chicago, IL: University of Chicago Press.

Boellstorff, T., B. Nardi, C. Pearce, and T. Taylor. 2012. *Ethnography and Virtual Worlds: A Handbook of Method*. Princeton, NJ: Princeton University Press.

Bourgois, P. 2002. *In Search of Respect: Selling Crack in El Barrio*. 2nd ed. Cambridge, UK: Cambridge University Press. https://doi.org/10.1017/CBO9780511808562.

Bowen, E. Smith. 1964. *Return to Laughter: An Anthropological Novel*. New York, NY: Anchor.

Boyer, D. 2008. "Thinking Through the Anthropology of Experts." *Anthropology in Action* 15 (2): 38–46.

Briggs, C.L. 2007. "Anthropology, Interviewing, and Communicability in Contemporary Society." *Current Anthropology* 48 (4): 551–580. https://doi.org/10.1086/518300.

Briggs, J. 1970. *Never in Anger: Portrait of an Eskimo Family*. Cambridge, MA: Harvard University Press.

Burgos-Debray, E., ed. 1981. *I, Rigoberta Menchú*. London, UK: Verso.

Cannella, G.S., and K.D. Manuelito. 2008. "Feminisms from Unthought Locations: Indigenous Worldviews, Marginalized Feminisms, and Revisioning an Anticolonial Social Science." In *Handbook of Critical and Indigenous Methodologies*, edited by Y.L. Denzin, Y. Lincoln, and L.T. Smith. Thousand Oaks, CA: Sage Publications Inc.

Carter, D. 2005. "Living in Virtual Communities: An Ethnography of Human Relationships in Cyberspace." *Information Communication and Society* 8 (2): 148–167. https://doi.org/10.1080/13691180500146235.

Chagnon, N. 1968. *The Yanomamo: The Fierce People*. New York, NY: Holt, MacDougal.

Charmaz, K. 2002. "Stories and Silences: Disclosures and Self in Chronic Illness." *Qualitative Inquiry* 8 (3): 302–328. https://doi.org/10.1177/107780040200800307.

Charmaz, K. 2006. *Constructing Grounded Theory: A Practical Guide Through Qualitative Analysis*. London, UK: Sage Publications Inc.

Chase, S.E. 2011. "Narrative Enquiry: Multiple Lenses, Approaches, Voices." In *The Sage Handbook of Qualitative Research*, edited by Norman K. Denzin and Yvonna S. Lincoln, 651–680. London, UK: Sage Publications Inc.

Choy, T.K., L. Faier, M.J. Hathaway, M. Inoue, S. Satsuka, and A. Tsing. 2009. "A New Form of Collaboration in Cultural Anthropology: Matsutake Worlds." *American Ethnologist* 36 (2): 380–403. https://doi.org/10.1111/j.1548-1425.2009.01141.x.

Clifford, J. 1983. "On Ethnographic Authority." *Representations* 2 (1): 118–146. https://doi.org/10.1525/rep.1983.2.1.99p0010p.

Clifford, J. 1990. "Notes on (Field)notes." In *Fieldnotes: The Makings of Anthropology*, edited by R. Sanjek, 47–70. Ithaca, NY: Cornell University Press.

Clifford, J., and G. Marcus. 1986. *Writing Culture: The Poetics and Politics of Ethnography*. Berkeley, CA: University of California Press.

Coffey, P. 1999. *The Ethnographic Self*. London, UK: Sage Publications Inc. https://doi.org/10.4135/9780857020048.

Collier Jr., J., and M. Collier. 1967. "Interviewing with Photographs." In *Visual Anthropology: Photography as Research Method*, edited by J. Collier Jr. and M. Collier, 99–116. New York, NY: Holt, Reinhart and Winston. Reprinted in 1986 by the University of New Mexico Press.

Collier Jr., J., and M. Collier. 1986. *Visual Anthropology: Photography as Research Method*. Albuquerque, NM: University of New Mexico Press.

Collins, S.G. 2014. "Poor Data, Rich Data, Big Data, Chief." *Anthropology News* 55 (9): 20.

Cool, J. 1993. "The Experts of Everyday Life: Cultural Reproduction and Cultural Critique in Antelope Valley." MA thesis, Visual Anthropology, University of Southern California, Los Angeles, California.

Cool, J. 2001. "Strange Distance: Reading Walden in Suburbia." *Etnofoor* 14 (1): 61–74.

Cool, J. 2014. "Gardening Metadata in the New Media Ecology: A Manifesto (of Sorts) for Ethnographic Film." *American Anthropologist* 116 (1): 173–178.

Cool, J., and S. Mulcihy. 2015. "Working Out the Kinks: Anonymous Subjects in Ethnographic Film." *Anthropology Now* 7 (2): 69–79.

Darnell, R. 2008. "North American Traditions in Anthropology: The Historiographic Baseline." In *A New History of Anthropology*, edited by H. Kuklick, 35–51. London, UK: Blackwell.

Darnell, R., and L. Valentine, eds. 1999. *Theorizing the Americanist Tradition*. Toronto, ON: University of Toronto Press.

Deloria, P.J. 2004. *Indians in Unexpected Places*. Lawrence, KS: University Press of Kansas.

Deloria Jr., V. 1988. *Custer Died for Your Sins: An Indian Manifesto*. Norman, OK: University of Oklahoma Press. (Original work published 1969.)

Denzin, N.K. 2001. "The Reflexive Interview and a Performative Social Science." *Qualitative Research* 1 (1): 23–46. https://doi.org/10.1177/146879410100100102.

Denzin, N.K., Y.S. Lincoln, and L.T. Smith. 2008. *Handbook of Critical and Indigenous Methodologies*. London, UK: Sage Publications Inc. https://doi.org/10.4135/9781483385686.

Driscoll, C., and M. Gregg. 2010. "My Profile: The Ethics of Virtual Ethnography." *Emotion, Space and Society* 3 (1): 15–20. https://doi.org/10.1016/j.emospa.2010.01.012.

Dudley, K.M. 1994. *The End of the Line: Lost Jobs, New Lives in Postindustrial America*. Chicago, IL: University of Chicago Press.

Dudley, K.M. 2000. *Debt and Dispossession: Farm Loss in America's Heartland*. Chicago, IL: University of Chicago Press.

Dudley, K.M. 2014. *Guitar Makers: The Endurance of Artisanal Values in North America*. Chicago, IL: University of Chicago Press.

Edwards, E. 2001. *Raw Histories: Photographs, Anthropology and Museums*. Oxford, NY: Berg Publishers.

Edwards, E. 2005. "Photographs and the Sound of History." *Visual Anthropology Review* 21 (1-2): 27–46.

Ellis, C., T.E. Adams, and A.P. Bochner. 2011. "Autoethnography: An Overview." *FQS— Forum: Qualitative Social Research* 12 (1). http://www.qualitative-research.net/index.php/fqs/article/view/1589/3095.

Emerson, R., R. Fretz, and L. Shaw. 2011. *Writing Ethnographic Fieldnotes*. 2nd ed. Chicago, IL: University of Chicago Press. https://doi.org/10.7208/chicago/9780226206868.001.0001.

Eriksen, T.H. 2015. "The Paris Massacre and the Syrian Refugee Crisis." *Eriksen's Blog*, https://thomashyllanderiksen.net/2015/11/14/the-paris-massacre-and-the-syrian-refugee-crisis/.

Evans-Pritchard, E.E. 1940. *The Nuer: A Description of the Modes of Livelihood and Political Institutions of a Nilotic People*. Oxford, UK: Clarendon Press.

Evans-Pritchard, E.E. 1951. *Kinship and Marriage Among the Nuer*. Oxford, UK: Clarendon Press.

Evans-Pritchard, E.E. 1956. *Nuer Religion*. Oxford, UK: Clarendon Press.

Flaherty, R. 1922. *Nanook of the North* [film]. Buffalo, NY: Pathé Exchange.

Flaherty, R. 1950. "Robert Flaherty Talking." In *Cinema 1950*, edited by R. Manviel, 10–29. London, UK: Pelican Publishers.

Fluehr-Lobban, C. 1994. "Informed Consent in Anthropological Research: We Are Not Exempt." *Human Organization* 53 (1): 1–10. https://doi.org/10.17730/humo.53.1.178jngk9n57vq685.

Fluehr-Lobban, C. 1998. "Ethics." In *Handbook of Methods in Cultural Anthropology*, edited by H. Russell Bernard, 173–202. Walnut Creek, CA: Altamira Press.

Fluehr-Lobban, C. 2008. "Collaborative Anthropology as Twenty-First Century Ethical Anthropology." *Collaborative Anthropologies* 1 (1): 175–182. https://doi.org/10.1353/cla.0.0000.

Forsey, M.G. 2010. "Ethnography as Participant Listening." *Ethnography* 11 (4): 558–572. https://doi.org/10.1177/1466138110372587.

Forte, M. 2011. "The Human Terrain System and Anthropology: A Review of Ongoing Public Debates." *American Anthropologist* 113 (1): 149–153. https://doi.org/10.1111/j.1548-1433.2010.01315.x.

Forte, M. 2015. "Human Terrain System (United States): Critique." In *International Encyclopedia of the Social and Behavioral Sciences*, edited by J.D. Wright. 2nd ed., 2:392–399. Oxford, UK: Elsevier. https://doi.org/10.1016/B978-0-08-097086-8.64112-0.

Foucault, M. 1975. *Discipline and Punish: The Birth of the Prison*. New York, NY: Random House.

Foucault, M. 1990. *The History of Sexuality*. Translated by R. Hurley. New York, NY: Vintage Books. (Original work published 1976.)

Garcia, A., C. Standlee, J. Bechkoff, and Y. Cui. 2009. "Ethnographic Approaches to the Internet and Computer-Mediated Communication." *Journal of Contemporary Ethnography* 38 (1): 52–84. https://doi.org/10.1177/0891241607310839.

Gibbs G.R., and C. Taylor. 2005. "How and What to Code." *Online QDA*. June 30. http://onlineqda.hud.ac.uk/Intro_QDA/how_what_to_code.php.

Gill, S. 1979. "Whirling Logs and Coloured Sands." In *Native Religious Traditions*, edited by E. Waugh and R. Prithipaul, 151–162. Waterloo: Wilfrid Laurier Press.

Ginsburg, F. 2002. "Screen Memories: Resignifying the Traditional in Indigenous Media" In *Media Worlds: Anthropology on New Terrain*, edited by F. Ginsburg, L. Abu-Lughod, and B. Larkin, 41–44 Berkeley, CA: UCP Press.

Glesne, C. 2010. *Becoming Qualitative Researchers: An Introduction*. 4th ed. Toronto, ON: Pearson Education.

Gmelch, G. 2006. *Inside Pitch: Life in Professional Baseball*. Lincoln, NE: Bison Books.

Gobar, A. 1990. *Gobar Report*. Lancaster, CA: Alfred Gobar Associates, Inc.

Goodson, I. 2001. "The Story of Life History: Origins of the Life History Method in Sociology." *Identity* 1 (2): 129–142. https://doi.org/10.1207/S1532706XID0102_02.

Gordon, A.F. 1997. *Ghostly Matters: Haunting and the Sociological Imagination*. Minneapolis, MN: University of Minnesota Press.

Gruber, J.W. 1970. "Ethnographic Salvage and the Shaping of Anthropology." *American Anthropologist* 72 (6): 1289–1299.

Gubrium, A., and K. Harper. 2013. *Participatory Visual and Digital Methods*. Walnut Creek, CA: Left Coast Press.

Gupta, A., and J. Ferguson. 1997. *Anthropological Locations: Boundaries and Grounds of a Field Science*. Oakland, CA: University of California Press.

Gusterson, H. 1997. "Studying Up Revisited." *Political and Legal Anthropology Review* 20 (1): 114–119. https://doi.org/10.1525/pol.1997.20.1.114.

Harper, D. 2002. "Talking about Pictures: A Case for Photo Elicitation." *Visual Studies* 17 (1): 13–26. https://doi.org/10.1080/14725860220137345.

Harrison, J., and R. Darnell. 2006. "Historicizing Traditions in Canadian Anthropology." In *Historicizing Canadian Anthropology*, edited by J. Harrison and R. Darnell, 14–21. Vancouver, BC: UBC Press.

Hastrup, K. 1995. *A Passage to Anthropology: Between Experience and Theory*. New York, NY: Routledge.

Heider, Karl G. 2006. *Ethnographic Film*. Revised ed. Austin, TX: University of Texas Press.

Hendrickson, C. 2008. "Visual Field Notes: Drawing Insights in the Yucatan." *Visual Anthropology Review* 24 (2): 117–132. https://doi.org/10.1111/j.1548-7458.2008.00009.x.

Henley, P. 1998. "Film-Making and Ethnographic Research." In *Image-Based Research: A Source Book for Qualitative Researchers*, edited by J. Prosser, 42–59. London, UK: Routledge.

Hine, C. 2000. *Virtual Ethnography*. Thousand Oaks, CA: Sage.

Hinsley, C. 1983. "Ethnographic Charisma and Scientific Routine: Cushing and Fewkes in the American Southwest, 1878-1973." In *Observers Observed: Essays on Ethnographic Fieldwork*, edited by G.W. Stocking, Jr., 53–69. Madison: University of Wisconsin Press.

Ho, K. 2009. *Liquidated: An Ethnography of Wall Street*. Durham, NC: Duke University Press. https://doi.org/10.1215/9780822391371.

Holstein, J.A., and J.F. Gubrium. 1995. *The Active Interview*. Thousand Oaks, CA: Sage Publications Inc.

Holt, N.L. 2003. "Representation, Legitimation, and Autoethnography: An Autoethnographic Writing Story." *International Journal of Qualitative Methods* 2 (1): 18–28. https://doi.org/10.1177/160940690300200102.

Howes, D., and C. Classen. 1991. "Conclusion: Sounding Sensory Profiles." In *The Varieties of Sensory Experience: A Sourcebook in the Anthropology of the Senses*, edited by D. Howes, 329–334. Toronto: University of Toronto Press.

Huber, M.T. 2011. "Oil, Life, and the Fetishism of Geopolitics." *Capitalism, Nature, Socialism* 22 (3): 32–48. https://doi.org/10.1080/10455752.2011.593883.

Hurworth, R. 2004. "Photo-Interviewing." *Qualitative Research Journal* 4 (1): 73–79.

Hutchinson, S. 1996. *Nuer Dilemmas: Coping with Money, War and the State*. Berkeley, CA: University of California Press.

Ingold, T. 2014. "That's Enough about Ethnography!" *HAU: Journal of Ethnographic Theory* 4 (1): 383–395. http://sed.ucsd.edu/files/2014/09/Ingold-Thats-enough-about-ethnography.pdf.

Jackson, J.E. 1990. "'I Am a Fieldnote': Fieldnotes As a Symbol of Professional Identity." In *Fieldnotes: The Makings of Anthropology*, edited by Roger Sanjek, 3–33 Ithaca, NY: Cornell University Press.

Jenkins, N., K.R. Woodward, and T. Winter. 2008. "The Emergent Production of Analysis in Photo Elicitation: Pictures of Military Identity." *Forum: Qualitative Social Research* 9 (3). http://www.qualitative-research.net/index.php/fqs/article/view/1169/2582#g21.

Jermyn, L. 2009. "B.A., M.A., McJob: The Student Debt Bubble, The Shrinking Middle Class, and the Future of Postsecondary Education." *Briarpatch Magazine* 38 (5). https://briarpatchmagazine.com/articles/view/ba-ma-mcjob.

Jones, S.E., T. Adams, and C. Ellis. 2013. "Introduction: Coming to Know Autoethnography as More than a Method." In *Handbook of Autoethnography*, edited by S.E. Jones, T. Adams and C. Ellis, 17–48. Walnut Creek, CA: Left Coast Press.

Jordan, B. 2009. "Blurring Boundaries: The 'Real' and the 'Virtual' in Hybrid Spaces." *Human Organization* 68 (2): 181–193. https://doi.org/10.17730/humo.68.2.7x4406g270801284.

Jorgensen, J.G. 1971. "On Ethics and Anthropology." *Current Anthropology* 12 (3): 321–334. https://doi.org/10.1086/201209.

Kolb, A.Y., and D.A. Kolb. 2005. "Learning Styles and Learning Spaces: Enhancing Experiential Learning in Higher Education." *Academy of Management for Learning and Education* 4 (2): 193–212.

Kozinets, R.V. 2010. *Netnography: Doing Ethnographic Research Online*. Thousand Oaks, CA: Sage Publications, Inc.

Kuklick, H. 1997. "After Ismael: The Fieldwork Tradition and Its Future." In *Anthropological Locations: Boundaries and Grounds of a Field Science*, edited by A. Gupta and J. Ferguson, 47–65. Oakland, CA: University of California Press.

Kvale, S. 1996. *InterViews: An Introduction to Qualitative Research Interviewing*. London, UK: Sage Publications, Inc.

Lawson, M. 2009. *Dammed Indians Revisited: The Continuing History of the Pick-Sloan Plan and the Missouri River Sioux*. Pierre, SD: South Dakota State Historical Society Press.

Leavitt, J. 2014. "Words and Worlds: Ethnography and Theories of Translation." *HAU: Journal of Ethnographic Theory* 4 (2): 193–220. https://doi.org/10.14318/hau4.2.009.

Leech, B.L. 2002. "Asking Questions: Techniques for Semi-Structured Interviews." *PS: Political Science & Politics* 35 (4): 665–668. https://doi.org/10.1017/S1049096502001129.

Leibing, A., and A. McLean. 2007. "Learn to Value Your Shadow!: An Introduction to the Margins of Fieldwork." In *The Shadows of Fieldwork: Exploring the Borders Between Ethnography and Life*, edited by A. McLean and A. Leibing, 1–28. Oxford, UK: Blackwell. https://doi.org/10.1002/9780470692455.ch.

Lowry, P. 2009. *Green Cathedrals*. London, UK: Bloomsbury Publishing.

Macdonald, G. 2003. "Photos in Wiradjuri Biscuit Tins: Negotiating Relatedness and Validating Colonial Histories." *Oceania* 73 (4): 225–242. https://doi.org/ 10.1002/j.1834-4461.2003.tb02822.x.

MacDougall, D. 1999. "When Less is Less: The Long Take in Documentary." In *Film Quarterly: Forty Years—A Selection*, edited by B. Henderson and A. Martin, 291–305. Berkeley, CA: University of California Press. Available online at http://ark.cdlib. org/ark:/13030/ft5h4nb36j/.

MacPhail, T. 2015. "Data, Data Everywhere." *Public Culture* 27 (2): 213–219. https://doi. org/10.1215/08992363-2841820.

Madden, R. 2010. *Being Ethnographic: A Guide to the Theory and Practice of Ethnography*. London, UK: Sage Publications, Inc.

Maier-Lorentz, M.M. 2008. "Transcultural Nursing: Its Importance in Nursing Practice." *Journal of Cultural Diversity* 15 (1): 37–43.

Malinowski, B. 2014. *Argonauts of the Western Pacific*. New York, NY: Routledge. Originally published in 1932.

Mannik, L. 2013. *Photography, Memory and Refugee Identity: The Voyage of the SS Walnut*. Vancouver, BC: University of British Columbia Press.

Maranhao, T., and B. Streck. 2003. *Translation and Ethnography: The Anthropological Challenge of Intercultural Understanding*. Tucson, AZ: University of Arizona Press.

Marcus, A. 2006. "Nanook of the North as Primal Drama." *Visual Anthropology* 19 (3–4): 201–222. https://doi.org/10.1080/08949460600656543.

Marcus, G. 1995. "Ethnography in/of the World System: The Emergence of Multi-Sited Ethnography." *Annual Review of Anthropology* 24 (1): 95–117. https://doi. org/10.1146/annurev.an.24.100195.000523.

Marcus, G., and M. Fischer. 1986. *Anthropology as Cultural Critique: An Experimental Moment in the Human Sciences*. Chicago, IL: University of Chicago Press.

Marks, D. 1995. "Ethnography and Ethnographic Film: From Flaherty to Asch and After." *American Anthropologist* 97 (2): 339–347. https://doi.org/10.1525/ aa.1995.97.2.02a00110.

Matthew, J., and C. Price. 2009. "Coding: Selective Coding." In *Encyclopedia of Case Study Research*, edited by A.J. Mills, G. Durepos, and E. Wiebe, 157–158. London, UK: Sage Publications Inc.

McCracken, G. 2011. *Chief Culture Officer: How to Create a Living, Breathing Corporation*. New York, NY: Basic Books.

McCurdy, D., J.P. Spradley, and D.J. Shandy. 2004. *The Cultural Experience: Ethnography in Complex Society*. Long Grove, IL: Waveland Press.

McGarry, K. 2015. "Ethnographic 'Frictions' and the 'Ice Scandal': Affect, Mass Media, and Canadian Nationalism in High-Performance Figure Skating." In *Reclaiming Canadian Bodies: Visual Media and Representation*, edited by L. Mannik and K. McGarry, 61–88. Waterloo, ON: Wilfrid Laurier University Press.

McIntosh, P. 1989. "White Privilege: Unpacking the Invisible Knapsack." *Peace and Freedom Magazine*, July/August, 10–12. Available online at https:// nationalseedproject.org/white-privilege-unpacking-the-invisible-knapsack.

McMurray, D.A. 2005. "Censorship, Surveillance, and Middle East Studies in the Contemporary United States." In *Auto-ethnographies: The Anthropology of Academic Practices*, edited by A. Meneley and J. D. Young, 173–186. Peterborough, ON: Broadview Press.

Mead, M. 1928. *Coming of Age in Samoa.* New York, NY: William Morrow.

Meyer, M.A. 2008. "Indigenous and Authentic: Hawaiian Epistemology and the Triangulation of Meaning." In *Handbook of Critical and Indigenous Methodologies,* edited by N. Denzin, Y. Lincoln, and L.T. Smith, 217–232. Thousand Oaks, CA: Sage Publications Inc. https://doi.org/10.4135/9781483385686.n11.

Munthali, A. 2001. "Doing Fieldwork at Home: Some Personal Experiences Among the Tumbuka of Northern Malawi." *African Anthropologist* 8 (2): 114–136.

Myerhoff, B. 1992. *Remembered Lives: The Work of Ritual, Storytelling, and Growing Old.* Ann Arbor, MI: University of Michigan.

Nader, L. 1972. "Up the Anthropologist: Perspectives Gained from Studying Up." In *Reinventing Anthropology,* edited by D. Hymes, 284–311. New York, NY: Pantheon Books.

Nahm, S., and C.H. Rinker. 2015. *Applied Anthropology: Unexpected Spaces, Topics and Methods.* New York, NY: Routledge.

Narayan, K. 1993. "How 'Native' is a Native Anthropologist?" *American Anthropologist* 95 (3): 671–686. https://doi.org/10.1525/aa.1993.95.3.02a00070.

Narayan, K. 2014. "Ethnographic Writing with Kirin Narayan." *Savage Minds,* February 3. Interviewed by Carole McGranahan. https://savageminds. org/2014/02/03/ethnographic-writing-with-kirin-narayan-an-interview/.

Nardi, B. 2010. *My Life as a Night Elf Priest: An Anthropological Account of World of Warcraft.* Ann Arbor, MI: University of Michigan Press.

Nikiforuk, A. 1999. "It Makes Them Sick." *Canadian Business* 72 (2): 46–51.

Nikiforuk, A. 2001. *Saboteurs: Wiebo Ludwig's War Against Big Oil.* Toronto, ON: MacFarlane Walter & Ross.

O'Reilly, K. 2005. *Ethnographic Methods.* London, UK: Routledge. https://doi.org/ 10.4324/9780203320068.

O'Reilly, K. 2012. *Ethnographic Methods* 2nd ed. London, UK: Routledge.

Orwell, G. 1946. "In Front of Your Nose." *Tribune,* March 22. Reprinted in 1968 in *The Collected Essays, Journalism, and Letters of George Orwell.* Vol. 4, edited by S. Orwell and I. Angus, 122–125. New York, NY: Harcourt.

Pink, S. 2001. *Doing Visual Ethnography.* London, UK: Sage Publications Inc.

Powdermaker, H. 1950. *Hollywood, the Dream Factory: An Anthropologist Looks at the Movie-Makers.* Boston, MA: Little Brown.

Powdermaker, H. 1966. *Stranger and Friend: The Way of an Anthropologist.* New York, NY: W.W. Norton & Co.

Pratt, M.L. 1992. *Imperial Eyes: Travel Writing and Transculturation.* London, UK: Routledge. https://doi.org/10.4324/9780203163672.

Prosser, J., and D. Schwartz. 1998. "Photographs within the Sociological Research Process." In *Image-Based Research: A Sourcebook for Qualitative Researchers,* edited by J. Prosser, 115–129. London, UK: Falmer Press.

Rabinow, P. 1977. *Reflections on Fieldwork in Morocco.* Oakland, CA: University of California Press.

Radcliffe-Brown, A.R. 1940. "On Joking Relationships." *Africa: Journal of the International Africa Institute* 13 (3): 195–210. https://doi.org/10.2307/1156093.

Read, C. 1892. "Part II–Ethnography: Prefatory Note." In *Notes and Queries on Anthropology,* edited by J. Garson and C. Read, 2nd ed., 87–88. London, UK: Anthropological Institute. (Original work published 1874.)

Richardson, L., and E.A. St. Pierre. 2005. "Writing: A Method of Inquiry." In *The Sage Handbook of Qualitative Research*, edited by N.K. Denzin and Y.S. Lincoln, 3rd ed., 959–978. London, UK: Sage.

Rosaldo, R. 1980. *Illongot Headhunting, 1883–1974: A Study in Society and History.* Stanford, CA: Stanford University Press.

Rosenthal, G. 2003. "The Healing Effects of Storytelling: On Conditions of Curative Storytelling in the Context of Research and Counselling." *Qualitative Inquiry* 9 (6): 915–933. https://doi.org/10.1177/1077800403254888.

Ruby, J. 1975. "Is an Ethnographic Film a Filmic Ethnography?" *Studies in the Anthropology of Visual Communication* 2 (2): 104–111. https://doi.org/10.1525/var.1975.2.2.104.

Russell, B. 2006. *Research Methods in Anthropology: Qualitative and Quantitative Approaches.* New York, NY: AltaMira Press.

Rylko-Bauer, B., M. Singer, and J. Van Willigen. 2006. "Reclaiming Applied Anthropology: Its Past, Present, and Future." *American Anthropologist* 108 (1): 178–190. https://doi.org/10.1525/aa.2006.108.1.178.

Ryan, G.W., and R.H. Bernard. 2003. "Techniques to Identify Themes." *Field Methods* 15 (1): 85–109. https://doi.org/10.1177/1525822X02239569.

Seremetakis, N.C. 1994. *The Senses Still.* Chicago, IL: University of Chicago Press.

Shandy, D.J. 2008. *Nuer-American Passages: Globalizing Sudanese Migration.* Gainesville, FL: Florida University Press.

Shannon, J. 2012. "On Working with the National Taiwan Museum." *Taiwan Natural Science* 31 (3): 10–17.

Shannon, J. 2014a. *Our Lives: Collaboration, Native Voice, and the Making of the National Museum of the American Indian.* Santa Fe, NM: SAR Press.

Shannon, J. 2014b. "Projectishare.com: Sharing Our Past, Collecting for the Future." In *Museum as Process: Translating Local and Global Knowledges*, edited by R. Silverman, 67–89. New York, NY: Routledge.

Simonelli, J., and J. Skinner. 2016. "Applied and Public Anthropology in the United States and the United Kingdom." In *The Handbook of Sociocultural Anthropology*, edited by J.G. Carrier and D.B. Gewertz, 553–569. London, UK: Bloomsbury Academic.

Simpson, A. 2007. "On Ethnographic Refusal: Indigeneity, 'Voice' and Colonial Citizenship." *Junctures* 9: 67–80.

Simpson, J. 2014. "Do Police Departments Need Anthropologists?" *Anthropoliteia,* December 8. https://anthropoliteia.net/2015/02/02/a-response-to-do-police-departments-need-anthropologists/.

Simpson, L., W. Nanibush, and C. Williams. 2012. "The Resurgence of Indigenous Women's Knowledge and Resistance in Relation to Land and Territoriality: Transnational and Interdisciplinary Perspectives." *InTensions* 6. http://www.yorku.ca/intent/issue6/.

Singer, M. 2008. "Applied Anthropology." In *A New History of Anthropology*, edited by H. Kucklick, 326–340. Oxford, UK: Blackwell.

Singer, N. 2014. "Intel's Sharp-Eyed Social Scientist." *New York Times*, February 15. http://www.nytimes.com/2014/02/16/technology/intels-sharp-eyed-social-scientist.html?ribbon-ad-idx=5&rref=technology&module=Ribbon&version=ori

gin&region=Header&action=click&contentCollection=Technology&pgtype=arti
cle&_r=0.

Skinner, J. 2012. *The Interview: An Ethnographic Approach*. London, UK: Berg Publishers.

Smith, C. 2005. "Decolonising the Museum: The National Museum of the American Indian in Washington, DC." *Antiquity* 79 (304): 424–439. https://doi.org/10.1017/S0003598X00114206.

Smith, L.T. 1999. *Decolonizing Methodologies: Research and Indigenous Peoples*. New York, NY: St. Martin's Press.

Smith, L.T. 2005. "On Tricky Ground: Researching the Native in an Age of Uncertainty." In *The Sage Handbook of Qualitative Research*, edited by N.K. Denzin and Y.S. Lincoln, 3rd ed., 85–108. Los Angeles: Sage Publishing Inc.

Smith, L.T. 2006. *Decolonizing Methodologies: Research and Indigenous Peoples*. London, UK: Zed Books. (Original work published 1999.)

Snodgrass, J. 2014. "Ethnography of Online Cultures." In *Handbook of Methods in Cultural Anthropology*, edited by H.R. Bernard and C.C. Gravlee, 465–496. London, UK: Rowman & Littlefield.

Spradley, J. 1980. *Participant Observation*. New York, NY: Holt, Rinehart and Winston.

Spry, T. 2001. "Performing Autoethnography: An Embodied Methodological Praxis." *Qualitative Inquiry* 7 (6): 706–732. https://doi.org/10.1177/107780040100700605.

Stevenson, L. 2014. *Life beside Itself: Imagining Care in the Canadian Arctic*. Berkeley, CA: University of California Press.

Stewart, K. 1991. "On the Politics of Cultural Theory: A Case for 'Contaminated' Cultural Critique." *Social Research* 58 (2): 395–412.

Stewart, K. 2007. *Ordinary Affects*. Durham, NC: Duke University Press. https://doi.org/10.1215/9780822390404.

Stillitoe, P. 2007. "Anthropologists Only Need Apply: Challenges of Applied Anthropology." *JRAI: Journal of the Royal Anthropological Institute* 13 (1): 147–165.

Stocking, G. 1983. "History of Anthropology: Whence/Whither." In *Observers Observed: Essays on Ethnographic Fieldwork*, edited by G.W. Stocking Jr., 3–12. Madison, WI: University of Wisconsin Press.

Strauss, A., and J. Corbin. 1991. *Basics of Qualitative Research: Grounded Theory, Procedures, and Techniques*. Newbury Park, CA: Sage Publications Inc.

Swadener, B.B., and K. Mutua. 2008. "Decolonizing Performances: Deconstructing the Global Postcolonial." In *Handbook of Critical and Indigenous Methodologies*, edited by N. Denzin, Y. Lincoln, and L.T. Smith, 31–43. Thousand Oaks, CA: Sage Publications Inc.

Taussig, M. 1997. *The Magic of the State*. London, New York, NY: Routledge.

Taussig, M. 2011. *I Swear I Saw This: Drawings in Fieldwork Notebooks, Namely my Own*. Chicago: University of Chicago Press. https://doi.org/10.7208/chicago/9780226789842.001.0001.

Tsing, A.L. 2005. *Friction: An Ethnography of Global Connection*. Princeton, NJ: Princeton University Press.

Tsing, A.L. 2015. *The Mushroom at the End of the World: On the Possibility of Life in Capitalist Ruins*. Princeton, NJ: Princeton University Press.

Tuck, E., and W. K. Yang. 2012. "Decolonization is Not a Metaphor." *Decolonization* 1 (1): 1–40.

Turner, V. 1987. *The Anthropology of Performance*. New York, NY: PAJ Publications.

van den Hoonaard, W.C., and A. Connolly. 2006. "Anthropological Research in Light of Research-Ethics Review: Canadian Master's Theses, 1995–2004." *Journal of Empirical Research on Human Research Ethics: An International Journal* 1 (2): 59–69. https://doi.org/10.1525/jer.2006.1.2.59.

Van House, N. A. 2006. "Interview V: Visualization-Assisted Photo Elicitation." *CHI EA '06: Extended Abstracts on Human Factors in Computing Systems*, 1463–1468. http://dl.acm.org/citation.cfm?doid=1125451.1125720.

Van Willigen, J. 2002. *Applied Anthropology: An Introduction*. Westport, CT: Greenwood Publishing Group.

Walther, J. B. 2002. "Research Ethics in Internet-Enabled Research: Human Subjects Issues and Methodological Myopia." *Ethics and Information Technology* 4 (3): 205–216.

Walton, S.P. 1993. "Jean Brigg's *Never in Anger* as an Ethnography of Experience." *Critique of Anthropology* 13 (4): 379–399. https://doi.org/10.1177/0308275X9301300406.

Wang, T. 2013. "Big Data Needs Thick Data." *Ethnography Matters*, May 13. http://ethnographymatters.net/blog/2013/05/13/big-data-needs-thick-data/.

Weber-Pillwax, C. 2003. "Identity Formation and Consciousness with Reference to North Alberta Cree and Metis Indigenous Peoples." PhD diss., University of Alberta, Edmonton, Alberta.

WHO (World Health Organization). 2015. "Anthropologists Work with Ebola-Affected Communities in Mali." *WHO Features*, January. http://www.who.int/features/2015/anthropologists-ebola-mali/en/.

Williams, M. 2007. "Avatar Watching: Participant Observation in Graphical Online Environments." *Qualitative Research* 7 (1): 5–24. https://doi.org/10.1177/1468794107071408.

Wilson, S. 2008. *Research is Ceremony: Indigenous Research Methods*. Winnipeg, MB: Fernwood Publishing.

Wood, C. 2016. "Inside the Halo Zone: Geology, Finance, and the Corporate Performance of Profit in a Deep Tight Oil Formation." *Economic Anthropology* 3 (1): 43–56. https://doi.org/10.1002/sea2.12043.

Yee, N. 2014. *The Proteus Paradox: How Online Games and Virtual Worlds Change Us—And How They Don't*. New Haven, CT: Yale University Press.

Young, J.D., and A. Meneley. 2005. "Introduction: Auto-Ethnographies of Academic Practices." In *Auto-ethnographies: The Anthropology of Academic Practices*, edited by A. Meneley and J.D. Young, 1–21. Peterborough, ON: Broadview Press.

INDEX

CPSIA information can be obtained
at www.ICGtesting.com
Printed in the USA
BVHW061742110222
628346BV00002B/5